Praise for **THE AI-POWERED ENTERPRISE**

"AI promises to provide the next 'turn of the crank' in business automation. However, purely statistical machine learning alone won't achieve this on its own. This book provides prescriptive guidance in the context of real business case studies to drive success instead of disappointment. It's a great resource to separate the hype from the reality and a practical guide to achieve real business outcomes using AI technology."
—**Peter N. Johnson,** MetLife Fellow, SVP, MetLife

"AI and its various meanings bring a whole new dimension to how enterprises operate. In his book *The AI-Powered Enterprise*, Seth has honed in on the methodology behind how AI impacts content—the one constant tangible for every enterprise. A must-read for any enterprise interested in what their content says about them—from a data miner to a taxonomist to a casual blogger. The clarity of the various aspects of content design is super impressive."
—**Eeshita Grover,** Director of Marketing, Cisco

"Artificial intelligence holds the power to transform your business and your career, but there will be plenty of challenges along the way. Earley demystifies the topic and provides a practical road map for applying smarter processes and technologies across the enterprise. Now is the time to explore AI, and this book is a great place to start."
—**Paul Roetzer,** founder and CEO, Marketing Artificial Intelligence Institute and author of *The Marketing Performance Blueprint*

"If you wonder where to get started in your company's AI journey, Seth lays out a playbook for a flexible, scalable, and tool-agnostic approach to AI implementation. The journey is difficult, but the rewards will enable businesses to compete and thrive in our complex and fast-changing technology world."
—**Ryan Miller,** Chief Digital Officer, First Investors Financial Services

"With every technology that comes knocking on our doorstep, the question we have to ask ourselves is, 'how will I use this to create value for my customers?' Businesses have weathered the turbulence of digital transformation and now AI is knocking on our doorstep. For executives, it can feel confusing, intimidating, and at times, downright dangerous. If you're in that mix, then you must keep Seth Earley's book close at hand. It delivers a practical approach to explaining AI as well as how to apply it to any organizational environment."
—**Carla Johnson,** international keynote speaker, bestselling author, and CMO

"For any leader considering ways to improve their business with advanced data analytics and artificial intelligence, this book is a must-read. Seth Earley has documented a recipe for your success."
—**Mark Loboda,** Senior Vice President of Science and Technology, Hemlock Semiconductor

"Read this book to learn how leaders and companies are using AI with structured data to transform business. Insight from real-world examples, combined with a proven methodology, will arm the reader with the knowledge and confidence necessary to drive AI in any organization."
—**Barry Coflan,** SVP & Chief Technology Officer, Schneider Electric, Digital Energy

"Success comes to those who plan ahead. And while AI has been in existence for a while, it's still not working at the level it should be. Why not? Seth's book provides the answer to that question and a clear path for everyone who want to hang ten the AI wave. Don't crash & burn, read this book!"
—**Jeffrey Hayzlett,** Primetime TV and podcast host, speaker, author and part-time cowboy

THE AI-POWERED ENTERPRISE

THE
AI-POWERED
ENTERPRISE

Harness the Power of Ontologies to
Make Your Business Smarter, Faster,
and More Profitable

SETH EARLEY

Cataloguing data available from Library and Archives Canada

ISBN 978-1-928055-50-1 (hardcover)
ISBN 978-1-928055-52-5 (EPUB)
ISBN 978-1-928055-51-8 (PDF)

Cover and interior design: Greg Tabor
Cover image: iStock/antoniokhr

Published by LifeTree Media Ltd.
LifeTreeMedia.com

Distributed in the U.S. by Publishers Group West and in
Canada by Publishers Group Canada

Printed and bound in Canada

CONTENTS

*To my wife Lisa, the love of my life,
for supporting me throughout this process
and for her support over the years
of building the business.*

FOREWORD

When I think of Seth Earley, I think of four things: knowledge exchange "salons" around the firepit at his home, a crazy-fast and small racing-power catamaran on which I risked my safety with him, knowledge management, and conversational artificial intelligence. I won't elaborate further on the first two, but the last two are highly relevant to this book. Like me, Earley spent a number of years consulting and writing about knowledge management. That topic isn't terribly popular now, but it has positively informed his approach to AI and this book.

The book is heavily focused on the importance of ontologies in conversational AI systems, and ontologies were also very important in knowledge management. Of course, the ontology Earley is addressing is not the metaphysical study of the nature of being. The other meaning of ontology is, to use Google's definition, "a set of concepts and categories in a subject area or domain that shows their properties and the relations between them." Earley is convinced, as am I, that you can't create an effective conversational AI system—a chatbot, an intelligent agent, or a virtual assistant—without an ontology. And if you want a practical introduction to ontologies and their application in conversational AI, you have come to the right place.

I have always liked Seth's favorite line of, "There is no AI without IA," where "IA" is information architecture—another term for ontology. It's both catchy and mostly true. Of course, as an academic (though a pretty practical one), I am inclined to look for exceptions to general rules, and I think there are some exceptions to that sensible rule.

You will note in this book that the primary examples of AI that Earley uses are the conversational approaches that organizations are widely adopting for interactions with customers and employees. His appealing rule about AI and IA is true for the great majority of conversational AI applications. Perhaps there are exceptions to it if you include, for example, statistical translation programs like Google Translate in the category of conversational AI. I'm not sure they belong in the category, but they do facilitate conversation with speakers of other languages.

The other exception domain is also debatable. I have argued with Seth that machine learning—statistical approaches to prediction and classification that many observers include as AI—doesn't necessarily demand an ontology. It requires data (often great heaping gobs of it) on multiple variables (also called features) in rows and columns, but we don't need to know the terminological relationships between them.

But Earley's counterargument is that if you are managing enterprise data, it is hugely beneficial to have an ontology that describes what data entities you have in your organization and how they relate. If you have a customer ID data element, for example, it's very useful to know that it includes current customers, former customers, and prospects, and that customer orders are aggregated by that ID. Earley has a particular passion for customer and product data, and I agree that they are perhaps the most important types for most organizations.

I am not a fan of massive projects to create enterprise-level ontologies (often known as "master data management" or "enterprise information architecture" projects), but there is no doubt that your organization should know what data elements you have access to, and how they relate to other data. And I believe that ontology efforts are of more value if they are relatively narrow in scope. So I partially concede the argument to Earley even for machine learning. And in the book he describes a "bottom-up, data- and content-centric" approach to creating ontologies, which I generally believe is more effective.

In any case, there is far more to this book than urgings about ontology. It also addresses such topics as the critical role of data in digital transformation, techniques like tagging data with metadata, organizational challenges for effective data, and the role of data in the customer experience. My favorite story in that regard involves granite countertop cleaners, but I won't spoil your suspense by relating it.

A great strength of the book is that it is replete with such examples from Earley's experience and the work of his consulting firm. He has worked with companies across many different industries—many of them very large and successful firms—that had problems with their data in the context of AI. His firm has built successful and sophisticated intelligent agent or chatbot systems for both customers and employees.

I have written two books on AI and read many more, and I do not know of any books that have such useful and detailed advice on the relationship between data and successful conversational AI systems. If that's what you need, read on.

Thomas H. Davenport

President's Distinguished Professor at Babson College, Research Fellow at MIT Initiative on the Digital Economy, and author of Only Humans Need Apply *and* The AI Advantage

CHAPTER 1

THE PROMISE AND
THE CHALLENGE OF AI

How will the future be different as a result of artificial intelligence? And what must your company do to stake its claim on that future? These questions are on the minds of every forward-thinking business leader, and they should be on your mind, too, whatever industry you are in. This book aims to provide you with answers to these questions so you can stop wondering what to do and get busy doing it.

When the web came along in the mid-90s, it transformed the behavior of customers and remade whole industries. New powerhouses like Amazon and Google arose and challenged established media and bricks-and-mortar retail companies. Even as Tower Records, Borders, and dozens of newspapers succumbed to the pressures of the digital revolution and the internet marketplace, other major players of that era—such as Home Depot and *The Wall Street Journal*—learned to thrive by capitalizing on the web's vast new marketing reach and economies of scale.

AI has been called the greatest invention in human history—greater than fire, greater than the Industrial Revolution.[1] That's hyperbole, but the magnitude of the change is indeed vast. AI is "reinventing the way we invent"[2] and will usher in a new era of human capabilities.

We *are* at an inflection point in human history.

That's all well and good, you say. AI will change everything really soon—I think—but meanwhile my customers want lower prices while venture-funded startups are trying to steal those customers from me, my call center agents are overloaded with support calls, my competition is getting more challenging . . . and it takes my organization weeks to onboard new products. Meanwhile, inside the company, my employees continually complain that they "can't find their stuff." How are we going to take advantage of all of this great new technology if they can't locate the marketing plan that worked so well last quarter or they have to recreate procedure documents yet again because they don't know which ones are up to date?

The question for realizing the promise of AI is, How do you get there from here? At the 30,000-foot level, there are books explaining how AI will solve world hunger, while others are saying it will throw half of all humans out of work. At the other end of the spectrum, there are technical books that require a PhD in data engineering to understand. My intention is to be more helpful. This book will help you address practical issues and show you how to make the incremental changes that will prepare your company to deliver AI's promise of revolutionary change. It will help you take the necessary steps down the path to transforming how your customers relate to your company. I will help you avoid career-limiting errors and I will show you how to set your BS detector for AI claims to "high." I will help you catch this wave, rather than be crushed by it. This book contains a number of practical approaches for solving information problems. Without them, your AI will not work the way it needs to for your organization.

To understand what it will feel like to be a customer in this new world, let's look in on a day in the life of one of those customers, an executive of a hypothetical manufacturer using hypothetical products from well-known brands, just a few years from now. (While Merrill Lynch, Grainger, and Expedia are real companies and may be working on chatbots, the bots in this scenario are invented representations of a fictional possible future.)

LIFE IN AN AI-POWERED WORLD

Allen Perkins feels powerful.

It is January of 2024. Perkins is the senior manufacturing manager for Hecker Heavy Locomotives, an Ohio company with a growing reputation for making the world's highest-quality passenger train locomotives. Perkins feels powerful not because of the massive machines he helps to build, but because of the web of information that accommodates his every decision, whether at work or at home. His adept management of artificially intelligent resources has earned him a promotion, and now he must deliver.

As his self-driving Tesla heads for his office, Perkins can use the time to focus on his personal finances. The markets have been volatile, and he wonders if he should make any changes in his portfolio. He taps a button on the Tesla's center console and speaks.

"Get me to Meryl," he says.

"Meryl here," a woman's voice answers. Meryl is the bot for Bank of America/Merrill Lynch, where Perkins's investments reside. "What can I do for you today, Allen?"

"I'm a little nervous about the choppiness in the stock market. How am I doing these days?"

"Your net worth with us has risen by 2% in the last twelve months," Meryl answers. "While the market has been going up and down by an average of half a percent a day for the last few weeks, we've got you in a pretty conservative mix of investments. So the value of your investments hasn't been moving quite as much."

"Are we on track with the kids' college funds?"

"The investments for Ray and Sarah are likely to be sufficient to cover their tuition when they start college a few years from now," Meryl replies. "I've been shifting those assets into more conservative positions because they'll be in college so soon."

"Is there a lot of cash in my account?"

"We're about 10% in cash right now, Allen."

"Can we invest some of that?"

"Sure, we could. But you're going to need cash for that remodeling project you told me about last month. There's not a whole lot lying around in your checking account right now. And don't forget you just bought a bunch of new suits to go along with your promotion."

"OK, leave the cash where it is," Perkins says. "But let's check back on this in a month or so. I may be getting a bonus."

"Sure thing, Allen," Meryl says. "Talk to you in February."

Perkins's Tesla pulls into a parking space near the front door and he strides into his office. After checking his emails, he begins the most important work of the day: selecting a new component supplier for six new locomotives for the California High-Speed Rail project.

He opens a browser and navigates to GraingerBot, a chatbot available from Grainger, one of the biggest suppliers to manufacturing companies like Hecker. He starts typing.

Hello, GraingerBot.

Hello, Mr. Perkins.

Let's continue ordering parts for the California locomotives.

I have opened the file that we were working on yesterday. What would you like to work on?

Suspensions. Can you locate the suspension springs in the 3-D model?

I see eight helical springs that are 36.3 centimeters high.

What suppliers make springs like that?

Several make the chromium-vanadium steel specified in the drawings. But I've found some research that shows a new material may allow you to get more durability for the same cost. Shall I show it to you?

Please.

The GraingerBot pops up a twelve-page document from the *International Journal of Engineering Research.* Perkins reviews it and confirms that the GraingerBot is correct—this new material appears to be superior for this part. He resumes the typed conversation.

How many manufacturers can make this part from the new material?

Seven. That includes one parts supplier that you've already used for six other components; they'll give you a discount if your order pushes the total over $35,000.

Get quotes on those, GraingerBot. And get a few quotes on the chromium-vanadium springs, too, just in case we decide to stick with them.

I'll have those answers for you by 12:30. I'm connecting with the bots for those parts suppliers right now.

Perkins signs off. This has been productive. While he would have liked to complete the order for the springs now, it looks like he might have found a more durable material—and with Hecker now doing the maintenance as well as the manufacturing, that would save the company some serious cash.

Perkins turns his attention to an upcoming business trip. He is going to Sacramento to meet with the California transit team that is buying these locomotives. He puts on his Bluetooth headset and connects with Pete, his virtual travel agent from Expedia.

"Pete, get me a flight to Sacramento for next Tuesday."

"Sure thing, Mr. Perkins," says Pete. "When will you be returning?"

"Wednesday or Thursday. Look into both."

"OK. I'm checking American Airlines, because that's where you have the best status. I have 18 possible flight combinations. I'm afraid you will have to connect."

"Yeah, nobody flies nonstop Dayton to Sacramento! Don't route me through Chicago or Denver. Too much snow this time of year," Perkins says.

"That leaves nine possible flights. Is this for the two o'clock meeting with the California rail project team?"

Perkins remembers that he has given Pete access to his schedule, and realizes the bot is figuring out flights that fit his existing appointments.

"Yes, that's the meeting," he says.

"I'll make sure your flight gets in well before that. I see that one of your manufacturing partners is based in that area. In fact, it looks like GraingerBot is connecting with them right now to check on some springs. Should I set up a meeting?"

"Definitely. See if you can get me in to see them on Wednesday. I'd love to tour that facility."

"Do you want to take a red-eye back?"

"No way," Perkins replies. "Better make it Thursday morning."

"OK, I see the best roundtrip now. It leaves at 7 a.m. on Tuesday and your return flight takes off at 8 a.m. on Thursday. Will you be staying at the Hilton at the airport again? They've got the best price for a three-star hotel."

"Go ahead and book it. And get me a rental car, too. Thanks, Pete."

Perkins muses for a moment about travel reservations. All that clicking and checking he used to do. . . . But the bots pulled it together in a way he never could have before. Perkins likes the feeling of control that gives him—and the efficiency, too.

Perkins doesn't need to think about what is going on behind the scenes to make investing, manufacturing, and travel so much easier than they used to be. But every time he interacts with a bot, he is drawn deeper into an ecosystem of artificial intelligence. He has grown to rely on the companies that were making his life easier—those that were ready with AI. Everybody else is working with those companies, too, and the competition is slowly fading into irrelevance.

WHAT IT TAKES TO SUCCEED IN THE AI FUTURE

We're on the verge of the future that Allen Perkins lives in. But not every company will make it into that future.

We know how we want our companies to work. Enterprises ought to be customer-focused, responsive, and digital. They should deliver to each employee and customer exactly what they need, at the moment they need it. The data and technology to do this are available now.

Any big company is likely to have an abundance of technology. It has systems for customers, inventory, and products, along with websites and mobile apps. These systems are spitting out data all day long. Within that data is exactly the information needed to make a business more responsive. The problem is, the data is often not used as it could (and should) be.

Artificial intelligence ought to take that data and turn it into effective execution, just as it did for Allen Perkins. IBM's Watson and Amazon's Alexa seem pretty smart. But despite the billions of dollars spent so far on bots and other tools, AI continues to stumble. Why can't it magically take all that data and make an enterprise run faster and better? Why can't it deliver the experience that Allen Perkins would expect?

Our organizations are up to their eyeballs in technology, and every venture capitalist believes that yet another tool is what the industry needs. But even after multiple generations of investments and billions of dollars of digital transformations, organizations are still struggling with information overload, with providing excellent customer service, with reducing costs and improving efficiencies, with speeding the core processes that provide a competitive advantage. Why is this happening? Because the foundational principles that I will discuss throughout this book are ignored, given short shrift, deprived of resources, or considered an afterthought. The elements that are required to make the shiny new technologies live up to their promise require hard work that is not sexy and shiny. There are new tools and approaches that make these efforts more efficient, and ways to embed new approaches to dealing with information and data, but they still require discipline, focus, attention, and resources.

Perhaps your organization has experimented with AI. An executive at a major life insurance company recently told me, "Every one of our competitors and most of the organizations of our size in other industries have spent at least a few million dollars on failed AI initiatives." In some cases, technology vendors have sold "aspirational capabilities"—functionality that was not yet in the current software. But in most cases, the cause of the failure was overestimation of what was truly "out-of-the-box" functionality, overly ambitious "moonshot" programs that were central to major digital transformation efforts but unattainable in practice, or existing organizational processes incompatible with new AI approaches. Leadership may have bought into the promise of AI without adequate support from the front lines of the business. Technology organizations may not have been adequately prepared to take on new tools and significant process changes. In many cases, the technology may have been potentially capable of functionality, but the data, locked in siloed systems, was inaccessible, poorly structured, or improperly curated.

Many AI programs attempt to deal with unstructured information and replicate how humans perform certain tasks, such as answering support questions or personalizing a customer experience. That may require pulling information from multiple systems and weaving together multiple processes, including some that have historically been done manually. To deliver on its promise, AI needs the correct "training data," including content, metadata (descriptions of data), and operational knowledge. If that data and corresponding outcomes are not available in a way that the system can process, then the AI will fail.

How do you make those data and outcomes accessible to power the AI? That's where the ontology comes in.

THE CENTRAL ROLE OF THE ONTOLOGY

AI cannot start with a blank page. It leverages information structures and architecture. Artificial intelligence *begins* with information architecture. In other words, there is no AI without IA.[3]

AI works only when it understands the soul of your business. It needs the key that unlocks that understanding. That's the science behind the magic of AI. The key that unlocks that understanding is an *ontology*: a representation of what matters within the company and makes it unique, including products and services, solutions and processes, organizational structures, protocols, customer characteristics, manufacturing methods, knowledge, content and data of all types. It's a concept that, correctly built, managed, and applied, makes the difference between the promise of AI and delivering sustainably on that promise.

Simply put, an ontology reveals what is going on inside your business—it's the DNA of the enterprise.

An ontology is a consistent representation of data and data relationships that can inform and power AI technologies. In different contexts, it can include or become expressed as any of the following: a data model, a content model, an information model, a data/content/information architecture, master data, or metadata. But an ontology is more than each of these things in themselves. However you describe it, the ontology is essential to and at the heart of AI-driven technologies. To be clear, an ontology is not a single, static thing; it is never complete, and it changes as the organization changes and as it is applied throughout the enterprise.

The ontology is the master knowledge scaffolding of the organization. Multiple data and architectural components are created from that scaffolding, so without a thoughtful and consistent approach to developing, applying, and evolving the ontology, progress in moving toward AI-driven transformation will be slow, costly, and less effective. The components of the ontology are the ones we have mentioned: metadata structures, reference data, taxonomies, controlled vocabularies, thesaurus structures, lexicons, dictionaries, and master data correctly designed into the information technology ecosystem. The ontology is at the heart of the information design of the AI-powered enterprise and it becomes an asset of ever-increasing value.

While it is true that some algorithms can operate on data without an external structure, they still operate based on the features programmed into the underlying system. Even if there is no structure to the raw data, the algorithm will perform better if more of that structure is provided as an input—as an element of the ontology.

Ontologies are a complex topic. For that reason, I've dedicated a whole chapter to them: chapter 2. For now, just know that the ontology is what makes the difference in whether AI drives your enterprise forward or just adds to the incompatible welter of technology that is slowing you down.

ORGANIZATIONS ARE LIKE BIOLOGICAL ORGANISMS

I like the economist Gareth Morgan's metaphor likening businesses to organisms living in an ecosystem competing for resources.[4] It explains so much about why AI projects go wrong.

An organism's survival depends on (a) perception of information from the environment (b) correct interpretation and processing of that information, and (c) communication of information as signals that are sent quickly to the parts of the organism that "need to know" and act. This process requires efficient internal communications and coordination so that resources can be deployed in response to the signal for a swift and appropriate response.

Just like organisms in an ecosystem, businesses consume energy and resources and then create solutions and structures from those resources. The resources and results primarily take the form of information:

businesses are living organisms that consume and produce information. Their agility and adaptability depend on how effectively they metabolize that information.

For example, consider how our brains and bodies act on signals from the environment and interact with the world based on integrated information systems and feedback loops. When the amygdala (the part of the brain that registers fear or desire) identifies a threat, our sympathetic nervous system (which controls the "fight or flight" response) reacts in a highly orchestrated way. Another part of the brain—the hypothalamus—instantly sends a signal throughout the body. This triggers the adrenal glands to release adrenaline, which causes a cascade of responses that we are all familiar with from instances when we are startled, such as if a car speeds toward us as we step into a crosswalk. The heartbeat increases, breathing becomes more rapid, and we feel a surge of energy. The brain also executes a new computational task—coming up with the appropriate expletives to hurl at the driver—and anticipates likely outcomes (Yikes, is he getting out of his car?). Everything works holistically to respond efficiently and effectively to the stimulus, with very little friction.

It's easy to see why holistic and synchronized information flows are essential to survival. It would not do us much good if the brain had to rummage around our past memories of speeding cars and try to decide what to do. The same kind of holistic, synergistic, and simultaneously integrated flow of information is also what's needed to create transformative AI solutions of the sort we read about in Allen Perkins's story.

For an organization to function effectively, the systems for managing information and the processes for supporting information flows have to be flexible, adaptable, and responsive to market conditions. This is the "organic" nature of the organization.

In this organic view of the enterprise, the subsystems within companies, such as business units and departments, are analogous to the organs and biological systems in an organism. For these departments and functions to operate smoothly, their information needs have to be met. Marketing needs product specifications and features from the enterprise's engineering and product development functions. Sales requires support collateral and leads from marketing. Finance needs customer and order information from sales. Each of these functions needs reliable information to achieve its objectives.

Let's take the metaphor further. Why does it matter how effectively information flows in the company? Because the entire economy is a collection of organizations interacting in an ecosystem that follows the same principles that living biological systems follow. Just as in a biological ecosystem, the economy is a collection of entities operating in interdependent networks and competing for resources. In the case of business, those resources include time, money, talent, expertise, and the attention that ultimately comes from customers. Information flows—both within companies and in the broader economy—are at the center of this activity. Our society and its associated value chains, knowledge networks, and information flows are endlessly complex, interrelated, and nuanced, containing layers of systems upon systems at every level of interaction—from the most basic to the most mind-bogglingly complex.

Just as environments select for the strongest organisms in a particular set of conditions, so too does the economy select for the strongest and best-adapted organization in a particular market sector or niche. Many companies will go extinct as our economic environment continues to change. Yours can be one of the survivors, but only if it can adapt to those changing conditions.

SERVING CUSTOMERS EFFECTIVELY IS WHAT MAKES COMPANIES SUCCESSFUL

In biological systems, organisms succeed because they can find food and reproduce (grow). What is the analogy to this in business? It is serving customers. The enterprise that best serves the customer grows and thrives at the expensive of its competitors.

While customer-centricity is ostensibly a major focus of most enterprises today, in many cases the understanding of customer experience is immature, or is siloed in parts of the organization that "own" one aspect of customer service or customer support. That understanding of customers is largely disconnected from other critical processes. Using the *entire* customer journey as the anchor to programs—whether traditional information projects or cutting-edge machine learning programs—is critical to success. (I describe the customer journey in more detail in chapter 3.) The customer journey is not a single thing; it encompasses everything that the enterprise does, directly and indirectly, that impacts how its customers perceive their interactions and the value they receive. If a system or process cannot be tied to value for the customer (whether that customer is an internal consumer of information or an external paying-end customer), then it cannot be justified.

The real challenge to delivering value occurs when systems are part of the foundation for a capability that can impact the customer, but customers don't interact directly with those systems. Infrastructure programs are notoriously difficult to justify because of the lack of a clear line of sight to their impact on the customer; but when the infrastructure is faulty, serving the customer becomes slow, complicated, or impossible. When the customer is internal, this is even more of a challenge. (I will discuss the "internal" customer in chapter 8 on productivity, but the same principles largely apply in that context.) In chapter 3, I will define an approach and framework that will show you how to establish the linkage between systems and customer value and how to communicate the value any project in the enterprise has for the customer experience.

Some of these linkages are indirect. Others may be difficult to measure. However, they all should be traceable to activities and capabilities that produce customer value. Everything that an organization does needs to improve how it serves its customers and how the enterprise creates value; each program, project, investment, and decision should be linked to a metric that impacts the customer's perceptions of their experience and the value that they receive from their relationship with your organization. High-fidelity customer journeys (described in chapter 3) are the key to successful AI initiatives such as personalization and campaign optimization, which can transform the customer experience and deliver new efficiencies and capabilities from human augmentation and machine-enabled automation.

AGILITY AND ADAPTABILITY DETERMINE COMPETITIVE SUCCESS

It's not enough to be customer-centric. You must also operate quickly. Speed matters in the biological world (ask the early bird that gets the worm), and increasingly, speed and agility are the factors that differentiate successful enterprises from those that lose the race.

Every enterprise needs to adapt to changing conditions in the environment (including customer needs, competition, changes in technology, and macroeconomic shifts). The faster it can do so, the better it can serve customers and beat the competition. Getting products and solutions to market faster requires faster decision-making, faster feedback, faster iterations, and faster experimentation—and each of these requires faster information flows. Friction in processes, systems, and technologies impede the flow of information and therefore slows decision-making.

Unfortunately, the speed of business change is inherently faster than the speed at which complex enterprise systems can adapt. When systems have data in incompatible formats, or when that data is of poor quality due to manual processes and conversions, making the data compatible adds another layer of friction. Friction comes from many sources, including out-of-date information, lost content, incorrect or poor quality data, disconnected processes, incorrect measures, inconsistent communications, excessive meetings, overcommunication, and undercommunication. These sources of friction become impediments that inexorably slow information flows.

The challenge is that this happens in myriad incremental ways that are difficult to pinpoint, hard to quantify, and challenging to remediate. In most cases, this friction is accepted as business as usual or as the nature of the beast—"that's just the way things work." Or leaders decide that it is too expensive to fix and that adding some people to deal with the issue is the most economical (short-term) solution. The problem is that these incremental friction points, which individually do not make sense to address, are never considered as a whole—or if they are, they become too difficult and disruptive (not to mention costly) to tackle.

AI projects can provide incremental value by addressing these friction points. As Tom Davenport points out in his book *The AI Advantage*, AI and cognitive technologies augment human work and provide incremental value in many areas that accumulate to transform the enterprise.

Since organizations operate on information flows, the leadership of the enterprise needs to invest in the things that smooth, speed, and improve the efficiency of those flows. The problem is knowing what to invest in and how to harvest the benefits of investments. When executed correctly and based on a solid ontology, investments in data and configuration of the infrastructure through which data flows can lead to enormous value. One implementation that I will describe led to a $50 million annual savings from a $1 million investment. Another digital transformation, the core of which was built on investments in data, data architecture, and technology infrastructure, led to an $8 billion increase in market value from a $25 million investment in the foundational principles that I will discuss throughout this book.

Things are accelerating as new entrants arrive that are "born digital"— like Airbnb in the lodging business, Tesla in the automotive business, Google in media, or Uber in transportation. Such businesses have the luxury of reinventing the end-to-end value chain and building integrated processes that speed the flow of information and data using a green field/ clean sheet approach. It's a huge competitive advantage—like the speed that warm-blooded animals tapped during the evolution process to allow them to compete effectively with sluggish reptiles.

THE PROBLEMS THAT KEEP BUSINESSES FROM MOVING FASTER

Businesses know all of this. So why can't they get out of their own way? Let's review the three most common problems that stop corporate organisms from competing effectively in the economic ecosystem.

Problem One: Friction and Siloed Communication
Companies, especially those born in the pre-digital age, are created not

holistically but in a piecemeal fashion. Departments and functions operate independently. When a signal comes in, it doesn't instantly go everywhere it needs to go; it must be routed from one place to the next. Internal communications, databases, and other systems act as messengers to relay a signal throughout the organization. Imagine if the brain told the legs to run, then the legs had to go and ask the adrenals for some energy to execute the movement, and the adrenals had to then go and verify that the decision was authorized by the brain. Before you could move, you'd be run over.

In most companies, there is a lot of friction along the way. Challenges like differing or competing priorities, incomplete understanding of the big picture, dropping the ball, and double-checking all create drag as information makes its way through the organization. That's not fatal when the information being handled is human brain–sized, which is why manual systems and processes have worked for companies so far. But it collapses under the weight of the enormous data sets required for AI and high-tech interventions and for the rapid response required in a digital economy. The key to making AI work is reducing that friction and speeding the flow of information.

Problem Two: Incompatible Data and Language

From time to time, every organization needs to do housekeeping on its digital working files, archived data, and other forms of information. But how do you do that consistently and cleanly when every process or function uses different terminology or a different way of organizing things? Too often, the various groups within an organization are speaking their own languages—or at least their own dialects. Information is stored differently, and teams use different terminology that speaks to their needs and processes but that doesn't consider the broader organization. This leads to manual workarounds and to information getting lost in translation. As I'll show in more detail in chapter 8, technology companies designed collaboration tools to make it easy for people to create and use data, not to make the data effective in the context of a corporation. The result is an information environment full of poorly designed, fragmented, and disconnected systems. It's not a surprise that many of these systems don't share a consistent set of data language.

Problem Three: Junk Data

Entropy is another fact of the physical world mirrored by the digital one. Every system tends from order to disorder, and reestablishing order requires energy. We all experience this in our day-to-day lives: our desk gets messy and we need to put energy into organizing it. The house gets dirty and requires energy to clean. Information gets messy, too, and organizing it also takes energy. For example, we have to delete or label our email messages, put files into folders, or cleanse a document repository of any out-of-date material. Productive activity seeks to reduce the amount of disorder and therefore reverse the entropy of a local system through the application of energy.

Most organizations today are drowning in junk data as the incredible volume of digital information produced massively outstrips the energy available to manually practice good data hygiene habits. This book will show you how to get your digital house in order so the robots can keep it clean for you.

TAGGING UNCLOGS THE FLOW OF INFORMATION

Tagging is a central part of what makes ontologies able to speed the performance of enterprises.

A manager's objective is to give employees direction; provide resources and the information necessary to solve problems; and allow creativity, hard work, and expertise to generate solutions that have value to customers and the marketplace. All of this activity is fueled by knowledge, and the way that knowledge flows through the organization's networks is key to its efficiency and effectiveness. Important information needs to be flagged, tagged, and held up as meaningful. This information includes, for example, the needs of customer segments based on market research, solutions to engineering problems, the current quarter's strategic objectives, and the features of a new product and how it is different from the competition. These are all signals that need to be separated from the noise of day-to-day communications.

The separation comes from tagging that identifies the information as important. Then someone can take that important piece of data and use it to solve their problem. (As I will describe later, that tagging, or separation of signal from noise, can happen at multiple levels—from manual information and data curation performed by humans through AI and machine learning approaches.)

Not having the right tags causes meaning to be lost—the noise drowns out the signal. Inefficiencies in information flows, lack of consistent terminology, and systems that don't talk to one another bog down operations and create waste. We've all seen what this looks like and felt the pain: for example, folder structures on shared drives that are redundant or nonsensical, or that contain labels meaningful only to individuals ("Joe—Important docs"), along with excessive translation and manual manipulation of data because systems do not use the same terminology or data standards.

Constraints can be liberating. The enterprise adapts and thrives when simple tagging rules that speed information flows create value through emergent behaviors within the system. Artificial intelligence is a mechanism that, properly designed and applied, speeds information flow and enables those emergent efficiencies, including tagging. It can therefore help every part of your organization do its job more quickly, efficiently, and consistently. To succeed over the long term, you must allocate resources in a sustainable way to build AI-ready assets of increasing value—including the ontologies and data structures that will serve all aspects of the business. The business needs to use continuous feedback to develop these structures, apply them to the production of value, fine-tune systems and processes, and adjust and make course corrections.

What does such a solution look like? There are three areas in which your company needs to rethink its resources, focus, and attention so it can exploit the power of artificial intelligence. My systematic plan that you can follow to prepare for an AI-powered enterprise includes these elements:

1. **Data.** This includes how data is architected, managed, curated, and applied. You must wrangle your messy and inconsistent data into a refined asset for high-precision, high-leverage activities.

The organizations with the most agile architecture, highest-quality data, and best algorithms for applying that data to address customer and employee needs will win.

2. **Technology.** To deliver personalized experiences to customers (whether internal or external), appropriate technologies must scale processes by relying on detailed enterprise knowledge. They must also remain adaptable as tools, approaches, and information sources evolve and change.

3. **Operationalization.** Just as with the reengineering transformation of the '80s, these improvements require a commitment to new forms of organizational discipline, with new accountabilities and metrics. This includes rethinking how the organization delivers value through end-to-end digital processes.

Let's examine each of these three requirements in detail.

Data: The DNA of the Organization

Most executives reflexively nod their heads when discussing the value of data. "Data is extremely valuable to our enterprise," they say. "We are undergoing a data-driven digital transformation." According to this thinking, good data is good, and bad data is not good. But when it comes to creating ontologies—which means fixing the foundational data issues in a sustainable way—and they see the price that the enterprise needs to pay, these same executives deprioritize projects like fixing the data-quality issues. "It's not *that* valuable" is the message that is communicated to the organization. Because data issues are not addressed properly at a fundamental level, tens or hundreds of millions of dollars will be spent on digital transformations that will fail in the long run.

High quality, findable, and usable data is an essential part of the AI-powered enterprise. Machine learning can find patterns in unstructured data, but it cannot make sense of information that is of poor quality or missing. Data needs to be contextualized; you cannot simply "point the

AI at all of your data" as some in the industry have claimed. Depending on the application it can also require curation and structuring for ingestion into many classes of AI tools, including cognitive systems. More structure will allow the algorithm to function more precisely.

For cognitive applications such as chatbots, the required training data is the same information that humans need but with a different structure and format. Predictive modeling AI needs training data to build recognition patterns and examples to learn from. Data is more important than the algorithms, and bad data will provide bad results.

Perhaps technology vendors have assured you that their AI will fix your data. That's optimistic.[5] In fact, many of the AI technologies on the market are actually Band-Aid solutions that try to make up for our sins in data and content curation. Because of a lack of resourcing and poor data hygiene, organizations are paying the price, and that price includes trying to fix data with AI, even though it's the organization's own data processes and governance that are at fault. Yes, AI can help, but there's more to it than what the large systems integrators are telling you.

The way to fix this problem is to harmonize your data with consistent data structures and models, creating a Rosetta Stone that helps your systems communicate and provides a waypoint so your AI can navigate your messy, fast moving, diverse, unstructured and structured data universe. That Rosetta Stone is the ontology.

While many master data types are challenging and prone to failure, the approaches we will discuss will increase your chances of success and will move the needle on multiple projects. Rather than striving for a "single source of truth," the goal is to increase the consistency and quality of information so that there is less friction throughout the organization. There will be differences in organizing principles and structures, but rather than being accidental, they will be intentional. The ontology becomes a reference point to inform where information structures need to be harmonized and where there can be (intentional) differences.

Technology: Having the Right Tools to Serve Customers (Internal and External)

Choosing the right technologies and integrating them successfully is a critical part of building out your AI program. It is not simply about adopting machine learning tools and technologies that are labeled as "AI," because, these days, every technology vendor says what it does is "AI."

Forget AI for a moment. Recognize that knowledge workers of all types, from engineers to marketers to designers, interact with technologies to accomplish their day-to-day tasks that directly or indirectly support the ways that customers interact. These workers work with systems on their smartphones, laptops, tablets, and intelligent connected appliances and devices. Having the correct technologies integrated in an adaptable, flexible way allows for processes and functionality to evolve in parallel with customer needs and the competitive landscape. Having the right tools enabled and enhanced by AI to serve each stage of the customer journey makes the business run faster, better, and in a way more aligned with customer needs.

The real challenge is that, if you're like most organizations, you probably have a patchwork of systems, technologies, and processes that have evolved organically over time. These have inevitably led to messy and complex integrations, manual processes, and workarounds that make things more difficult in the long run. Some people refer to this as technical debt—the shortcuts taken in the hope of deploying technology more quickly. But just like debt in the real world, this approach is costly, and you have to pay for the shortcuts, sometimes at interest rates that would be classified as usury if they were on a consumer's credit card. What appears to save time and money in the short run, when accumulated over numerous projects and multiple years, hamstrings the business and prevents adaptation as each leader kicks the can down the road for the next person to deal with. And now that person is you.

Adapting legacy systems built on a patchwork of different platforms and technologies to changing conditions is a slow and laborious process. But it's essential to making the tools and technology effective and the data actionable.

Operationalization: Leading with Vision and Managing Change

Every project, whether a departmental reorganization or a ten-year growth plan, begins with vision and strategy. What is different about an AI strategy is that the possibilities are entirely new, which means you will have to look at the business and customer relationships in entirely new ways. Whenever there are fundamental shifts in technologies, what becomes possible is not just an extension of where we are but an entirely new way of being or interacting. If you don't know what is possible, you cannot think about those possibilities and consider what they mean for the business.

In the early days of the web, organizations were just thinking about how they might use it to get their marketing materials in front of more consumers. They were not thinking about the capabilities of iPhones to carry the equivalent of shelves of compact discs or every photo album owned, or about what it might be like for consumers to carry a digital bank teller in their pocket. They certainly weren't imagining entirely new business models like ridesharing services. Those capabilities evolved and required the concurrent evolution of various supporting components. Some organizations were ahead of the curve and disrupted industries, while others underinvested and were left behind. Still others overinvested before the market was ready and wasted resources.

The other operational challenge is that the different parts of the organization—internal systems and processes—move at different speeds and change at different rates. For example, enterprise resource planning (ERP) systems are relatively stable and do not change frequently. A long development cycle is required to add or evolve core modules and functionality. At the other end of the spectrum are social media applications and programs that change extremely rapidly. Inherent mismatches in these clock speeds in the organization exacerbate the data and architecture challenges (see Figure 1-1). As the AI landscape evolves, governance structures, processes, and decision-making need to allow for adaptability and to support cultural change that will be part of the new organization dynamics.

The challenge is that business always changes at a faster pace than the internal IT organization can support, and technology changes faster than

Figure 1-1: Varying Clock Speeds throughout the Organization

CLOCK SPEEDS   SLOW → FAST

Application	ERP, Accounting	Ecommerce	Knowledge Repositories	Web Content	Site Search	Email Marketing	SEO	Social Media Marketing	Chat Virtual Agents	Chat Live Agents
Analytics	Financial reporting	Shopping patterns, segmentation	Content utilization	Web metrics, click streams	Search analytics	Promotions engagement	Rankings	Sentiment analysis	Learning algorithm, customer feedback	Quality, customer satisfaction
Architecture	PIM, MDM	PIM, customer master data	Knowledge content models	Static and dynamic web content models	Merchandise categories	Latest attribute models	Editorial standards, attribute precoordination	Product thesaurus	Component content modeling, expertise models	Knowledge and expertise models
Driver	Stability reporting	Scalability	Support management	Personalization, dynamic content	Product/solution findability	Outbound engagement	Inbound engagement	Community engagement	Support cost containment	Customer retention
Governance Challenges	Mission criticality, high cost of change	Cross functional constituencies	Tacit knowledge capture, curation standards	Model immaturity, technical complexity, flawed construct	Merchandizing vs. usability vs. SEO	Departmental merchandizing vs. objectives vs. customer attention	Dynamic, fast evolving, continuous tuning/decision-making	Compliance and authority vs. responsiveness	Resource intensity of process	Cost and logistics of live agents

humans and organizational processes can absorb. But even if IT could keep up with the best-of-breed tools for the business, people would not have the capacity to absorb change that quickly.

Decisions about the pace of change need to be methodical and data driven, not based solely on opinions. A metrics-driven framework for managing decision-making and resource allocation removes guesswork and ensures that your investments will produce value. Sustainable, metrics-driven governance is the single determinant of successful AI programs. Throughout this book, and especially in chapter 10, I'll show you how to set up a governance playbook that can be updated and evolve as the capabilities of your AI-powered enterprise continue to mature.

Governance is built around organizational structure and reporting models, aspects that need to evolve and be updated as capabilities mature in AI-powered organizations. For example, old school "spray and pray" mass marketing approaches and skill sets need to be updated with data-driven digital marketing precision. The workforce will have a new makeup in the AI-powered enterprise, and just as machinery amplified physical human strengths, machine intelligence will amplify cognitive human strengths.

In this chapter, we began to explore in broad brushstrokes how your organization needs to transform foundational processes and further evolve fundamental capabilities as you embark on your AI-powered path forward. Decisions in each of the three areas—data, technology, and operationalization—need to be grounded in the organization's strategy for how it will serve the customer, and must be based on data-driven approaches, not trial and error.

Ontology Supports Everything

All of these elements—data, technology, and operationalization—relate to having consistent fundamental organizing principles reflected in the ontology. Ontologies capture more than data representations. These structures begin at the level of concepts that are important to the business and are then translated into processes, systems, navigational constructs, applications, and yes, data structures. In addition to allowing systems to talk to one another, these naming conventions, organizing constructs, conceptual relationships, and labels speed information flows; enable data, content, and information to be integrated; streamline end-to-end processes; permit the aggregation of data sources; and stimulate faster adaptability in a rapidly changing ecosystem. They allow for the contextualization of insights, the cataloguing of metrics, and the creation of feedback mechanisms for continual improvement.

In the end, the foundation of an enterprise ontology captures the intelligence of the organization and becomes the scaffolding that guides and optimizes information flows, powers and contextualizes insights from AI systems, and becomes the brains behind tools like chatbots and cognitive search.

COGNITIVE AI AND ONTOLOGIES

Many of the examples in this book are from a group of applications referred to as "cognitive" AI. This class of AI seeks to improve how humans interact with computers and requires an intentional approach to building out the underlying knowledge architecture—or, as we discuss throughout the book, the ontology.

There are other classes of machine learning and analytics types of AI whose algorithms may not depend as extensively on this knowledge engineering approach. However, I want to make two distinctions here. While this book focuses a great deal on cognitive types of AI, I will show how other types of AI that leverage a range of purely data-centric approaches (deep learning and neural networks, for example) can also work better with defined data structures—including knowledge architectures and ontologies.

For example, machine learning algorithms may not need an ontology to function, but applying the results to the business does require the consistency and efficiency provided by an ontology and the resulting knowledge architecture. Similarly, while a neural network may not require an ontology to perform the analysis, application of that analysis does.

Many of the approaches in this book are part of a technology-agnostic tool kit for making changes and improvements that lead to greater efficiencies, increased revenue, and greater differentiation in the marketplace. In many organizations, these approaches have not reached their full potential with current technology. Many of the problems that organizations are turning to AI for are in part due to the fact that the correct approaches have not been operationalized using existing technology. In other words, we are using AI (or trying to do so) to make up for our past sins in poor information hygiene. This is the nature of the industry—fast-changing tools and the inability to absorb and manage change effectively over generations of technology adoption. These approaches are even more critical in today's competitive landscape.

YOUR CHARGE FOR THE FUTURE

This is a practical book for CEOs, CMOs, and technology executives who want to transform their business to get a jump on the opportunities of the AI future. It's not just about the technology of AI. It's about how to manage the change, step by step. It's also about understanding where to get the money and where the quick wins are. In short, it's about learning what a business driven by ontology-powered artificial intelligence can do and how to make that happen.

Gaining this edge depends on establishing a foundation that includes pieces of the organizational and technology puzzle. Some of these are likely familiar—such as having the right people supported by the right tools and processes—but they will require new approaches, while others are entirely new (such as fresh ways of looking at how technology can support your customers). In some cases, the missing ingredients will be a new sense of discipline and an increased level of resourcing and commitment applied to known approaches to problems.

To get this edge, executives at your enterprise must create a vision that empowers AI to uniquely deliver your value proposition in support of your customers' experience, as well as a strategic plan for differentiating from your competitors. It will require developing new supporting processes and new competencies. I will outline the steps for benchmarking the maturity of each of these components and developing a plan for bridging gaps between where you are and where you need to be.

No twenty-first-century executive can succeed without understanding the role of AI in enterprises and how to make this technology work effectively. It's time to go beyond clouds, big data, and mobile fantasies. It's time to learn what it takes to power your enterprise with AI, now.

TAKEAWAYS FROM CHAPTER 1

In this chapter, I've described how AI will change the priorities for enterprises and how ontology can play a critical role in taking advantage of those opportunities. These are the main points in this chapter:

- AI marks an inflection point in human history.
- AI initiatives fail if the information they depend on is not properly structured.
- The ontology—a central repository of data terms and relationships—is what makes it possible for AI projects to succeed.
- Organizations are like organisms that depend on freely flowing information to survive.
- Agility and adaptability are the qualities that enable organizations to thrive in their broader ecosystem.
- The failure of holistic communication, data incompatibility, and junk data prevent companies from operating effectively.
- Tagging speeds the flow of information.
- Competitive advantage arises from the ways that organizations manage data, technology, and operationalization.

CHAPTER 2

BUILDING THE ONTOLOGY

I t costs over a billion dollars to build a "fab"—a semiconductor fabrication plant. At a price like that, it had better be up and running every possible hour of the day and night.

That's the problem that Applied Materials was struggling to manage. The company bills itself as "the leader in material engineering solutions used to produce virtually every new chip and advanced display in the world."[1] Its field service technicians are tasked with getting fabs running after problems have taken them offline. A down fab can cost its owner millions of dollars per day in lost business. If Applied Materials can't fix the problem quickly, it can end up on the hook for large penalties for failing to deliver on its service-level agreements—not to mention the damage to its reputation. It's a tough job, because semiconductor manufacturing processes are mind-bogglingly complex.

The know-how to keep a semiconductor fab running was spread throughout so many systems and processes within Applied Materials that up to 40% of its field service technicians' time was spent searching for the information they needed. Each plant was unique, so technicians needed to be able to locate the exact configuration of the equipment and procedures for any plant they were working in. The technicians work in dust-free, ultraclean environments and have elaborate and time-consuming processes for getting in and out of the plants. Some fabs even prohibit laptops or tablets, so technicians had to equip themselves with all the information they would need to solve any suspected problem before entering the plant.

Techs in this environment hedged their bets. They stocked their service vehicles with a wide variety of costly components, since not having the right part ready would lead to expensive additional delays. With 3,000 technicians in the field, this practice tied up tens of millions of dollars of inventory. Technicians became frustrated with attempting to locate service information across 14 different systems. Adding complexity, Applied Materials technicians working for one customer might have to maintain trade secrets for that customer, making it impossible for them to share all their information with other technicians.

Because this challenge threatened Applied Materials' brand and reputation, it's no surprise that the company tried to solve the problem on three separate occasions over a five-year period. All three attempts failed.

When Applied Materials brought my company in to help them, it became clear that the missing piece of the puzzle was how to organize diverse sources of information and unify the field technician experience. The key was finding ways to remove friction from the process of accessing exactly the information that was needed to solve the problem at hand. The magnitude of the problem seemed overwhelming because the company had so much information in so many places

We discussed the problem with one of the company's senior finance executives and outlined a solution, including an ontology and its subsidiary classification systems, known as taxonomies. The ontology would enable an AI-powered semantic search approach to organize the information for retrieval in the context that a technician would need when servicing a fabrication plant. The finance executive was dubious. He asked, "Why do we need taxonomies? Why don't we just get Google?"

I responded to his question with one of my own: "Do you have a chart of accounts for your finance organization?" Naturally, he did. So I asked, "Why don't you get rid of your chart of accounts and just get Google?" He laughed at such a preposterous idea. "Well," I responded, "what we want to build is like a chart of accounts for field service knowledge. It organizes information far better than a random search ever could. It will help the service people locate exactly what they need when they need it."

Consider the parallels for a moment. A chart of accounts organizes financial information for the accounting department and helps financial managers identify patterns in the numbers, make predictions about the future, and decide how to allocate resources. It provides the organizing principles to eliminate noise (such as irrelevant trends, anomalies, one-time events, or variations that are immaterial) and identify the important signals (trends in leading indicators like leads, success of promotions, effectiveness of advertising, and the impact of pricing changes). By providing a structured way to interpret corporate data, an ontology does for knowledge what the chart of accounts does for financial information.

We helped Applied Materials create the required ontology. Once the company had identified the multiple vocabularies, hierarchies, and relationships that comprised the ontology, the next step was to integrate it with the organization's technologies and apply it to the data. Various elements of the techs' experience needed to be designed to reflect the organizing principles of the ontology. Information about parts had to be tagged consistently: a part could not be called by a short name in one system and a stock number in another. Similarly, documents for troubleshooting had to be reclassified using a form of AI called "text analytics." Text analytics starts with example documents that have been tagged with information from the ontology, and then automatically applies the same tags to documents containing similar text.

It took a lot of work to implement the ontology in multiple systems and processes; incorporate it into workflows for content publication and approval; connect it to enterprise resource planning and digital asset management systems for visual part identification; and incorporate dozens of content libraries by ingesting them, automatically classifying content, and manually mapping relationships.

But once this work was complete, the architecture of the Applied Materials solution allowed field technicians to get the information they needed when they needed it. It helped them locate exactly what would be most useful by building logical groupings of content—surfacing the troubleshooting guides according to the process the tech would be troubleshooting, for example. The ontology enabled this by creating hierarchies—lists of concepts that are grouped logically—so that technicians could scan groupings and infer what they needed just by scanning the list. These hierarchies also allowed ambiguous queries to be clarified by asking questions about the parts and their applications. When they searched, the search results were grouped in a way that made sense to the technician—that fit their "mental model" of the problem and solution. These changes enabled the computer to give the technicians what they were seeking using the terms they were likely to be thinking about, rather than forcing them to root through masses of information with terms they might not recognize, organized in incompatible ways more accessible to computers than to humans. The result was a system that reduced the time that field technicians spent searching for information by half. The company estimated their savings at tens of millions of dollars per year. We enabled technicians to reduce their component and replacement part inventories and speed turnaround time for down fabrication plants.

And Applied Materials was able to live up to its reputation as a global leader in chip manufacturing, an essential element for its future business success.

WHY ONTOLOGIES MATTER

With the speed and effectiveness of the company at stake, building an ontology is not just an IT project. It is one that should matter to every CEO, CMO, and senior manager inside your company. Once you create the framework for the ontology, you can get more from your current investments in technology and apply emerging artificial intelligence techniques to drive your business. The ontology is the tool that teaches intelligent machines how your business runs. Without it, neither your systems nor your employees can truly understand how to access and organize the lifeblood of the business—the knowledge and information that provides value for your customers and the marketplace.

Ontologies are the secret weapon that will bring you victory in the battle for customers by transforming your company into an AI-powered enterprise. AI capabilities, supported by an ontology, will allow employees and the systems they use to function faster than ever before. It becomes a supercharger for your business. It helps you get products and services to market faster, serve customers more efficiently, and take advantage of quickly emerging opportunities in the marketplace. With the streamlined information flows that the ontology supports, both automated systems and humans can make better decisions.

Your ontology has the potential to accelerate your enterprise whether you work in retail, finance, health care, government, or any other sector. Once ontology-powered AI is in place, you can create:

- apps that suggest exactly the right product for each customer, based on history, context, inventory, and even the weather;
- tools that facilitate team meetings by suggesting the best solutions to your toughest problems;
- audience insights based not on superficial attributes like age but on people's secret motivations—along with product improvements that match those motivations;
- sales improvements that prioritize the leads that are most likely to generate more profit and make this determination more quickly than any other method now available;
- systems that predict when equipment will fail and proactively order maintenance before disaster strikes;
- virtual assistants that provide new capabilities and levels of service at a lower cost than previously possible; and
- bots that will help engineers solve challenging design and manufacturing problems by embodying the knowledge and expertise currently in the heads of your own experts—much as Applied Materials did.

Ontologies speed the information metabolism of the enterprise, forming the foundation for improved search, information management, and digital asset retrieval. They support mechanisms that improve communication among systems by acting as the Rosetta Stone of system integration.

Think of an ontology as a "knowledge chart of accounts" for marketing, engineering, finance, human resources, operations, and sales. Ontologies form the source of features for predictive analytics programs to improve their performance. They are the source of labels for navigational elements on an ecommerce website. They are the foundation for improved customer service since they contain knowledge of customers, problems, processes, and solutions. They provide improved business insights and intelligence by allowing for consistent analysis of products, revenue, costs, efficiencies, and metrics across the enterprise. They are the source of rights-management attributes and can help manage risks, exposures, and compliance.

Since the virtual world is entirely composed of data, victory will go to the organizations that can best control, manipulate, and exploit that data to attract customers and provide what those customers need, sometimes before they know they need it. Companies that do this will gain an edge in the AI future, while other companies will suffer competitive losses. Organizations cannot gain this edge and do so successfully, cost-effectively, and at scale without investing in the foundation of correctly designed and applied ontologies.

Why is it important to have a framework for organizing information? It can provide a competitive advantage based on how you envision your business, and you can differentiate your company by anticipating what your customers will need and by doing some of the heavy lifting for them. If your company is dependent on an individual for facilitating customer interactions, developing an effective ontology can buffer the impact if the individual leaves the company, or it can help you scale up to reach more customers.

In the rest of this chapter, I'll show you more about why ontologies matter, what they include, and how to build them.

UNDERSTANDING ONTOLOGIES

The term *ontology* refers to a domain of knowledge and the relationships among different concepts. The idea originally comes from philosophy, where ontology is the study of the nature of relations and being.

An ontology allows people and systems to understand relationships between concepts, just as a reference librarian can guide someone looking for information at a library. Someone seeking information may not know that valuable information about a subject can be found in a particular section of the library, or they may not know the best place to locate information that is less commonly available. This is similar to a book index, in which the "see also" entries guide the reader to another location that they might not have otherwise found or looked at.

Ontologies are built up from *taxonomies*. A taxonomy is a clearly defined hierarchical structure for categorizing information. Most people are familiar with the taxonomic classification system for animals, which includes invertebrates and vertebrates, and within the vertebrate category, birds, fish, reptiles, amphibians, and mammals. Similarly, the Dewey Decimal System is a taxonomy for categorizing books.

Taxonomies and ontologies have different purposes and uses. On a website for home products, a taxonomy could classify different departments such as lumber, tools, lighting, and appliances. Within each category, there could be subcategories such as hand tools and power tools, or refrigerators and stoves. In many cases, a taxonomy like this is sufficient for prospective customers to locate the items they need. However, a different level of sophistication can be achieved by overlaying this information with an ontology that adds richer information on products. This step would be required to respond to answers to questions such as "What are you trying to do?" If the answer is "Build a deck," then the store could present a suggested list that included supporting posts, decking lumber, deck screws, and a circular saw. Ontologies are a key ingredient for personalization and proactive marketing.

Ontologies Power Meaningful AI Capabilities

Ontologies begin as a holistic understanding of the language of the business and the customer, and are then designed into processes, applications, navigational structures, content, data models, and the relationships between concepts. They contain language variations, alternative spellings, translations, acronyms, and technical terms. They can describe "is-ness" and "about-ness"—this *is* a contract, it is *about* a services engagement, it is also *about* this vendor, for example. Ontologies can also support advanced capabilities to drive intelligent virtual assistants (bots). They can form the basis for inference engines—mechanisms to essentially answer a question that has not been preprogrammed into the bot. Bots powered by ontologies are faster to deploy, more scalable, and more cost-effective. Every aspect of business requires contextualized knowledge. The role of AI is to use the ontology to assist with this contextualization.

Here's an example scenario. Imagine a bot that answers questions about support problems.[2] For this to work, the bot needs to understand "intent"—the thing that the customer is trying to achieve. According to P.V. Kannan's AI book *The Age of Intent*, intent is the fundamental concept that drives all intelligent virtual agents. As Kannan defines it, "Intent is a determination of what a customer wants from an interaction with a company."[3] Once an AI determines that, it can supply an appropriate answer.

For example, a customer may not be able to connect a printer to the network. The troubleshooting bot can determine the customer's intent by first extracting the elements of the problem from the customer statement (called the utterance). "I cannot connect my printer to the network" contains the entity "printer" and "network" and the symptom "cannot connect." These elements are captured in the ontology along with synonyms and variations such as "unable to connect" or "not connecting." The intent, which the bot determines from this information, is "fix printer connection problem." Having determined the intent, the bot can walk the user through steps to solve the problem.

There is also a relationship between the symptom and a solution. The solution may require more information, which the bot can request from the customer. If the customer is logged in, the bot can look up information from the list of equipment they own. With this knowledge, the system can better identify and present the appropriate troubleshooting steps.

Each of these elements and the relationships that associate them form the knowledge graph—that is, a knowledge structure that contains related elements. You may be familiar with graphs of relationships from Facebook, where you may find new friends via different connections and follow those connections to another group of acquaintances based on factors like school, group membership, or interests. The movie database IMDb shows a similar set of graph relationships—you can choose a movie and look up the actors and directors to see which other movies they were in and which other actors they costarred with (useful for the game Six Degrees of Kevin Bacon[4]). The ontology becomes a knowledge graph for your organization, with the ability to answer a limitless number of questions over time.

How Ontologies and Taxonomies Worked at Applied Materials

In the case of Applied Materials, the taxonomies described every aspect of the chip manufacturing process, including these concepts:

Account	Geography	Partner	Solution
Application	Code	Platform	Status
Assembly	Security	Process	Subject
User	IP	Equipment	Technology
User Interest	Owner	Product	Units of Measure
Division	Language	Published To	Substrate
Document Type	Business Unit	Region	Sub-assembly
Plant	Configuration	Severity	

(Representative list of vocabularies. Concepts and names changed or omitted for confidentiality.)

More than 30 taxonomies described Applied Materials' world, and each taxonomy had a relationship to others—for example, Platform to Process, Assembly to Product, Partner to Region, Solution to Plant, or Severity to Status. These knowledge relationships could be mapped across content processes, allowing automated "reference librarians"—AI—to suggest resources and answers. These embedded relationships enriched the ontology to create a conceptual representation of a domain of knowledge. Taken together, all these taxonomies and all of their tens of thousands of terms and hundreds of thousands of relationships represent the semiconductor fabrication world: the knowledge domain of semiconductor fabrication equipment and methodologies.

These various organizing systems and vocabularies allowed all 14 different knowledge, content, and data systems to be unified under a semantic layer that translated inconsistent information structures into a common framework. This information architecture (or knowledge architecture) also guided the development of the technicians' experience: in this case, a search interface that let technicians navigate and retrieve their desired content using their mental model of how they thought about the problem.

This allowed many different types of users with different problems to locate what they needed in the context of their problems. Taxonomies functioned as navigational filters and provided "see also" constructs to guide technicians to their answer. They consolidated multiple information sources from disparate systems using terminology that was mapped through the ontology.

But the ontology did more than organize content and make queries more effective. It allowed the business to use AI approaches to classify content, identify security and IP issues, and automate some aspects of relationships among parts. The same ontology allows for analysis of anomalies, powers predictive maintenance, and identifies reliability issues and field usage patterns. The data it generates feeds upstream design and manufacturing processes to further improve products and innovate in semiconductor manufacturing—and to sustain Applied Materials' leadership in that space.

To Be a Source of Truth, Ontologies Must Be Comprehensive and Architectural

The ontology becomes a reference point for the organization that provides consistent naming, structures, and standards for applications and new technologies. It becomes a source of truth.

The ontology represents knowledge of the information structures and processes that drive information flows throughout the organization. The ontology is representative of products, services, processes, problems, tasks, intents, interests, user types, roles, content, data types, reference architectures, navigational structures, security classifications, applications, and every other entity, whether virtual or physical, in the enterprise. Any entity that someone interacts with can be part of the ontology.

But it's not just the elements of the data that count. The ontology reflects the architecture of that data. Data fundamentally has an architecture. It has to. Financial systems have charts of accounts. They have to. Algorithms can do a great deal with messy or missing data, but they must have a reference point containing the labels and information as a basis to find patterns. Pattern matching is inherently about classification, and the ontology forms the core structure for classifications of all sorts. Data dictionaries are part of the ontology; product catalogs are part of the ontology; financial charts of accounts are part of the ontology. The ontology represents the knowledge domain of the enterprise.

Before we can apply AI, we need two things: a core understanding of the business problem we are attempting to solve and a mechanism for identifying the important signals contained in the data. The ontology contains an overall set of labels for important business concepts—product names and descriptors. Marketing, for example, must track campaigns with categories for types of promotions, events, audiences, targets, personas, segments, assets, media, channels, and so on. Engineering uses classifications for techniques, materials, designs, problems, and specifications. Ecommerce websites allow customers to shop according to the classifications that are meaningful for them, such as brand, product type, size, color, and style.

If the ontology includes all of these different types of structures throughout the enterprise, then how can it be practical? The answer is that ontologies provide a consistent reference point to capture knowledge relationships. We make an ontology practical by building it piece by piece for particular purposes and to solve specific problems. The value of the ontology continues to increase as it is further refined and applied to organizational processes. Over time the ontology matures and is applied to solve customer problems and improve information flows.

Most organizations have costly and hard-to-manage problems with data quality. Because of this, technology integrations are brittle, making it slow to deploy changes to customer-facing functionality. This friction inexorably slows down the information metabolism and reduces the speed of product, service, and value creation. The ontology has the potential to vastly reduce these challenges.

The key to building a practical ontology is to focus on application and usage. Ontologies require consideration of focused problems and specific contexts. They become the North Star for new applications and systems, for new technology deployments, and for new products and services. Ontologies provide a guide point and are aspirational—they are never complete. If an ontology is not developed within an application-centric framework, it will become an academic exercise—a science project—with no end and little value.

ONLY A DELIBERATE APPROACH WILL WORK

Some AI experts actually frown on the idea of explicitly and carefully building an ontology to solve AI-related problems or power AI technologies. They imagine that the answer lies strictly in the data, and that statistical algorithms can analyze that data and automatically create a structure from it. But as you can imagine from what I've described so far, this approach is inadequate. A machine cannot read a random collection of data and understand the goals of the business. Though AI can help identify patterns, only a comprehensive human-driven review of the data, systems, and processes can create the Rosetta Stone that the whole business will run on.

That doesn't mean you must start from scratch. Organizing principles and architectures are already embodied across multiple systems and embedded throughout the organization's processes. In practice, these architectures tend to be fragmented, lacking consistent, standard ways of managing different levels of detail. This effectively makes them "accidental" ontologies. Accidental ontologies result from changes that are not governed or managed, business units that do not collaborate, vendors with inconsistent architectures, and developers who create technologies without reference standards. They can also arise from integration of acquisitions, consolidation of data sources, architecture layers evolving at different rates of change, and other changes in day-to-day operations. Frequently, they are haphazard and inconsistent because there is little awareness of how they should be integrated, cross-mapped, unified, or managed. They present many varied views of the truth, in contrast to the unified view represented by a deliberately created ontology.

How do these incompatible views develop? As I described in chapter 1, different parts of the organization have varying process clock speeds and rates of change. Social media marketing requires fast turnaround and fast responses to customer issues. The social media technology also changes rapidly within the already fast-evolving digital marketing technology ecosystem. Because the functionality of those systems will constantly evolve, the underlying architectures, organizing principles, and models will never be completely aligned.

While they may try, IT staffs rarely have the resources or skills to solve these problems in a systematic way, by applying end-to-end principles combined with metrics-driven feedback loops in ways that are appropriate to the problem. A carefully developed comprehensive ontology can help. If the social media marketing technology needs to interface with an ecommerce system, which will have slower-changing components, the ontology will provide a translation layer between faster- and slower-moving layers. The ecommerce system may sit on top of an enterprise resource planning (ERP) system that changes at an even slower rate and, once again, the ontology can act as a shock layer between those systems.

Ontologies Vary from Industry to Industry and from Business to Business

You could imagine a world in which a single organizing principle would allow all data structures to interoperate. While there are many standards to improve interoperability, a perfectly interoperable world does not exist, because businesses and their processes are diverse. The concepts and processes that comprise the world of a commercial insurance company, for example, are fundamentally different from those of a life sciences company. Insurance is about risks and regions, types of businesses, exposure, and so on. A life sciences company deals with diseases, treatments, indications, generic compounds, drug brands, mechanisms of action, and biochemical pathways, among other things. In each case, the ontology describes the various concepts and buckets of information along with relationships between those concepts—for example, "risks in a region" or "treatments for a disease." Taxonomies describe each concept, and the ontology consists of all the taxonomies and all the relationships among them. But even for companies within the same industry selling to the same customers and with similar products and services, there are differences. Their competitive differentiation comes from differences in how they interact with their customers and how they present solutions, communicate, and position their brand in the marketplace. Their ontologies will reflect those differences and embody their competitive advantages.

BUILDING AND APPLYING THE ONTOLOGY

Ontologies have to solve specific, meaningful business problems. It takes time and money for organizations to develop the necessary detailed use cases and scenarios with the associated content models and ontology. However, building ontologies using a holistic approach that correctly identifies information flow dependencies can solve many related problems at little additional cost. I will describe two ways to begin building an ontology: a "user- and problem-centric" approach, which focuses on the users and their challenges, and a "data- and content-centric" approach, which focuses on organizing the data. Enterprises have to use both approaches to some degree or another; user challenges deal with information and data, and data has to be organized around a user need or context.

The User- and Problem-Centric Approach to Creating an Ontology

The user- and problem-centric approach, focusing on users and their challenges, includes nine steps:

1. **Observe and gather data (pain) points.** Many of the world's greatest thinkers have stated that identifying the problem constitutes most of the work toward finding a solution.[5] Identification of the main problem establishes the context for the ontology and relates it to any other problems you're working on. When solving a problem, one gathers observations and data points from multiple perspectives. Problems have symptoms, and grouping those symptoms together and identifying the root cause for that grouping provides the context for the ontology. The symptoms (data points/observations) can come from anywhere, including customer complaints, interviews with people at the front lines, executive interviews, surveys, journey maps, call logs, search logs, working sessions, strategic plans, competitive analyses, quality problems, usability metrics, and heuristic evaluations. Identifying the source of each observation or data point is important so that executives and other stakeholders (especially the owners of a

process that may not be functioning optimally) can see the source and the observation or symptom can be justified. This is part of the audit trail of the ontology.

2. **Summarize into themes.** Since we don't solve one issue at a time and multiple issues can have the same cause, you must group and categorize the problems. (Categorization is a major part of ontology and this is the first categorization exercise!) Themes are a step toward diagnosing a problem; finding the root cause of as many problems as possible is the objective of this part of the exercise. The categorization process also helps people in the organization understand how problems and processes are related and how addressing one class of problem will make many others disappear.

3. **Translate themes into conceptual solutions.** Developing conceptual solutions by considering all the possibilities gets people thinking creatively and without constraints. A solution can be as obvious as asking, "Wouldn't it be great if we could . . . ?" and answering the question with the absence of the problem. For example, my problem is that I can't find things. Wouldn't it be great if I could find the document I wanted within 30 seconds? But of course, we need more detail than that—what things are we trying to find? During what process? To accomplish what task?

4. **Develop scenarios that comprise solutions.** This is getting to the next level of detail. What does the solution look like? What do people need to do? What would a day in the life of a worker look like if this new capability were in place? How exactly would people go about solving their problem or doing their job?

5. **Identify audiences whom the scenarios affect.** Sometimes the scenario involves just a few audiences (e.g., customers and marketing), while at other times, it has an effect on every department. When the solution or problem impacts many other groups, that means the value of the new capability extends beyond solving the

initial problem. This step also identifies other potential stakeholders, decision-makers, process owners, funding sources, operational bottlenecks, constraints, benefits, and dependent processes.

6. **Articulate tasks that audiences execute in scenarios.** This is another layer of granularity to the context and solution scenarios. Now we are at the ground level of detailed tasks that people have to accomplish. As we go deeper, we are uncovering more layers of detail and more nuances.

7. **Build detailed use cases around tasks and audiences.** Use cases are the next layer of detail. These are the testable assumptions about what an individual has to do to achieve the outcome described in a step-by-step manner. This level of detail is not always needed and can become painstakingly elaborate. However, after you develop use cases, you can categorize and generalize them so that one type of use case can become a model for dozens of similar ones.

8. **Identify content needed by audiences in specific use cases.** We are finally at the level of understanding what people need. Where do they go for answers, information, or inputs? What piece of information do they need? What do they call it? What do others call it?

9. **Develop organizing principles for data and content.** Now we can describe a piece of information. Imagine that I hand you a document or fact. What is it? Is it a contract? A policy? A risk profile? A customer record? That is what we call the "is-ness." The next question you need to ask is, If I had one thousand pieces of that thing, how would I tell them apart? If they are contracts, what kinds of contracts? What piles would I put them in? How many different types of piles could I create? For example, I could classify them by contract type, by region, by customer type, by issue, by topic, and so on. These characteristics are what we call

the "about-ness" of the information. Is-ness and about-ness are the metadata descriptors of the content. Each kind of is-ness forms a vocabulary. Each kind of about-ness also forms a vocabulary. Those vocabularies are also organized into hierarchies—taxonomies. When you have created the relationships among taxonomies and described all of the different types of information and ways of describing that information, you have developed your ontology. Table 2-1 summarizes this method.

The Data- and Content-Centric Approach to Ontologies

The user- and problem-centric approach to ontologies is more generally applicable, but it doesn't always create a complete picture. The data- and content-centric approach can be helpful as well.

Sometimes the ontology problem is presented as a pile of data that needs to be better organized—perhaps a website, an intranet, a knowledge base, or a content or document repository. This approach, while starting with the data, still needs a context, though that context can be quite broad. A starting point for analyzing that context is to gather groups of stakeholders together and provide packages of sticky notes and markers to each person in the room. The objective is to write down, as quickly as possible, everything that they work with on a day-to-day basis. You must be thinking, "Seriously? That would take forever." This is actually a speed-and-volume exercise. Recall that I started with context—the context could be a department, such as marketing, sales, engineering, or finance. Each of these groups will be able to write down at least 20 or 30 items on sticky notes that represent their information interactions.

The exercise can be very revealing. Sometimes people stay at too high a level and say things like "documents," "email," or "communications." In that case, we go back and say "Try again": What kinds of documents? What are the emails about? The goal is to get as granular as possible. Then the group places their sticky notes on a wall of flip-chart pages and tries to group them into logical groupings. Sometimes they end up with very large buckets, a result that reveals a group of "lumpers"—people who like to combine things. At other times they are split into numerous categories—a characteristic of "splitters," who like to separate things. You need

Table 2-1: Steps in the User- and Problem-Centric Method of Creating an Ontology

Process Step	Answer the Following	Examples
1. Observe and gather data (pain) points	What are the specific problems and challenges that users are identifying?	"We can't locate information about policies for specialty coverage." "We need to look in multiple systems to find prior experience data when underwriting new policies in high risk areas." "Different terminology is used in different systems, which makes queries difficult."
2. Summarize into themes	What are the common elements to observations? How can symptoms and pains be classified according to overarching themes?	Inability to locate policy and underwriting information using common terminology
3. Translate themes into conceptual solutions	Wouldn't it be great if we could . . . ?	Wouldn't it be great if we could access all policy and prior experience data across multiple systems using a single search query and return consistent results?
4. Develop scenerios that comprise solutions	What would a day in the life of a user look like if this solution were in place?	At a high level, describe how underwriters go about their work in writing policies for specialty and high-risk clients. Describe each potential situation and how they would go about their work.
5. Identify audiences whom the scenarios affect	Who are the users that are impacted?	Risk managers; underwriters; sales personnel
6. Articulate tasks that audiences execute in scenarios	What are the tasks that need to be executed in each scenario?	For a given scenario, articulate tasks (research options, review loss history, locate supporting research, etc.)
7. Build detailed use cases around tasks and audiences	What are the specific steps to accomplish tasks?	For a single task, list the steps to execute (this level of detail is not needed in all cases). Step 1: Log on to claim system. Step 2: Search for history on the coverage type in geography. Step 3: . . .
8. Identify content needed by audiences in specific use cases	What content and information is needed at each step in the process?	Claims data; policy information; underwriting standards; actuarial tables; fraud reports; etc.
9. Develop organizing principles for data and content	Arrange the things audiences need according to process, task, or other organizing principle	Begin with "is-ness." What is the nature of the information? Then determine "about-ness," the additional characteristics of the information. How would you tell apart 1,000 documents of that type?

to repeat this exercise with multiple different groups to get a sense of the elements and classifications they consider to be important. This process can inform the mental model of the user and then lead to the development of organizing principles that can be applied to knowledge bases and document repositories.

This is not the only data- and content-centric approach. Here are some others:

- Start with a body of content and ask people to come up with labels.
- Come up with labels and ask people to group them within existing categories.
- Ask people to group labels into new categories.
- Sample all of the existing terminology lists and have people reconcile them.
- Hand out sample content and have people classify it with existing labels.

Each of these approaches informs the mental model of the user and helps create language and terminology that can label and tag products, services, and reference content for easier access.

The challenge with data- and content-centric approaches is that they lose the understanding of the user's goals. The challenge with a user- and problem-centric approach is to prevent it from becoming a laundry list of user challenges. A combination of approaches is often the best way to crack the problem.

Checking the Box versus Validating the Work

How do you know when an ontology is sufficient to be useful? Here's a story that may illustrate that question.

The head of knowledge and search at a large global services firm was having challenges with information management across the enterprise. The company's program for searching for answers to employees' questions was held up as a model of exemplary practices at conferences; numerous attendees would crowd around the presenter after her talk and ask questions about how her team did it. Each week, the group reported positive results and metrics showed steady improvement in measures such as improved search accuracy and precision of results. But as a head of one of the business units confided to us, "People still can't find what they need." The company wanted to understand why, so they hired my consulting firm.

At first, it appeared that the company had already achieved a high level of success. My consultants and I listened to their approach, and our first thought was, "They really know best practices and understand how content, knowledge, taxonomies, and ontologies work. They are applying them and following all the steps."

But our main contact at the company suggested that we dig deeper. "Go to the end users and look at what they are trying to do," they advised. "Evaluate their taxonomies and ontology and how they got there."

The rest of the week was quite revealing indeed. Even though the steps that the global services firm followed were valid, problems emerged. Use cases were vague: "Users must be able to access the information they need when in the field." That type of use case is not testable. What information? For what purpose? From where? None of the details were specified.

When it came time to build the taxonomies and ontology, a manager sent out a spreadsheet that people added terms to, and then the head of the group added his own terms and deemed the taxonomy complete. There was no validation or testing with actual users or measures of usability. The firm had not followed best practices and heuristics for ontology development. There were too many overly broad terms (such as "documents" and "content"— what is the difference between a document and content?) and too many detailed terms that had insignificant differences ("exemplars" and "examples"). Hierarchies were six or seven levels deep in some parts and one level deep in other areas, making it nearly impossible to establish a mental model of how the information was organized. And there were many other violations of accepted practices (such as large "general," "miscellaneous," and "other" categories—which are useless individually and nonsensical when combined).

Ontologies should not be a matter of individual opinion. They should not be deemed complete by business leaders, based only on their judgment or developed in a vacuum. Everything should be testable and measurable. No one at the global services firm tried ingesting information using the system and then measuring how people located the information on an end-to-end, holistic basis.

An even larger mistake in many organizations is a lack of a clear understanding of the customer at a level of detail that truly informs decisions and provides enough of the features that both humans and machine learning algorithms can interpret and act upon. Achieving this level of understanding and insight begins with humans applying consistent, repeatable, testable methodologies, because machines cannot understand human needs without a reference point. What is it about your services, products, and offerings that appeals to your customers? When do customers seek them out and how do they make decisions? What is most important to them and why? What exactly do they need to do from moment to moment when they are interacting with different parts of the organization? That understanding is critical and all too often insufficient, lacking in important detail, or just plain wrong.

AI can be a powerful way to contextualize the customer experience by seamlessly serving up the information, products, services, and solutions they seek, but it cannot make sense of bad data and it cannot substitute for an understanding of the customer. AI cannot make up for your sins of poor information practices and bad customer experiences. Some of the tools can help, but they need a structure, a scaffolding in which to operate and in which to contextualize information. Successful AI programs require that the organization has its data house in order and that it understands what customers and end users need.

The Promised Land: Applying the Ontology

There are thousands of ways to apply an ontology.

There is a sculpture on my desk (the inspiration for the cover image on this book) that represents the infinite ways of applying an ontology while also representing the structures within it. The piece is made of glass of varying types with different refractive characteristics. There is an easily seen cubical structure within it; it is complex but not mysterious. But when light goes through the sculpture, it creates infinite representations of that light. The ontology is the cube. The ways of using the ontology are the light that goes through it. It changes depending on perspective but in predictable ways. It is infinite in its output but made of a finite number of elements.

The ontology is the foundation of language and business terminology and concepts that are important to the organization. It becomes the knowledge scaffolding and reference point for building various applications and powering AI tools. It has to be designed into the downstream systems and be the starting point for any data definitions. For example, it contains the lingua franca and golden record for product information in an ecommerce system. It does not always house the product information, but it holds the categories of products that would also be used in marketing tools, in customer engagement applications, in analytics programs, in internal knowledge and content bases, and so on. It can be used in search to provide conceptually related results that might otherwise come from a reference librarian. Every information system should begin with consistent language, concept relationships, terminology, and organizing principles; the ontology supplies these.

Now you know what an ontology is. What's it good for? We'll explore the uses of ontologies in many contexts in the chapters that follow, starting with the way an ontology improves the most fundamental process of any company: delivering an excellent customer experience.

TAKEAWAYS FROM CHAPTER 2

In this chapter, I've described what an ontology is, how it's useful, and how you can create one and put it to use to power your enterprise. These are the main points in this chapter:

- Ontologies help deliver the right information at the right moment, faster, and more accurately, which will give you an edge in the battle for customers.
- An ontology describes all the knowledge and data within your company and the relationships among different concepts.
- The main building blocks of ontologies are taxonomies— hierarchical classifications of various domains of knowledge.

- Ontologies power AI capabilities like chatbots by delivering a core understanding of the business problem and a mechanism for identifying reference signals within the company's data.
- To be valuable, ontologies must reflect the architecture of the data within a company.
- Creating useful ontologies demands a careful, deliberate approach—you can't just turn a machine loose on your data; nor can you stitch together "accidental" taxonomies that have developed throughout the business.
- Ontologies vary across industries and are unique for every business.
- One of the best ways to develop an ontology is with a nine-step user- and problem-centric approach that includes identifying problems, collecting them into themes, and developing solution scenarios.
- You can enhance ontology development by adding a data- and content-centric approach—for example, interviewing employees about the various data elements they use and how they use them.
- An ontology isn't done until it has been tested for validity and with actual user scenarios.
- Once created, an ontology can power a limitless number of AI-driven improvements within the business.

CHAPTER 3

CUSTOMER EXPERIENCE: THE FRONT LINE OF THE BATTLE

What is customer experience? What makes it good . . . or terrible? Let's take a look at three experiences I recently had with different companies. In each case, ask yourself, How did the information systems or data within these companies create—or destroy—the opportunity to deliver an experience that would make me a loyal customer?

Experience the first: I needed to clean my granite countertops. The local store stocked only the brand I didn't want. I found an online retailer that stocked the brand I wanted and I purchased a bottle. Unfortunately, the online retailer delivered the same undesirable brand stocked at my local store. When I called to complain and say that the return was not even worth my time, the service rep assured me that it would not take any of my time: UPS would come to pick it up with a label and all I had to do was give them the package.

When I put the package out, my local mail carrier (USPS, not UPS) tried to help by taking it. When UPS showed up, the package was gone, so they did not leave the label. Then the post office called to tell me I had to pick it up or they would throw it away. I drove to the post office, picked up the package, and then called UPS—spending 30 minutes on hold and leaving a voice mail—only to receive a callback from a rep who told me to call the retailer and promptly hung up the phone! Somebody at the retailer emailed a label, and I then had to find a drop-off location for the package after I printed the label. It took four hours of my time to process a return for a $12 purchase.

In this instance, the breakdown in customer experience happened at many points in the process. There were data issues at the point of purchase, a lack of clear explanation of the process, a breakdown at the local post office, and a disconnect at UPS. Do you think I will go back to that online retailer?

Experience the second: I received a mortgage refinancing offer from my bank. It was a great deal. But I was already in the process of refinancing with the same institution, a process I'd started a month before I received *that* particular offer. The bank's marketing organization was trying to sell me something that I had already purchased.

Experience the third, which restored my faith in companies' ability to do customer experience properly: My wife is an avid cook, as well as a fan of any and all quality cooking tools. I had heard good things about Kamikoto chef's knives, but I assumed they were very costly.

I clicked on an offer in my Instagram feed and found a deal for a Kamikoto knife set at a savings of several hundred dollars. This engaged me enough to take the next step and continue exploration. I researched the knives a bit more by reading web reviews and comparisons and decided to buy them for my wife (okay, they were really for me). The purchase process allowed me to use my Amazon account, which made it simple since Amazon already knows my credit card number and shipping address. After the purchase, the retailer enabled me to track my shipment (text or email) and a mechanism for returning it for any reason to reinforce the wise choice that I had made to purchase these fine knives.

The knives arrived in a beautiful wooden display case, along with certificates of authenticity and information about the history of the company, its manufacturing process, the high grade steel it used, the precisely balanced ratio between the handle and blade to allow for effortless cutting and chopping, and instructions on how to best care for the knives (wipe with a clean damp cloth and *never* put them in a dishwasher or toss them into the sink with dishes and silverware).

At each stage of the process of buying the knives, my customer experience was seamless and easy. Very little got in the way of my becoming a satisfied customer. I like these knives. My wife likes them, too. And I like the company that sold them to me—unlike the retailer who drove me nuts returning $12 worth of granite cleaner, or the bank that tried to sell me on a financing offer I'd already taken them up on.

CUSTOMER EXPERIENCE SUCCESS DOESN'T HAPPEN BY ACCIDENT

Customer experience (CX) is hard to get right and easy to get wrong. It's not a question of will: everyone wants to be good to the customer (except maybe Ryanair). It's not even a question of investment. It's a question of the proper integration of technology. A well-designed customer experience accounts for the customer's needs and all possible events the customer may experience (as the Kamikoto knife ads and delivery did). It allows for the possibility that things can go wrong and delivers an acceptable experience accounting for those cases (as the granite cleaner retailer didn't). And it leverages all the knowledge that the company has about an individual, even if it's held in different information systems (as the bank's system obviously didn't).

Customer experience is the sum total of all of the experiences related to your brand. It starts with the first marketing impression; expands with the customer's increasingly detailed understanding of the features, benefits, price points, style, and other selection considerations; and continues through the actual purchase, acquisition, usage, maintenance, and post-purchase relationship.

During this lifecycle, in which prospects become first-time customers, then repeat customers, and then loyal brand advocates, they will have a series of interactions online and off-line. They may talk to friends or colleagues, conduct research, look for recommendations and online reviews, talk to customer service reps and salespeople, visit stores, test products, and investigate competitive products. In this process they also experience a range of emotions: they may become confused on a website or by instructions, read conflicting reviews, become excited by the prospect of purchase, become disappointed, get frustrated, feel happy about getting a good deal, or become angry about not getting a better deal. They may experience regret at missing an opportunity, or buyer's remorse after making a purchase. They may be delighted by an unexpected level of customer service or attention to their needs, or they might be freaked out by overly personal service that feels intrusive. All of these emotions, interactions, perceptions, and events are part of the customer experience.

For CX design to work right, the brand must avert countless opportunities to fumble the sale by using comprehensive planning and immaculately consistent messaging that eliminates all potential friction. AI can help, but if the supporting processes and systems are not solidly aligned and integrated, no AI can enable a friction-free experience.

There are now many more dimensions to a successful engagement strategy than there were before people went online, including social media, content marketing, cross-channel customer experience, big data, and analytics. We'll touch on digital marketing as well, because much of the data used to power these experiences comes from new marketing technologies. (We'll explain the role of the digital marketer in more detail in the next chapter.)

In this chapter, we'll explore how problems can get in the way of a systematic approach to customer experience and describe the eventual solution: the high-fidelity journey map and the plan for applying it to your technology. The result is a technique for applying the ontology to customer experience in your marketing technology stack and making more thoughtful decisions about technology. We will show you how to use the customer journey to make marketing technology plans, blueprints, and investments.

Let's get started by looking at the fundamental challenge: how can you move quickly and personalize experience at the vast scale that's necessary in the enterprise?

Ontology Enables Agility and Scalability to Coexist

Enterprises interacting with customers pursue two conflicting goals: agility and scalability. The newly integrated worlds of customer experience and marketing demand the ability to react and respond quickly and efficiently across departments, tools, platforms, and business functions. They also require organizations to globally manage a significantly larger volume of personalized and localized content than ever before. The customer experience emerges from this, since it is the sum total of all interactions: with marketing, with sales, with customer service, and throughout the organization.

The first goal is agility—or more specifically, agile execution. Agility is crucial as the pace of business and markets accelerate. Organizations must keep up with changing priorities, strategies, and execution challenges. What is working and what isn't? Where are resources focused? What do market research and customer data tell us, and how should organizations respond, adapt, and evolve? What tools are most appropriate to solve engagement problems?

The second goal is scalability. Enterprises must be able to scale sophisticated and nuanced marketing, product, and service initiatives across platforms and channels, and operate them efficiently to support customers at every stage. This goal conflicts with agility in that it typically entails coordination of many tasks and processes that cannot be completed quickly.

How can you harmonize these two goals? The correct governance structure combined with consistent organizing structures provided by the ontology is the key. A fully integrated, holistic, cross-department execution perspective is most effective with digital technologies based on a consistent architecture—and managed with reference to the ontology. Agility is based on reacting and adapting. Scaling requires consistency and standardization. It is only through the use of an ontology that the two goals are no longer at odds with each other.

Complexity and the Customer Experience

As more customers transact most or all of their business online, organizations are forced to stitch together a seamless customer experience from what in many cases is a series of disparate systems.

For example, we once conducted a customer experience project for a financial firm using more than 50 platforms for managing customer investments. Customers could conduct some transactions predominantly online. For more complex investment redemptions, changes in beneficiary, or transactions with tax implications, the customer needed to call and speak with a customer service representative. Of these tasks, some required transfers to specialists for callbacks, and others required the call center agent to interact with a back-office transfer agent. In extreme cases, the transfer agent required support from a special "hotline" of top-tier specialists who had even greater levels of training, expertise, and system access.

Imagine the customer experience this generated: beginning a process online, running into a roadblock, searching for help, sending an email request, calling in, being transferred, getting placed on hold, leaving messages, calling back, having to provide basic identifying information repeatedly, and so on. Rather than a smooth paved highway, that journey was filled with bumps, detours, and side ramps that slowed the process, increased support and transaction costs, and damaged the customer relationship. Each step and task could require a different department, system, process, technology, cost center, or procedure. So much for a smooth, seamless journey. Disconnected internal systems and processes destroyed it.

This type of poor experience will likely result in customer ill will, higher support costs, missed opportunities, and lost business.

Reducing the Customer's Cognitive Load

We have all been transferred from department to department and have had to repeat account information and security questions. We have all dealt with confusing and maddeningly unhelpful call trees (press 1 to be annoyed, press 2 to be really annoyed, press 3 to be really, really, annoyed . . .) while yelling "Operator!" and frantically pressing "0". Some of us have even tried to return granite cleaner and wasted fruitless hours on the task.

In theory, the customer experience can be drastically improved in almost any organization. However, the groups that are typically tasked with improving customer experience (for example, call center operations) do not always have the resources to get to the root of the problem and fix issues upstream. Call centers are incented to maximize productivity, not to actually solve the problems that are causing customers to call in the first place.

To solve the problem, eventually the root cause needs to be addressed. But all too often, the organization lacks the discipline to make the investment in finding the root causes of experience problems. Or the organization has tried solutions before but has been burned due to the complexity of the problems, the number of systems involved, interdepartmental dependencies, a lack of overarching governance, incorrect metrics, outdated or poorly selected technology, or an insufficient application of resources to the problem.

Many customer experience improvements are rooted in reducing the cognitive load on the customer—by simplifying menus, understanding customers' intent, and finding a way to cut directly to the chase. If I had been presented with hundreds of choices for chef's knives rather than one or two options, I likely would not have purchased any of them. The "paradox of choice" states that providing too many options increases anxiety and leads to second-guessing decisions and unrealistic expectations.

This is why simple interfaces presenting just the information needed in a particular situation reduce the mental work and allow for faster, easier decisions with higher levels of satisfaction. But it's not at all easy to figure out how to best simplify the experience. The key lies with exercises that map the customer's journey with the company and attempt to understand the customer, including their decision criteria, values, and considerations, along with the features, functions, and characteristics that are important to them. These components become a subset of the data attributes that represent the customer; those attributes must be included in the ontology so that systems can align the correct content with the signals gathered during their journey.

Just as a great salesperson reads verbal and nonverbal cues and body language to gauge what a customer needs, our digital customer engagement technologies read the customer's digital body language and present what they need—no more, no less. We understand those needs and digital signals through journey mapping.

TOWARD A HIGH-FIDELITY MAP OF THE CUSTOMER JOURNEY

Executives believe they understand their customers and their customers' needs. They most likely have groups of employees tasked with understanding and researching this exact topic. They may run focus groups, conduct user studies, analyze data in voice-of-the-customer surveys, and organize research teams.

One goal of all this activity is to develop a journey map: a high-level description of the steps the customer takes on the way to achieving their objectives. The customer journey:

- traverses multiple channels and touch points;
- interacts with every part of the business (throughout the product or service lifecycle);
- is supported by multiple departments;
- includes transactions across many systems and applications;
- is governed or managed through various processes and organizational structures;
- leverages models of the customer to varying degrees, including attributes, characteristics, and preferences from the ontology; and
- extends well beyond marketing, sales, and support and depends on all the other parts of the organization.

Maps of customer journeys are typically developed at a high level; the details of moment-to-moment needs are difficult to analyze, understand, and serve. Many customer journey maps are based on what the organization *thinks* its customers experience rather than what they actually experience. The reason for this is that primary research (talking to, interviewing, and observing customers in their actual environment) is expensive. Even when organizations undertake costly customer research, there can be biases in what the researchers are looking for or interpreting.

One revealing exercise is to compare a hypothetical understanding (getting executives in a room to chart out how they believe their customers interact with their organization) with one that is validated by actual users in as close to a real-life circumstance as possible. Many organizations employ usability testing labs, and although those environments attempt to simulate real-world conditions, they are, by nature, a simulation.

AI-powered customer experience takes this approach to an entirely new level. It does so by considering customers' needs in their specific contexts as they go about their tasks and building from this information data models that represent *moment-to-moment* needs of the customer. We all play different roles throughout the day—parent, employee, boss, colleague, and customer of a range of businesses. Our needs change as our role and our immediate objective changes.

The High-Fidelity Journey Map Is the Keystone of a Better Customer Experience

Preparing for AI-powered customer experience demands a new kind of journey map: a high-fidelity journey map. While you may think you know your customer, you'll know them a lot better with a high-fidelity journey map informed by AI.

No doubt your organization has developed customer journey maps at some level of detail from your research activities, testing, user focus groups, and internal working sessions. To keep things manageable, people who create these maps tell me things like this: "We are keeping it simple. We don't want to overcomplicate things." That is not a bad idea. "Don't make it the Mardi Gras," as a colleague of mine was fond of saying.

However, in practice, many customer journey maps lack enough specificity—they are oversimplified. Not only do they fail to include enough detail in the tasks that the customer needs to execute, *but they lack a way of representing the customer stages and objectives in ways that computers can understand and act upon.*

The solution is to create what I call high-fidelity customer journeys. Why "high-fidelity"? Well, beyond sounding cool and different and buzzwordy, the term actually means something. High-fidelity customer journeys are representations of the customer's needs in data terms. The map of the high-fidelity customer journey models customers' "attributes"— the descriptors and identifying features indicate their role, buying stage, interests, demographics, goals, and even state of mind.

Developing customer journeys that can convert what the customer is trying to achieve into things that the technology can present back to the customer presents a problem. We have to think through the "So what?" question. What does it mean when we say that the customer is from a particular industry or that they are trying to select one product or another? How do we represent (and how does it matter) when our customer is at the "choose" stage in trying to decide what to purchase? The process is logical and objective, but there is art along with the science.

Oftentimes, internal research groups and external agencies can miss the critical linkages of the customer experience to attributes that your systems can interpret and act upon. These linkages are mechanisms that allow the journey map to come alive within the systems and technologies within your organization. They inform the machine learning and AI tools and are defined as elements within the enterprise ontology.

To complete the high-fidelity journey map, you must *validate* the journeys through primary research—that is, through actual observations of customers, interviews, and simulations that prove out your assumptions and insights about what the customer wants and how they think about the world.

High-fidelity journey maps are validated models. They are distinct from other customer journey representations because they include a detailed, nuanced, and multidimensional understanding of various aspects of the customer. The high-fidelity journey map requires new and evolved ways of thinking. It also takes into consideration variations in use cases and makes those part of the ontology. This data allows AI and machine learning programs to assemble and optimize offers by recognizing signals that indicate the customer's intent and context.

When high-fidelity journey maps are combined with customer attribute models (descriptors that represent the customer's interests, needs, tasks, objectives, role, history, propensity to buy, and so on), these representations tell our AI technologies how to enhance weak signals like a simple keyword search with more contextual clues that piece together what the customer really needs. (We will explore how to model customer attributes in chapter 5 as we explore ecommerce and personalization.)

SIX STEPS TO CREATING AND APPLYING A HIGH-FIDELITY JOURNEY MAP

With this mental model in place, the ultimate solution to customer experience challenges is to create a high-fidelity customer journey map and implementation blueprint that goes along with it. This is an exercise that addresses how customers interact with all the company's systems throughout their journey—the relationships between the customer journey and your company's stack of technologies. The purpose of this six-step exercise is not just to identify how those technologies are affecting the customer experience, but to build a roadmap for making technology improvements that will optimize that experience.

These are the six steps in that process:

1. Understand and map the customer lifecycle.
2. Define customer engagement strategy at each step of that lifecycle.
3. Survey and assess existing tools and approaches.
4. Assess the maturity of your supporting processes.
5. Assess tools, technologies, and internal processes with regard to engagement strategy and technology landscape.
6. Develop the implementation roadmap based on enterprise maturity and high-value areas of opportunity.

The process begins with understanding the customer lifecycle.

Start at the Highest Level by Mapping the Customer Lifecycle

This is the first step in creating a high-fidelity journey map. Ask yourself, where do customers come from? How do they go from not knowing anything about your product or service to becoming a loyal, repeat customer and market advocate? Answering these questions leads to mapping your customer lifecycle.

What are the stages your target customers experience, such as learning about your organization and value proposition, determining which products and offerings they need to evaluate, making a choice and purchasing your product, using the product, getting support, maintaining the product, and becoming an advocate? Each industry has prototypical customer journeys, but the precise journey will vary from organization to organization (see Figure 3-1). The nuances of messaging, engagement, experience, and interactions are what differentiate your organization and comprise the character of your relationship with your customers.

Figure 3-1: Industries' Unique Stages of Customer Engagement

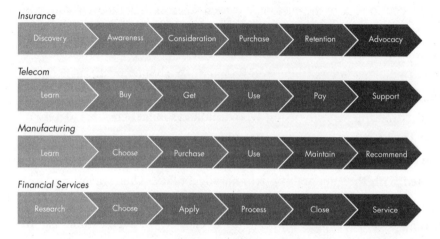

Insurance

Discovery | Awareness | Consideration | Purchase | Retention | Advocacy

Telecom

Learn | Buy | Get | Use | Pay | Support

Manufacturing

Learn | Choose | Purchase | Use | Maintain | Recommend

Financial Services

Research | Choose | Apply | Process | Close | Service

All these lifecycles have similar elements. If people don't know anything about you, they need to be informed that you exist and that there is a reason for them to continue the exploration. Some industries call this stage "research," others call it "learn," still others call it "discovery."

In the pre-digital era, the learn or discovery stages were mostly the purview of marketing organizations, whose job ended once the customer walked through the door or picked up the phone, responded to a mailing, and so on. Each subsequent stage was handled by a different department, and therefore issue resolution could require multiple handoffs.

Organizations are still structured in discrete processes, but with end-to-end digital experiences available, customers do not see the organization in this way. They care about solving their problem and don't want to be bounced around from one group to another.

Define Customer Engagement Strategy at Each Step of the Lifecycle

This is the second step in the application of the high-fidelity journey map. At each stage in the customer lifecycle, you can differentiate your company from the competition with the positioning of your message, the approach to reaching your audience, the way you describe your value, the nuances of your message, and the character of the relationship.

Aligning the right content with an effective customer engagement strategy allows you to engage the customer at each stage of their lifecycle with content and information to move them down the path toward purchase or solving their problem. That's what happened in my story about the Kamikoto knives—the marketers understood something about me through understanding my behaviors and they optimized their offers based on large numbers of experiments with people who exhibited similar behaviors to mine.

The right customer engagement strategy helps customers make a decision by providing exactly the information they need at that point in time, aligned with their mental model and vocabulary. Their *mental model* is how they think about their problem and how they think about solving it. Engagement happens on multiple levels and has various dimensions. Engagement is about meeting the user's needs, which may be emotional or logical. It is dependent on their context and perspective. It can change from moment to moment and from step to step.

How can an organization anticipate and meet the needs of the prospect or customer with content data, knowledge, products, functions, or services? The first step is to describe the customer in terms of everything we know about them. This "customer model" is represented according to the ontology, and it changes as the user goes through their day. We can think about metadata swirling around us describing what we need and when we need it. If I am hungry and want pizza, that can be represented by elements in an ontology. If I am in the role of parent, boss, husband, or colleague, each of these can be represented by data and the ontology. We can use explicit descriptors: facts and history such as the products I own or where I live, or we can infer and derive data about who I am and my behaviors. These are the implicit descriptors that can either be predicted by other indicators or can be based on the knowledge or judgment of an expert (see Figure 3-2).

Figure 3-2: Customer Descriptors at Different Stages in the Customer Lifecycle

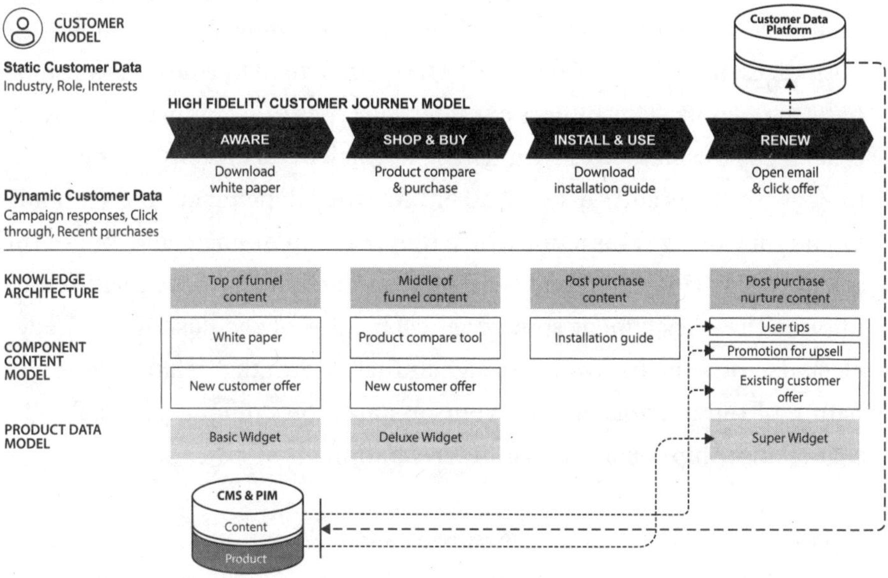

These descriptors tell our systems and technologies who we are at any given point in our journey and role, and what we may need at that point in time. Just like that great customer service rep who knows your needs and helps you solve your problem, the marketing technology engagement stack, informed by the ontology, can assemble messaging components and content aligned with your digital body language to anticipate what you need at each step of the journey.

These various descriptors comprise the scaffolding for knowledge and content and the signals that form a detailed interpretation of needs. Machines can deal with as many variables as we can come up with. If a "feature" of a customer can be identified, it can be associated with reference data and inform the algorithm. The question is whether meaningful distinctions can be made between the terms used to describe some aspect of that customer at a particular state in their journey and whether we can derive meaning from that descriptor that will help identify a pattern. To use a made-up example, is there a correlation between the age of someone's car and how responsive they are to a credit card offer? If the data can show that there is, then that feature may be a useful signal.

Finally, recognize that different customers will want different types of relationships. In a *Harvard Business Review* article, Jill Avery, Susan Fournier, and John Wittenbraker describe customer relationships with businesses in the same terms that are used to describe relationships between people. The authors consider the types of relationships in terms that are, by business world standards, unusual. Does the customer want "a fling" with the brand? A secret affair? Are they dependent on the brand? Or are they being transactional? Do they want an intimate and long-term relationship? Understanding the character and nature of the relationship informs the engagement strategy at each stage of the customer's lifecycle and allows the harvesting of signals that inform that relationship. The nature of the relationship and your organization's unique personality in that relationship is part of your differentiation.[1]

Survey Existing Tools and Approaches

The third step in mapping application of the high-fidelity customer journey to the tools that enable that journey is to survey the technologies that are currently in place.

Each stage of the customer's experience is supported by a set of internal processes that are in turn supported by corporate technology applications. For example, at one large retailer, there were 600 different systems supporting customer-related processes. However, relying on dozens or hundreds of different systems that are not well integrated slows down the flow of signals that determine the customer experience. When those applications don't talk to one another and slow batch processes are used to move information from one system to another, the system contains too much friction to respond effectively and in a timely fashion.

The organization learns about customer needs at multiple levels. Humans use judgment to formulate offerings and understand the needs of customers. Processes—the embedded habits and organizational learnings—also change in response to customer needs, but at a slower pace. Dynamic content enables faster responses to customer signals, but those responses must be correctly designed to identify what is important and present that information appropriately. When organizations do not hear their customers' voices and respond to their needs—either by adjusting products, pricing, and offerings or by correcting lapses and disconnects in their experience—they lose out to competitors who are better at doing so.

For example, when my bank sent me the offer to get a loan I was already applying for, there was a disconnect in systems and in processes that caused them to waste resources and damage their brand in my mind. I was told by the same bank that they did not provide auto loans, only to learn that the car dealer I selected used that same bank to service their customer financing. Again, there was a disconnect in process and data. It's a scenario where everyone loses—but they don't have to, if things are done right.

Tools and technologies are a deep topic. For now, the objective is to understand what you have in place throughout the enterprise to support the customer experience. This may be a very long list of home-grown, legacy, hosted applications and rogue systems on people's desktops. Later in this chapter, I explain how to examine and score them in more detail.

Assess the Maturity of Supporting Processes

Assessing the maturity of supporting processes is the fourth step in leveraging high-fidelity customer journeys within your marketing ecosystem. It will help you set priorities and determine where to focus resources.

Let's look at the example of one large manufacturer of communications equipment that was recognized for the quality of its stack of marketing technologies. Its customer engagement tools included more than 20 applications, displayed in its marketing technology stack diagram as an arrangement of various objects arranged around the central customer. Multiple tools served each stage of the customer journey, with various parts of the organization handling a slice of the relationship. This elaborate arrangement is in part due to the complexity of the company's product offerings, but it's also due to the range of different customer types and industries that an organization of its size and scale must serve.

Though its suite of technologies was well integrated and mature, this equipment vendor's challenge was to bring the supporting processes to the same level of maturity. Customer engagement technology does not magically understand what customers need. Technology cannot automate processes without insights from humans who understand the needs of the customer. Feedback from engagement strategy provides additional insights that humans can act upon by adjusting offers, messaging, and tactics for further improving engagement. The dilemma for this organization was that, because of the complexity of its technology in comparison to the relatively less mature supporting processes, it was difficult for its salespeople and marketers to act on insights that came from transactional and behavioral data. In most cases, it took two weeks or longer for the data to be retrieved, and then another two weeks to act on it. The company's goal was to remove the time lag following feedback and provide a more dynamic and personalized user experience that better anticipated the needs of audiences.

In an enterprise as large and complex as this one—encompassing tens of thousands of products and hundreds of markets and customer types—scaling digital, personalized, seamless marketing across channels was not possible without automation and orchestration of data, content, product information, and technologies. In a perfect world, the technology stack is bound together by ontology-driven knowledge of detailed customer needs at every step and stage of the customer journey, anticipating every need and interpreting and acting on every buying signal and digital nuance. But this is not a perfect world, and what is possible in theory has limitations in practice. Having the best technology without maturity in supporting processes is like having a Ferrari in the garage and only having rutted dirt roads to drive on. You are unlikely to experience the power and capabilities of this state-of-the-art technology without a deep understanding of the customer, modeled in an ontology, just as you will not experience the power and handling of a supercar while driving on dirt roads.

Take a Deeper Dive into Assessing Tools and Technologies

This is the fifth step in practically applying the high-fidelity journey map to technology decisions. The best way to analyze the value of the tools and technologies that your organization already has in place is to determine exactly what stages of the journey a particular tool supports and to assess how well that tool is being deployed. At a minimum, your company has a website that allows you to educate and communicate with your customers. Your sales organization has some mechanism for documenting the interactions with prospects and customers. Three components—a content management system (CMS), an email marketing technology, and a customer relationship management (CRM) system—form the bare minimum, and in some organizations they may be all that is in place. If utilized to their fullest capabilities, these classes of technology can be very effective in engaging with customers. Most organizations have more than those basic tools, and some have dozens of tools. For each stage in the customer lifecycle, you may have multiple tools with overlapping functionality, or you may be using multiple tools but in such a way that there are still gaps in how the customer is being served.

How do you know whether your organization has the right technologies to support customer engagement with your brand? First, you need to understand how your customers want your company to communicate with them and what their preferences are. Then look outward and think about the ways that your company differentiates itself in the market through its engagement with customers. (We describe this process in more detail in chapter 4.)

The appropriate applications depend first on the customer lifecycle and next on your strategy for attracting customers. The customer engagement strategy will then determine how important a particular tool is, and how much time, money, and resources your company should apply to the care and feeding of the technologies in your high-fidelity customer journey.

You need to evaluate each tool according to how inherently important that class of tool is in a particular stage of the customer journey. The level of importance is not just about the capability of the technology but about how you plan on using it. The question is how to most effectively serve the customer at each stage and what tools to deploy to do so in a manner most closely aligned with your value, type of relationship, and customer preferences.

For example, if the business emphasizes product selection and ease of online purchase, then the ecommerce catalog and product data must be highly optimized and aligned with the things that the user finds most important and appealing.

Understanding how well complex technologies are deployed does require a degree of technical expertise, but you can begin with questions your company should consider about its business strategy, such as:

1. How do we attract customers?
2. How do we increase their knowledge of our solutions?
3. How do they make a selection?
4. How do they acquire or purchase our products or services?
5. How do they get usage information after they purchase the product?
6. How do they get maintenance for their product?
7. How can they become advocates?

Table 3-1 shows the most common AI technologies and the stages at which they're typically applied.

If the selection of products is very narrow, a technology like on-site search may be less valuable than the technology that helps the customer compare a limited number of selections. Or the customer may find the most value in choosing and combining product options to come up with a custom version with the help of a product configurator. The answers to the first three questions in the list above will determine the type of technology that will be needed and its importance to the process.

You don't need to be an expert in a particular technology to know how well the technology is serving the customer—whether those customers are internal or external. You can learn a great deal by asking the people who are using or managing it. Have them show you how a business user accomplishes a task. Customer engagement technology should make sense and be explainable. You may not understand the technical principles of how the tool does what it does, but you should understand its purpose and business value. Does search work? Can people find what they need if they come to your site? Can email campaigns be created, managed, and targeted at specific users without acts of heroics? Can new products be onboarded and appropriate support and sales content be uploaded to the site without someone writing custom software?

To extend the analysis further, test the usability of technology with use cases and scenarios. Do users need to resort to work-arounds during setup and configuration? Are the processes efficient and clear? Can they be documented simply, in a way that is understandable to a non-specialist?

Table 3-1: Technologies Used at Different Stages in the Customer Lifecycle

Engagement question	Lifecycle stage	Approach	Use of AI Technologies
1. How do we attract customers?	Awareness	Email and ad campaigns, promotions, sales outreach	Personalized offerings, prioritized outreach, targeted email campaigns based on demographics and response analytics
2. How do we increase their knowledge of our solutions?	Awareness	Finding the right content on the web site or seeing an ad in the context of a task, getting recommendations from friends	Semantic search, personalized landing pages, Q&A bots, text analytics of social media
3. How do they make a selection?	Selection	Product comparisons, social media reviews, web research, on site search	Configuration bots, search-based merchandizing, solution bundles, recommendations, text analytics of social media
4. How do they acquire or purchase our products or services?	Purchase	Purchase on company web-site or through a marketplace, direct sales promotions, inbound calls	Recommendation engines, pricing optimization algorithms, shopping basket analysis, target prospect prioritization
5. How do they get usage information after they purchase the product?	Use	Content on the website, in application help, customer service center calls, knowledge bases	Q&A bots, troubleshooting bots, customer support bots, helper bots, semantic search
6. How do they get maintenance for their product?	Maintain	Product manual downloads, software updates, dealers, third-party maintenance, troubleshooting guides	Q&A bots, troubleshooting bots, customer support bots, helper bots, semantic search, sensor-based diagnostic tools, predictive maintenance based on IoT data
7. How can they become advocates?	Recommend	Social media promotions, newsletters, customer stories, contests	Text analytics of social media, personalized email messaging

Functions should be understandable in terms of how they provide value for the customer and how internal users enable them. At one organization I worked with, onboarding customers required more than 100 steps. The process was overly complex and failed to create commensurate value.

Avoiding Imaginary AI Functionality

Ordinary tools often do what they're supposed to do. AI tools sometimes don't. They're "promiseware."

Tool vendors owe you clear explanations of their capabilities. If a vendor says, "That's proprietary," or characterizes a tool as a "black box" that only data scientists can understand, you are either speaking to the wrong person or asking questions at the wrong level. Even the most esoteric tool needs to have a clearly stated impact on business value and its delivery to customers.

Sometimes the value is just, shall we say, *aspirational*. The functionality that you were sold doesn't exist yet. For example, when researching virtual assistants—AI-powered chatbots for conversing with customers—Brett Knight at the financial services giant USAA spent many cycles searching for "purple unicorns" whose promises were matched by actual capabilities. "I have the battle scars to prove it," he remarked. "They would all say just give us all your data and a boatload of money and we'll give you the finished product." While experiments with these services would sometimes provide some insight, Knight found that the vendors did not have a secret sauce or magic algorithm to do all of the hard work necessary to train the virtual assistant and process the data and content needed to make the system work.

When technology is leading edge, it may not yet have been applied to your exact situation, which is why the purchase and evaluation process needs to be rigorous and structured. You have to take control of the purchase process—*not be controlled by the sales process*. The key to evaluating technology is defining how that technology will be used when applied to solving your problems or serving your customers. Ask for proof that it will work in your circumstances, using your data, and in the context of your processes in your environment. This is why understanding the high-fidelity customer journey—as well as the internal use cases to support that journey—is so important. This understanding provides the foundational use cases against which you will evaluate software and which you will use to measure its effectiveness once it is deployed. This understanding will also form the foundational data sources for making future decisions and resource allocations. It will form the basis for metrics-driven governance.

An Implementation Roadmap Based on Enterprise Maturity and Opportunity

This is the final stage in the application of the high-fidelity journey map. At each step in the lifecycle, depending on the engagement strategy, you can rate the importance of the technology as low, medium, or high. If the importance is high, then you need to further rate its deployment on a scale of 1 to 3, with 1 being excellent and 3 being terrible.

What's the point of this exercise? It allows you to figure out where the customer experience challenges and opportunities are. They come from areas of high importance that are being supported by poorly deployed technologies. (Obviously there's more to it than that, but this approach will show you where the hotspots for improvement are.) Table 3-2 shows a sample of how such ratings are made.

We can add more layers of sophistication by including other parameters in a prioritization matrix. For example, we can rate cost (1 = high cost, 3 = low) and complexity (1 = highly complex, 3 = less complex). The idea is: the higher the score, the higher a project priority. Focus your time and resources on parts of the technology that are important to your engagement strategy and that are *not* well deployed.

Other parameters to take into account could be whether the benefits can be easily measured, are hard or soft, have high or low visibility, are already instrumented, reach a broad audience or a narrow one, have an internal or external focus, require a high or low degree of change management, require process redesign or not, have good or poor quality data sources, require new tools or can be done with existing tools, cross departments or not, support greater or fewer numbers of users, support numerous processes or few, and have or lack executive sponsorship.

This matrix also reveals where AI can have the most impact. Once we understand what is important and where we need to focus our attention—and provided that an ontology is present—we are able to ask: Can we automate a process using AI and machine learning? Where can we augment what humans do in serving the customer? What is important about engaging with the customer at each stage of the journey? What is the relative value of each process on the scale described in Table 3-2?

Considering these factors will help an organization determine where

Table 3-2: Rating Technologies Show Where Changes Will Matter Most

Stage	Goals	Technologies	Importance of Stage 3=High 1=Low	Deployment Health 1=Excellent 3=Poor	Score (Importance + Health)
Learn	Increase awareness and enable research: build aware-ness through advertising, campaigns, word of mouth, website content	Content management	3	1	4
		Campaign management	3	2	5
		SEO	3	3	6
		Email	3	3	6
		Social Media	3	1	4
Choose	Educate and demonstrate: help customers learn about the products and try to get them to a dealer for a test drive	Content management	3	1	4
		Site search	3	3	6
		Campaign management	3	2	5
		SEO	1	3	4
		Email	1	3	4
		Social media	1	3	4
Purchase	Streamline purchasing experience: transact with the customer or, since site does not transact today, get them to the dealer	Ecommerce	3	3	6
		Catalog	3	3	6
		Shopping cart	3	3	6
		Order management	3	3	6
		Chat	3	3	6

Table 3-2: (Continued)

Stage	Goals	Technologies	Importance of Stage 3=High 1=Low	Deployment Health 1=Excellent 3=Poor	Score (Importance + Health)
Use	Enable product usage: provide more personalized content based on the purchase, engage in social media, answer questions	Chat	3	3	6
		Personalized email	3	1	4
		Knowledge base	3	1	4
		Social media	3	1	4
		Content management	1	3	4
Maintain	Assist with maintenance: same goal as above, plus troubleshooting, automated diagnostics	Chat	3	3	6
		Personalized email	3	3	6
		Knowledge base	3	1	4
		Social media	3	1	4
		Web content	1	3	4
Recommend	Strengthen relationship: further support a positive experience with events, promotions, community development	Personalized email	3	3	6
		Social media	3	3	6
		Campaign management	3	2	5
		Knowledge base	1	1	2

to prioritize its resources and attention and build a prioritized marketing technology blueprint and execution roadmap. The result of well-deployed customer experience technology is the ability to provide the right information for the right customer at the right time to move them seamlessly through their journey. The approach we outlined is a methodical way to rationalize decisions and focus attention and resources in the areas that will produce the greatest impact for a given investment.

While this chapter has described systems across the entire organization, it should be clear by now that the biggest impact from changes in technology and AI appears in digital marketing. We look at how AI impacts digital marketers in the next chapter.

TAKEAWAYS FROM CHAPTER 3

In this chapter, I've described what customer experience is, how technology can get in the way of doing it right, and how to create and apply a high-fidelity journey map to figure out how you can best improve it. These are the main points in this chapter:

- An ontology is necessary to make improvements in both agility and scalability.
- Complexity of systems makes it hard to improve customer experience.
- An ontology is a key component to rationalize data across systems, enabling you to leverage insights in that data to improve customer experience.
- A detailed analysis of the customer journey can enable you to build a mental model of the customer at any given decision point.
- A high-fidelity journey map—one that accounts for how technology represents and enables elements of the customer's journey—is the keystone to making customer experience improvements.

- When surveying tools and technologies where AI and other improvements can take hold, focus on high-impact elements where deployment is less effective.
- Putting marketing stack technology decisions in the context of the customer journey, current tools, process maturity, engagement strategy, and effectiveness of deployment will pinpoint and prioritize areas of greatest impact and the opportunity to optimize using AI technology.

CHAPTER 4

MARKETING: AT THE CENTER OF THE DATA STORM

Search engine optimization (SEO) seems straightforward; you might think AI wouldn't be a big part of it. But marketers are beginning to think about AI as a tool that can be used not just for SEO but throughout the marketing process—and one that can make marketers far more efficient.

That's the lesson that a digital marketer named Linda Smith learned. Smith (that's a pseudonym, since she wants the name of her company kept confidential) is a strategist with over five years' experience at a company that serves law firms and optimizes their websites. Smith's job, on behalf of her client law firms, is to make their sites as effective as possible. A lot of that includes optimizing search. If a potential client is searching for a topic like nursing home abuse or truck accidents and a law firm specializes in those topics, it's part of Smith's job to make it as likely as possible that the client will find that law firm.

Taking into account the number of pages on any given firm's site—and the need for SEO specialists to identify appropriate terms and competing firms' positions in web searches—Smith estimated that a thorough approach could take 10,000 person-hours. But the firms she serves aren't often ready to sit around patiently while her team conducts a review like that. When Smith discovered MarketMuse, a platform for AI content intelligence and strategy, she recognized that it could make her job a lot faster and more effective.

MarketMuse analyzed a law firm's site to determine the most important topics. It then analyzed hundreds of thousands of pages on the web to dissect industry coverage of related topics, understand search intent, and identify high-impact opportunities for content creation. As David Juengst, senior content strategist for MarketMuse explains, "We use AI to identify what is being written and compare it to a giant corpus of data: not only what topics are important, but how relevant are they and how much content is required to cover each topic in a meaningful way. We identify the common topics, and also related topics that ought to be covered." MarketMuse creates a topic model to determine the words and their relationships that convey meaning to a person conducting a search.

Applying MarketMuse, Smith was able to recommend pages to add and wording to change on the site of her pilot client. Because attorneys are highly regulated, every potential change needed to be vetted. But once the firm followed her recommendations, there was an 890% lift in time spent on key pilot pages and a 35% improvement in the dollar value of the pages, as measured by how often they led potential law clients further down the marketing funnel.

In one case, the firm had a concentration of clients who were getting cited for DUI (driving under the influence) on a road that passed through a military base. MarketMuse was able to suggest the right terms, and Smith to suggest the right content, to get the firm's pages to rank on searches of "military DUI" and other related terms. Now the people with the citations could easily find the best representation, and the law firm could get itself in front of clients who needed its specialized skills.

What mattered even more than the improvement in marketing effectiveness achieved with MarketMuse was the speed the platform enabled.

Smith's team were able to create three new pages of content per month and to measure the impact of every change. The analysis that used to take 10,000 hours could be done in less than 300.

Smith's company is now figuring out how it can expand the MarketMuse AI content intelligence to its 115 premiere clients, and eventually to 1,700 other clients. When it comes to combining agility with effectiveness, AI is crucial. That's why AI-savvy digital marketers like Linda Smith are becoming central to the customer experience at such a wide range of companies.

DIGITAL MARKETING IS CENTRAL TO CUSTOMER EXPERIENCE

As we saw in the last chapter, digital marketing and the technologies that power it are woven through the modern customer experience. And as we saw in the above case study, even as seemingly basic a task as search engine optimization includes elements of artificial intelligence connecting to the ontology at the center of a company's information architecture.

Consider how customers begin the process of researching something that they need. Perhaps they begin with a keyword search or a product review. They may not know anything about your offerings and may have only a general idea of what they are looking for. They may not know that they have a need or want that you can satisfy. They may not understand the nature of their problem or may describe the symptoms and not the solution. They may be considering making a purchase but not know where to start. Or they may know what they want and be researching options.

The piece of information that is most appropriate at the beginning of the process of generating awareness will depend on where they are in their understanding and what they are trying to achieve. The right piece of information depends on how knowledgeable they are about the problem or type of solutions available. Marketing's job starts with building awareness. The purpose of a piece of content at any stage in the customer's awareness is to engage them in some way so they want to continue down the path to eventual purchase. Presenting exactly the right content that will engage the user depends on understanding their needs and context.

In the physical setting of a retail store, a sales associate reads signals from body language, such as where the customer is browsing, whether they are picking items up, how they are focusing their attention, and whether they are looking around for assistance. Sales staff can infer a great deal from clothing, age, how a person carries themselves, what they focus on, and other nonverbal communication clues. In the online world, there is an equivalent of physical body language: the digital breadcrumbs, cues, and clues that tell us about what our customers need, how we can meet those needs, and how to best present the content most likely to engage the customer at that moment in their journey.

AGILE DIGITAL MARKETING

Agile digital marketing is able to leverage data and content from diverse systems, processes, and organizations in a coordinated and synchronized fashion.

Many marketing organizations are still working in a fragmented way. Personalized content for a mobile campaign is typically modeled, tested, and deployed independently of print campaigns, which are managed by another part of the organization using a different set of resources and technologies. Omnichannel marketing programs in many cases are hand-crafted through customer focus groups and rolled out by agencies for each brand. Email marketing lives in a separate silo from web commerce. The traditional division of responsibilities, skills specialization, and varied technologies create a fragmented environment that makes it extremely challenging to scale well-coordinated digital marketing and customer engagement initiatives.

Marketing assets and programs are now "born digital." There are no more paste-ups and mechanicals. Assets must be proactively managed and leveraged across channels—not emailed from group to group. Upstream processes that are broken or slowed by organizational friction impede the ability to deliver value.

Orchestrating and Coordinating Marketing Messages

Marketers have many opportunities to fine-tune messaging using technology. They are also vulnerable to many pitfalls inherent in preexisting processes—some of which are carried over from analog days. These processes evolved from paper, to hand keying of data into legacy systems, and then to hard-coded integrations across systems and siloed departments.

Consider the challenge of providing consistent messaging and offers to customers across channels and devices. One building supply retailer used hundreds of systems covering every aspect of internal operations and external experience. Because in-house developers and a range of outside vendors developed these systems over the past several decades, they had to be wired together to talk to one another and share information through custom hard-coded integrations. Therefore, any changes in underlying technology entailed a difficult upgrade to multiple tools in the stack.

When the company wanted to build a smartphone app to help customers find products in its big-box-format stores, they had to bring in multiple vendors to tie together store layouts, merchandising systems, inventory management, and pricing systems. But the experience broke down when the company needed to tie regional and store-specific promotions to the in-store wayfinding application. The lag between updating an offer from a newspaper circular—big-box retail still uses old-school ad vehicles—to registering it in the smartphone app took days or weeks. Customers became frustrated when they could not locate specials and promotions that they learned about from traditional advertising channels.

Omnichannel messaging requires that the customer experience be the same across channels and devices—whether a customer learns of it from a promotion on a website or in an email message, a text message, a radio advertisement, a mailer, or a store display. When channels are not in agreement, customers may learn after making a purchase that they could have saved money. This damages the brand. Customers get frustrated and angry and call customer support, complain to managers, complain to store personnel, and return their items for refunds. A mature digital marketing function must develop "orchestration capabilities" that arise as a result of maturity across the dimensions of customer experience, content optimization, product information, and knowledge engineering. Only then can.digital marketing achieve its goal of optimal, financially sustainable engagement across audiences and segments.

Content marketing is one of the hottest trends in marketing, but it's challenging to integrate this process into the rest of a company's marketing. Content creation is still a human activity—and humans don't move at the speed of AI. Or at least they didn't used to. At the American Marketing Association, AI enabled the organization to notch a huge win with customers and reduce friction in its processes at the same time.

HOW THE AMA MADE PERSONALIZED MARKETING MORE EFFICIENT

The American Marketing Association (AMA) counts over 30,000 marketers in its membership. Those members need a reason to renew their memberships—and to patronize AMA's targeted events. The clearest way to retain them is with useful content.

But for Molly Soat, AMA's editor in chief, managing all that content was beginning to be a huge pain in the butt. AMA had a weekly email, as well as six monthly newsletters, focused on topics like health care and market research. That meant that her limited staff had to scramble to come up with enough individual articles to fill those newsletters and add value for subscribers. "It was taking up a massive amount of time to create all of these different content pieces, and we were only achieving one goal at a time," she recalled. When those newsletters fell short—or when they became too promotional—some people would unsubscribe, sometimes from all AMA emails. AMA needed a process to deliver more content and more value with less work.

Soat and her team settled on rasa.io, an AI-based newsletter-creation tool. Enabled with smart technology, rasa.io knows what readers are clicking on and uses that information to scope out what's important to them. Combined with the information AMA already had in its Salesforce database, these insights held out the possibility of a strategy that was never before possible: developing a newsletter that was fully personalized for each AMA subscriber.

The workflow of Soat and her team is now completely different. Each day, her content staffers create three pieces of original content. They also review about 100 other sources of marketing content, including content from marketing thought leaders. An AI highlights the most promising content pieces on any given day, based on keywords that indicate articles that marketers would be most interested in; Soat's staffers review those quickly and designate hundreds of possible articles for inclusion as links in the newsletter.

The algorithm generated by rasa.io then sends out the newsletter to 100,000 subscribers. Each subscriber sees the three original articles and links to seven others, but the seven additional articles are selected to match subscribers' interests as indicated by their past behaviors and what the customer database says about them.

The transition to AI-based technology was not an easy one for Soat. Anyone whose job title is "editor in chief" has a personal stake in creating the best possible content. But eventually, despite her journalistic instincts, Soat realized that the truth was, "It's not about our taste." She road tested rasa.io with internal users at AMA and proved that AI-created, personalized newsletters were not only possible, but were better and more relevant than what AMA had been creating before. "It was a kick in the pants; it forced us to take a big leap towards personalization," she said, while acknowledging, "It was scary in some ways, to wrest control of content from our own hands" and give it to a machine.

Once they rolled out the concept, it became very popular with readers. Unsubscribes went way down. Open rates for people in their database were 40%, double the industry average for newsletters. Click rates were 13.1%, five times what's typical for a newsletter. AMA's membership became more highly engaged, which will likely improve membership renewals and event attendance.

Now that all of AMA's subscribers are reading an AI-generated newsletter, Soat told us she had only one regret. "I wish I'd done this sooner," she said.

DIGITAL MARKETING IS INCREASINGLY RESPONSIBLE FOR THE CUSTOMER EXPERIENCE

The experience of being an AMA member is now different—better—because of AI. For AMA, digital marketing through the newsletter is a big part of the customer experience.

In larger companies, the experience is far more complex, but digital marketing is increasingly the aspect of the organization where AI catches on most quickly. As a result, rethinking the customer experience also requires rethinking roles that used to be distinct but that must now traverse areas previously outside of their purview. Marketing organizations are feeling the brunt of this shift since they have become owners of a technology stack that has to serve the customer throughout their experience. There is no longer a distinction between digital and marketing.

Many customer-facing systems are supported by disconnected internal applications, departments, and processes. This leads to continual gaps in detail about customers and an inability to see the full picture of customer experience. Many organizations are trying to achieve a 360-degree view of the customer—to the extent such a view is possible—but internal system disconnects are getting in the way. If any group is to take responsibility for this challenge, it is typically digital marketing.

Customers leave digital trails that contain the clues to building a responsive marketing system. However, those clues are typically dispersed among dozens of different systems and technologies. For digital marketing to be effective, it is necessary to develop the appropriate taxonomies and an ontology that organizes the data from these disparate systems to provide a more complete picture of how customers are responding to messaging and promotions.

New Roles for Digital Marketers

Because of the many pressures on digital marketers, the leaders of digital marketing are pressed into new roles: as knowledge enablers, champions of data quality, and eventually, architects of the digital data systems that power the shared view of the customer.

Marketing is about more than messaging as it expands to include collaboration and engagement. Customers want to have their problems solved, not to be marketed to. This may mean exposing the knowledge and expertise of engineers in a B2B organization, or it may mean enabling customers to have the insights they need to choose your product in a B2C context. This means that marketers have to be knowledge enablers; they are no longer limited to the role of messaging creator.

Marketing is now about scaling the machinery of communication, collaboration, and content processes, much as Molly Soat did at AMA. It is about enrolling deeper levels of the organization in the process. This means marketers must be involved in various aspects of governance and change management to get meaningful content created, managed, organized effectively, and presented to target customers in a consumable way. Marketers also need to be intimately involved in IT processes. They need to work closely with the CIO (chief information officer), and, if the role exists, the CDO (chief data officer). Marketing is increasingly data-driven, and data quality will be essential to marketing success. Digital agility means data agility. Therefore, marketers need to show the organization what can be done with high-quality data as well as demonstrate the impact of poor quality, difficult to access, or missing data. Marketing leaders can champion data quality to show the impact on the bottom line through metrics linked to customer acquisition and revenue growth.

I recently heard about an organization choosing a digital asset management system *without* the involvement of marketing. Marketing is one of the chief creators and consumers of non-text assets, and it should therefore be driving requirements for these types of systems, as well as systems including web/marketing content management, marketing automation, and customer relationship management (CRM).

Ultimately, digital marketers need to become digital architects. The marketing function leverages data assets from many parts of the enterprise—from customer purchase histories to call center feedback, survey responses, social media data, clickstream behaviors, campaign responses, external data feeds, mobile usage data, and search metrics. Deriving value from these sources means translating this "digital body language" into meaningful content, campaigns, and offers. Increasingly, this means translating data models from various systems into attributes managed in the ontology. Those attributes become inputs into personalization engines, web content management tools, collateral creation processes, campaign management systems, and various outbound demand-generation activities.

All of this leads to one conclusion: the ontology is very much the responsibility of the senior leaders in digital marketing. The digital marketing landscape is constantly changing, with thousands of vendors clamoring for attention to their "AI" technology. There is no shortage of white papers, books, and conferences on marketing technology, customer experience, or the analytics of engagement. Executives are getting advice from all quarters about what they need to do to have a successful digital marketing strategy.

What is conspicuously missing from these to-do lists is any reference to the foundational role of ontologies. Many systems are deployed in isolation or with a nod to integration using web services; however, very few marketing leaders are in a position to develop the foundational data infrastructure that is needed for success. If the enterprise is to have any hope of a positive outcome from all of the investments being made in advanced marketing technologies that are meant to smooth the customer journey, marketing leaders have to streamline marketing operations and supporting processes across all of their tools. They must pursue this effort in a holistic way that includes a framework so all of these systems can communicate.

The next chapter will provide a deeper dive into ecommerce and how maturity in product information and content processes will arm the organization for the ongoing battle for ecommerce wallet share.

TAKEAWAYS FROM CHAPTER 4

In this chapter, I've described how digital marketers play a central role in integrating customer-facing technologies and must connect them to a central ontology. These are the main points in this chapter:

- Marketing's job starts with awareness by delivering the appropriate piece of content at any moment to move the user to the next step in their journey.
- Agile digital marketing requires orchestrating messages across diverse systems, not all of which are controlled by marketers.
- Digital marketers must become knowledge enablers, champions of data quality, architects of digital systems, and keepers of the ontology that powers it all.

CHAPTER 5

MAKING ECOMMERCE SMARTER

Ecommerce used to be about finding what you wanted to buy. But there are so many possible things to buy—and so much information available about the people who want to buy them—that ecommerce has to be smarter than that now.

What does smarter ecommerce look like? Let's imagine, for a moment, that my wife is buying me a pair of hiking boots . . . and that she's interacting with a virtual sales assistant on a website. Virtual sales assistants can guide consumers in locating and selecting products and options, depending on a range of criteria. One method is faceted search, which allows the customer to narrow the selection according to criteria such as brand, style, color, price, and size. Here's how that conversation might go:

Virtual sales assistant: "What type of hiker is your husband—serious multi-day backpacking, or day trips?"

Her: "Day trips."

VSA: "What length boot does he prefer—ankle or calf?"

Her: "Ankle."

VSA: "Any special features?"

Her: "Very wide feet." [I have been told I could probably water ski without skis.]

VSA: "That limits some other choices. What type of weather?"

Her: "All seasons, I think."

This conversation could continue with more questions: Do you need something waterproof or insulated? Lightweight or heavy? Is there a price range you need to stay within? With a dialogue like this, the virtual assistant narrows the choices down to the exact boots she should buy for me.

Behind the scenes, powering this virtual sales assistant, is structured data about the features that are important to customers. This chapter is about how to prepare that data and tap artificial intelligence to enable a more interactive, customized, conversational approach to ecommerce.

ECOMMERCE IS WHERE AI HAS ITS BIGGEST IMPACT

As I described in chapter 3, customer experience is about the end-to-end process of acquiring, serving, and supporting the customer. It spans nearly every department and process in the enterprise.

Ecommerce, websites, and apps are a narrow slice of that experience, but that slice is crucially important. It's the most powerful place to improve the customer experience. It's connected to all the company's data systems, and even in companies from which people don't typically buy online, online is often where they make their buying *decisions*.

Even though ecommerce is just one aspect of the customer journey, it generates revenue directly. As a result, you can use it to justify investments that improve all aspects of the customer experience. Change an ecommerce site—whether through a redesign, new technology, changes to taxonomy, improvements in supporting content, or whatever—and you can directly measure the results. This means that ecommerce can create the foundation for metrics-driven governance, the decision-making playbook that is the cornerstone of a data-driven organization. (I'll discuss governance in more detail in chapter 10.)

In this chapter, I will share an in-depth exploration of the data, architecture, governance, and execution elements of successful ecommerce and interactive programs. I will refer to the web presence as "ecommerce" whether the site is transactional or not. Regardless of whether customers actually purchase on a site, design and execution are crucial when educating the customer about product features, specifications, availability, and where to purchase (if not online).

Here's how I'll tell that story. First, I'll show how search is giving way to smart, conversational, predictive forms of interaction as a way to help customers, based on solid product and customer data. Then I'll show you how such data can lead to highly personalized and customized sites that connect each customer as quickly as possible to their best possible offer, powered by the ontology. And finally, I'll describe how you can assess your tools to determine if your business is ready to deliver on the promise of smarter ecommerce.

HOW AI TURNS SEARCH AND SITE NAVIGATION INTO A CONVERSATION

Questions are ambiguous. To understand them, you need to know more about who is asking and the context.

For example, I once attempted a guided winter hike up Mount Washington—the highest mountain on the east coast of the United States—on the coldest day of the year. When the guide asked me about my experience, I inferred from the context that he was asking about my experience with winter mountain climbing, not my experience as an AI consultant. Similarly, in a business scenario, if I don't know anything about the person asking a question (perhaps at a networking event rather than during a sales call), I might ask a clarifying question in order to answer more precisely.

Search is now a conversation as well. Search terms are often short, ambiguous, and an approximation of the searcher's real information need. A generic set of responses is no longer the best choice. When you start to type a search into Google, the query box will begin to contextualize the query with suggestions and to customize the results based on your own personal search history. Why? *Because search is a conversation.*

On an ecommerce site, the same sort of thing happens. For example, if you visit MSC Industrial Supply's website, mscdirect.com, and search "tools," the site will try to anticipate the category of tool by presenting choices that clarify the question, What kind of tools are you looking for? If you select "power drills" from the set of resulting options (also known as facets), the site will then narrow down, attempting to determine "What kind of power drill?" by presenting a selection of air drills, cordless drills, coring drills, electric drills, and so on. Select "electric drills," and the site then narrows things down further by determining more details: brand, size, speed, handle, and so on. These clarifying choices appear as navigational elements. We are, you might say, drilling down into drills to get to the specific item that you need.

On-site search is a critical function on an ecommerce site, and one in which AI techniques can balance recall (the completeness of results) with precision (the most appropriate results). Recall and precision are typically at odds with one another, but AI that has the correct information architecture can increase both recall *and* precision. For example, a smarter search engine recognizes that when I search for "sushi," the results should match restaurants close to my location.

A smart site needs context to improve results. Consider a customer searching an industrial site for "mold stripping." They may be a plastics manufacturer who wants to clean an injection mold, an industrial reclamation contractor seeking to remove mold and mildew from damp surfaces, or a remodeler resurfacing the wooden molding on a ceiling. Depending on the customer's context, the correct search results might be release lubricants, cleaning chemicals, or abrasives. The search term itself is only one signal; add the industry or application and you have supplied another signal that the search engine can interpret to more precisely return the appropriate result.

Where does context come from? Each dimension that informs a search is part of the ontology: classifications of products and customers, the desired application, and the industry, for example. The search engine uses relationships contained in the ontology to contextualize industry and return the correct products.

Search has long depended on AI and machine learning techniques to contextualize vague or ambiguous queries. AI enables functionality like analyzing text, clustering and grouping content, creating search indexes, extracting entities from text (such as name, company name, dates, or part numbers), interpreting intent, correcting spelling, and presenting related items. AI can inform search results by weighing other signals about the customer's context, including whether or not the customer is new, technically sophisticated, or commercial, and what tasks, problems, objectives, and interests they may have.

Each of these concepts is modeled in the ontology, which contains the relationships that are important to the customer, industry, and engagement strategy. In the case of the "tools" search term, for example, Amazon, Lowes, Grainger, Gamut, and MSC all return different results and have different conversations with the user. An intelligent assistant can convert these queries into a conversational interaction:

User: "I am looking for tools."

Bot: "What kind of tools do you need? Power tools or hand tools?"

AI can take the various phrase variants ("I need tools," "I am looking for a tool," and so on) and interpret the customer's intent based on historical data (search logs or chat logs, for example) to return the correct tool categories and continue refinement from there.

Dynamic Navigation

Search and site navigation are two sides of the same coin; in a smart site, both processes improve incrementally based on context. In the ecommerce facet refinement scenario that I just described, each of the clarifications looked like navigational elements: links or checkboxes. The customer may have felt as if they were navigating, but behind the scenes, the system was executing a search. The navigation is dynamic, in that the order and detail of choices surfaces the most appropriate attributes and characteristics based on other signals from the user.

How should the questions the bot asks, or the options it presents, be ordered? What is the correct level of detail to show the user? A site can order navigational links based on rules (bestselling product categories first, perhaps, and then highest margin categories) or based on customer knowledge. If you know that this customer has always purchased sale items, you might display the best deals or clearance categories first. A navigation rule could vary what is shown based on what items the customer has previously clicked on or purchased. For example, if a customer browsed running shoes and then purchased outdoor wear, a subsequent search for shorts could present activewear at the top of the product listing.

Sites can go too far with this level of customization. Ever-changing navigation breaks the customer's mental model; people want a sense of the structure and organizing principles of the site, so when things are moved around or the same category is used in more than one place—a so-called polyhierarchical structure—the customer may have trouble grasping the site's organizational structure. (As an analogy, when you go to the hotel's breakfast buffet, you might find the spoons next to the cereal, next to the coffee, or with the other silverware—but are they where you expect them to be?) Polyhierarchy can reduce findability and increase the customer's cognitive load, as there is no longer a simple answer to the question, "Where would I find this thing I'm looking for?"

Whatever rules your site uses—according to merchandising priorities, the needs for a given customer, what's overstocked, or a combination of factors—those rules depend on an intentional design for elements captured and referenced in the ontology. An ontology containing customer interest categories can serve them up to the search engine when that customer comes back to the site, for example. AI search tools and mechanisms are endlessly configurable, but to be effective they require fine-tuning, an understanding of the customer, and an information architecture that contains the appropriate product features, functions, and details that are important to target customers. You should build the appropriate ontology to drive search over time, rather than purchasing a generic or off-the-shelf architecture or engagement approach. Search personalization isn't one size fits all.

Predictive Offers and Shopping Basket Analysis

Let's look at two of the most common mechanisms for presenting products and content that best serve a particular customer.

Predictive offers attempt to induce behaviors by anticipating a buying signal from a prospect and nudging them into a purchase. By testing the performance of similar offers on similar customers, the algorithm can fine-tune offer parameters and design elements to increase likelihood to buy.

Shopping basket analysis makes a suggestion based on what others have purchased along with the products that the customer has selected. This can be refined by comparing shopping baskets of customers who are most similar to the customer currently shopping, who share the same industry, who have similar problems, or who are in similar job roles.

The ontology is the reference point for defining these characteristics consistently across systems. These types of offers can be surfaced in the context of a user's search or presented as navigational choices. In either case, they work in similar ways—interpreting user intent and combining that intent with other signals to provide a targeted response. That response could be a recommended product, a more functional (and expensive) option, a related accessory, an offer of some sort, or a solution. Over time, algorithms can learn from customer behavior and present content and offers that are progressively more effective.

DATA POWERS ECOMMERCE

Since the ecommerce customer experience is made up completely of data, that data needs to be correctly designed, organized, and managed. While this sounds obvious, many organizations have immature product information processes. When they add new products (a process called "onboarding"), they don't manage product information in an adaptable, sustainable way.

An effective ecommerce experience begins with good product design principles and clean, well-structured product information, and then attempts to reduce the customer's cognitive load in navigating the site. What appears to be a simple customer experience on a site is, behind the scenes, quite complex. In fact, the role of the designer is to hide the complexity from the customers by thinking through the steps of their processes and the details of their mental models and presenting information in a manner meant to be intuitive. The information then makes sense to the customer. It is easy for the customer to find what they need, because the designer anticipated their need and provided a limited number of choices based on that need and the customer's journey stage.

The designer begins this process manually and uses AI technologies to help refine, tune, and scale individual experiences. This requires a deep understanding of customers and how they think about the world. AI-powered ecommerce allows for differences in how users perceive the world, and should be designed to adapt to their needs based on real-time signals and behaviors. However, the process must begin with a foundational design that the AI can adapt and improve.

The fuel for a customized ecommerce experience comes from two kinds of data: product data and customer data. Let's start by looking at product data and taxonomies.

Product Taxonomies Are the Foundation of the Ecommerce Experience

Managing a large product selection of thousands or even millions of products begins with a primary hierarchy called the product taxonomy. This is also called a navigational hierarchy or display taxonomy, and it is a critical foundation of the user experience. At first glance, one might think, "How hard is that?"

In fact, a number of years ago, when I was meeting with a new primary care physician, he asked me what kind of work I did. When I explained what taxonomies were—a way of organizing and navigating products, content, and knowledge—he responded with an incredulous, "You make a living at that?" I replied that I (along with 30 employees) indeed made a living at that. He could not comprehend why that would take any effort or how that could be a business. Similarly, many senior executives cannot understand why taxonomies would be costly or complex to develop or maintain.

Here's one way to think about the value of a taxonomy: The way products are organized within it is analogous to the way a physical store is designed. The taxonomy undergirds the virtual store and becomes part of the character, personality, and differentiation of your site.

Physical stores selling the same merchandise have different ways of presenting it. Products are arranged in different ways and merchandised to appeal to certain types of customers. The taxonomy is like virtual store shelving (and aisles and signage). Different users not only shop for different items, but they also walk through the store to navigate and find their way differently.

Retailers spend a lot of time and money designing store layouts and build "planograms" to show where products should optimally be displayed and merchandised. By powering the ecommerce site, the product taxonomy functions as a virtual planogram that can, unlike a physical store layout, adapt to the needs of a customer as they move through the site.

For large ecommerce websites, product arrangements need to be tested across different customer types or personas (as I explain later in this chapter). Machine learning can then adjust and fine-tune assortments, offerings, and arrangements, but these should begin with a well-designed and tested hierarchy: the product taxonomy. Your product taxonomy is not necessarily going to be the same as that of your competition, even if you carry the exact same merchandise. The foundation has to be tuned specifically to the needs of your users and adapted to their circumstances, goals, and objectives.

Another challenge is in the quality and design of product data, which is directly related to customer needs. Product data should reflect the product features that are important to different types of customers. If I like socks with thick, fuzzy soles, but that attribute was not modeled in the product architecture, I won't be able to find those types of socks as easily. Including a feature in the product data also enables analysis of purchases to inform promotions. I can send fuzzy sock offers to people who have purchased them or who are similar to people who have purchased them. A shallow understanding of the customer will impact the way that product data is architected and populated, resulting in missed opportunities.[1]

Product Relationships Must Be Included in the PIM System

PIM (product information management) systems hold information about products, including product relationships. Product relationships establish connections between products, helping users navigate and discover products and solutions. Product relationships may be simple accessory relationships or may reflect complex component assemblies and configuration rules. These relationships enable recommendations based on what products work best together or are used together as a solution. Recommendations about related products lead to higher revenue and more frequent returns to the site.[2]

Solution bundles can become quite complex; merchandisers, solution engineers, or subject matter experts may need to define them manually. But they can also be created using AI tools to mine information from maintenance manuals, product configuration content, and engineering specifications. Various product relationships can be captured and managed for presentation to users in the right context, including replacement parts, related parts and categories, kits and sets, competitor cross-references, distributor cross-references, compatible products, required components, optional accessories, and obsolete products. Your site can present these relationships to help the user choose what combination of products to buy, smoothing their journey.

Product relationships often already exist, but they need to be captured and normalized in a PIM. Product relationships can be discovered in static text, spreadsheets, folder systems, or existing PIM systems. Product managers and subject matter experts can help curate such product relationships. Understanding these relationships will help customer experience designers include the correct relationship for a particular use case. Best practices for managing product relationships include centralizing product relationships data, capturing and documenting the definitions of relationship types for consistency, creating processes for ongoing maintenance and governance, integrating relationship identification into the item onboarding process, and reporting regularly on product relationships by type (including usage metrics).

Standardize for Efficiency; Differentiate for Competitive Advantage

There's a fundamental question when it comes to product taxonomies: should we match industry standards or develop our own customized version?

A key principle here is that standardization leads to consistency and efficiency, whereas differentiation leads to competitive advantage. As I have described, the navigational taxonomy informs the front-end customer experience and guides how customers find the desired product on the site. Within your company, the taxonomy also influences how your merchandisers plan inventory and promotional strategies and how the finance organization predicts demand and tracks revenue and profitability.

In some cases, a manufacturer will want to use the same terminology, organizational structure, and navigation as their distributors—which may also mean that they are using the same conventions as their competitors. The upside is that this makes it easier for an organization to exchange information with trading partners and consistently track information as it flows through the supply chain.

Of course, if every competing site is based on a similar taxonomy, then a business needs to differentiate its products in another way. Ecommerce sites can still differentiate their offerings through such factors as price (larger sellers can offer bigger discounts), quality (premium products), or convenience (faster delivery, easier transactions, more intuitive site design, better suggestions, or more customized interactions).

Customer Scenarios, Personas, and Models

The taxonomy of product features is, of course, only half of the equation when it comes to an organization delivering the best possible site experience. Data about customers is the other half.

How do we gain a deep understanding of the needs of our customers and tailor their experiences appropriately? We do so by modeling our users through the use of *personas*. Personas are iconic representations of the different types of customers that we serve. Customer experience teams typically develop these representations with input from other departments that have customer knowledge and systems of record. Some designers define personas at a high level without personal details (some refer to this higher-level classification as an "audience"). Such broad personas have names like "first-time buyer" or "repeat customer." Other designers get into significant details about the wants and tastes of specific classes of customers.

Personas, while fictitious, can be developed with a lot of personal details that are meant to help the designer keep customer needs and preferences in mind. However, it is easy to get carried away and spend too much time on detailed persona development without spending enough time on what the personas are *trying to achieve* through customer stories. A solid understanding of what personas care about and value comes from an often undervalued activity: primary research interviews with actual customers. When executives and merchandisers imagine that they know their customers and how they interact with the organization, their teams may develop personas without costly in-depth customer interviews and research. They may make unquestioned assumptions about their customer, resulting in hypothetical personas that can turn out to be inaccurate.

When personas are developed through actual research, however, the results can be eye-opening. Consider an example persona: Liz, a procurement manager with a graduate degree and two high-school-aged children. (Some teams choose names as hints about the customer—for example, if Liz is price-sensitive, she might be called "Low Budget Liz.") Another persona might be Tom, a manufacturing line manager in his mid-fifties who likes to play golf and travel with his wife now that the kids are out of the house. Perhaps he is more technical and interested in quality and reliability—which is why he's "Techie Tom."

Modeling a persona puts the designer in the shoes of different types of customers, so they can understand those customers' habits, goals, values, and ways of thinking. The persona informs design for their specific needs. Personas with nuance—a name, hobbies, a family, a career, particular values, and a personality—help designers better understand the types of target customers the organization is focused on. Then the people who are designing the site experience can ask themselves, "Would Tom think like this? How would Liz react to this offer?"

Developing a persona involves the creation of what are variously called customer stories, user stories, scenarios, or use cases. A customer story gets into the details of common challenges and problems across various types of users. The stories can get more granular as the needs and experiences of different customer types diverge, including increasing detail about the problems they are trying to solve and the tasks they need to complete on the site. As user experience expert Kim Godwin said, "Personas without scenarios are like characters with no plot."[3] Personas and scenarios can also ensure that testing covers the range of customer types that are likely to use the site.

Testing Across the Customer Taxonomy

A large, diversified business serving a range of markets and types of buyers could have numerous audiences and personas defined by characteristics like background (business or technical), role (buyer or engineer), title (CIO or CDO), size of firm (over or under $1 billion in revenue), or buying authority (over or under $1,000). Personas can help more precisely define audiences and inform design and testing if there are significant differences among audience members that impact navigation, terminology, goals, or other aspects of the customer's mental model.

Whatever you call them—audiences, personas, or customer types (and we'll use the terms interchangeably from here on)—designers use these classifications to make taxonomy and customer experience decisions. During taxonomy and customer experience design, personas, along with their scenarios, determine the information needed at a particular stage of their experience. Designers recruit test participants to ensure that the design meets the needs of different types of customers. Personas may not cover every type of customer (there are always outliers), but they should be representative of a cross-section of the majority of your customers.

Use multiple personas to test a core design on the different mental models of your customers. Different types of customers are likely to use different terminology, which should be captured and represented in the ontology. The ontology can act as a Rosetta Stone for your customers and is especially valuable when a website is serving both a technical/professional audience and a lay audience. For a health care site that serves both physicians and patients, for example, the patient search term for "cardiac care" might be "heart health." The ontology must be responsive to both types of searches to meet the needs of both customer groups.

Terminology, Context, and Expectations

While this may seem to be splitting hairs, it is important for an organization to test both the terms and concepts that are represented (the taxonomy) and how they are presented (the customer experience). They are intertwined, and therefore both must be tested.

When serving many audiences, the same terminology can have multiple meanings and contexts (remember "mold stripping"?). Consider a search on a financial services site for "tax planning." The right answer depends on the customer's job: a financial planner may be looking for tax-free bonds, while an accountant is seeking detailed tax code rules governing financial instruments. Perhaps the site has a broad audience; it serves young people, older folks, and people of various demographic backgrounds and interests. What would be the point of describing all of these types of customers—is the experience really going to be that different for each? Instead, test performance across personas to identify differences, if any, in how people navigate. It may make sense to allow them to self-select (commercial versus individual) and then provide different terms, paths, and structures for each.

By recruiting test subjects for each persona, you can determine which elements work for all customers and which ones needs to be adapted for subsets of customers. Testing across representative audiences tunes design, informs a personalization framework, and is the foundation for metrics-driven governance.

Audience Attributes

Tracking audience attributes allows you to move from design to site personalization. Those attributes can become quite complex. You can describe a customer based on details of products or services they have purchased in the past, their history with customer service, the types of equipment they may own, their status as businesses or consumers, their demographic details, and the types of content they are interested in.

As we mentioned in chapter 3, you can infer other characteristics that are less clearly defined, that may be rapidly changing, and that arise from a combination of human judgment and AI. For example, loyalty may be a composite measure based on length of relationship and past behavior. Or the customer may be described as "high value" based on frequency or volume of purchases. Figure 5-1 shows how customer metadata can reflect both explicit and implicit characteristics.

Figure 5-1: Explicit and Implicit Customer Data

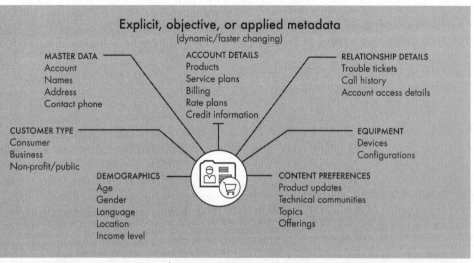

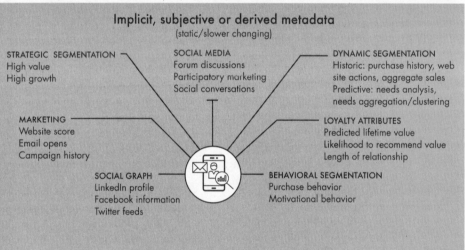

Customer Data Platforms and Customer Information Flows

Because so many different systems touch users, sites use a crucial piece of software that constantly takes in the "data exhaust" from other systems: the customer data platform (CDP). This software can make decisions about how to customize a site or aggregate signals for input to AI tools. In order for the CDP to function, the different systems have to consistently define attributes of the customer and their interaction using identical or analogous terminology.

The definitions of customer characteristics constitute an attribute model. Since each system has some representation of what customers are doing—whether clicking banner ads or opening email and searching on websites—these systems must use the same names for the same concepts. However, these tools typically come from different companies, so they inevitably will use different names for the customer attributes. For example, one system might track location as "geography" while another calls it "region." The model has to be defined to account for all customer data and how it flows among systems.

Some systems act on and change customer data—for example, when the customer orders a product. That new information goes into multiple systems, including the customer relationship management (CRM) system and the enterprise resource planning (ERP) system. A CDP might take that into account and then direct the content management system (CMS) to provide content more appropriate for a current customer rather than for prospects. The CDP may also cause the campaign management system to acknowledge that the target is a current customer. For example, if a customer responded to a campaign and filled out a form to download a white paper, the CDP could use that form to add profile elements such as "topics of interest." The campaign management tool would then communicate back to the CRM system, adding the topics of interest to the customer's record. The CDP and other systems would now have that data available to further inform future contact with the customer. Mapping information flow among technologies is a critical element of CDP deployment. For more detail, see the section on ontologies in ecommerce later in this chapter.

THE ESSENTIALS OF SITE CUSTOMIZATION

So far in this chapter, I've discussed the product and customer data that organizations collect and how sites customize search and navigation based on that data. But customization goes beyond navigation. So let's take a look at how sites will flex based on who's visiting and what they're looking for.

Consider how your organization reacts to the signals that indicate which kind of customer is visiting. For some organizations, data signals generate millions of customized audiences and offers, each one specifically tailored to exactly what that customer needs. Sites like wayfair.com use this mass personalization approach to optimize each user's experience on the site.

Designing for Automation: Begin with Artisan Processes

Automation is not magic. It starts with a complete understanding of the path humans follow and the ways a site can react.

When you set out to automate a personalized ecommerce experience, no system will know what a particular user or audience needs without the crucial factor of human insight. A marketing specialist who knows their customer will have to decide what message or part of a message they *think* will resonate—and then test it. They can then handcraft the message and try a variation, just as an artisan uses knowledge of their craft to create something that will engage with another human. The marketer will then try other variations and learn what other items might work and which ones do not.

Once you understand what drives messaging and design unique engagement components for it, you can experiment. Here is where the metrics and feedback allow for optimization—*handcrafted optimization*. This is not practical or scalable. But it is the beginning of understanding how to vary the design elements that can be recombined by a system and process and, ultimately, an algorithm.

One organization had 20 components that could be varied on a landing page: different images, offers, calls to action, phrasing, and headlines that could be rearranged and reassembled like Lego blocks. Suppose these elements could be arranged in five slots on the page, with four possible elements in each slot. The number of possible combinations of elements that could make up that page is four to the fifth power ($4 \times 4 \times 4 \times 4 \times 4$) or 1,024—over 1,000 possible variations of that page from those Lego blocks.

After breaking the messages up into reusable building blocks, the blocks need to be structured and organized through—as you probably guessed—the ontology. The ontology has the instructions for how the pieces fit together by virtue of its models of the content. Think of how tiles on a mosaic floor might fit together. The pieces have regular patterns that allow them to fit together within predetermined templates that have slots for each of the pieces.

What's the best way to assemble these hundreds or thousands of possible combinations? This is where machine learning algorithms come in. The input is the messaging architecture and a collection of components for each design element. The output is a random assembly of those components, which is then tested with audiences. The algorithm analyzes the data, picks the winning elements for that audience and journey stage, and then continues to experiment across other audiences, selecting winners in a Darwinian process. Over time, the system can generate hundreds or thousands of personalized experiences. Other algorithms can determine which products are presented once the customer clicks through on an offering. What that customer sees will depend on past purchase analysis, behaviors of similar audiences, and recent activity signals. You can do the same testing with ad copy, promotional offers, and sequences of messages.

This analysis is based on large-scale experimentation. It uses a form of AI called a *neural network*—a computing structure that "learns" patterns by observing the results of experiments. The neural network tests various weights to components and audience attributes until they produce optimal outputs. The network has a target of maximizing revenue and will experiment until it reaches the best performance possible with those components.

A Detailed Architecture Allows Customization at Scale

Personalization at this scale is a process of continually testing and recombining elements of design, messaging, and offerings. Marketers, of course, lack the bandwidth to customize messages across hundreds or thousands of audiences. What they need to develop is a messaging *architecture* that the AI can optimize across these audiences.

Even if the organization lacks the processes to develop a messaging and component architecture, there are many reasons to design potentially personalized content based on a large number of descriptors. If segment data is detailed, you can perform analytics to identify underserved markets and customers. As capabilities evolve, fine-tuning offers with machine learning will become a standard practice. Other tools in the organization's technology ecosystem will benefit from fine-grained audience definitions. New ways of interacting with customers will evolve quickly.

This level of detail also lends itself to revealing new insights about how the customer responds to offers and messaging. If you lump a large number of customers into one big bucket of "new customers," it will not be possible to understand their differences across other characteristics and descriptors. Remember that, ultimately, humans will not be selecting attributes and personalizing content based on them—algorithms will. A customer attribute model defines the data features that the machine learning algorithm will use. Machine learning algorithms perform best with a lot of variables; the more customer features we define up front, the better the algorithm can perform.

AI can actually help identify audiences with common responses to offers. Machine learning can look at all of the signals from customer characteristics and seek latent or hidden attributes that explain how offer characteristics relate to audience responses. The algorithms can predict who else might respond similarly to the same characteristics or identify new audiences based on subtle common details in prior audiences. Those esoteric customer features could depend on complex relationships with dozens of variables, but they indicate that two audiences are similar. The algorithm can identify these "look-alike" audiences through combinations of data gleaned from shopping patterns, demographics, industry, job role, interests, purchase history, and other user signals.

Initially your organization will not act on all of the signals. You can simplify your approach by customizing a broad model of the domain for a particular use case and application; the added granularity in the data will improve future flexibility and adaptability. The ultimate goal is for the system to read the customer's digital "body language," just as a star salesperson might use their knowledge of all the customer's past history and tendencies and behavior in the moment to adjust exactly how to best communicate with that customer.

ONTOLOGY FOR ECOMMERCE

If data is the foundation of a customized site experience, wrangling that data from multiple systems is increasingly the most difficult ecommerce challenge. The solution to that challenge lies with the one corporate element that ties together all the data: the ontology.

Each of the data elements that describe the customer needs to be harmonized with the other customer experience and engagement systems. To function together, the systems require common ways of describing these elements and organizing principles. The ontology is where these elements are synchronized.

Machine learning programs refer to these common elements as "features." Though the machine learning program figures out some of these categories and classes itself, those features are not sufficient. Defining the features that are unique to your organization is key to your differentiation and competitive advantage.

Product categories are part of the ontology, as are the various vocabularies that define features and specifications. Those relationships are often contained in specialized ontology management tools, or can be embedded in master data, metadata, and CRM systems. The important piece is to be consistent when possible, and to differentiate where necessary, depending on the application.

For example, as we've described earlier, product classifications have to be consistent across the ecommerce system, the CRM system, the content management system, and the enterprise resource planning (ERP) system. This does not mean they are exactly the same in each of those systems. The ERP system typically uses a structure that lends itself to financial reporting, while the CRM system may use a more territory-specific ordering or subject matter expert grouping. Merchandisers need a view of product collections that is different from the one that customers see, and product classifications for the merchandiser can provide that. Those variations need to be intentionally designed rather than left to independent groups making decisions as they develop, configure, or deploy their tools—and the ontology needs to rationalize and connect them.

What about the product information management (PIM) system? It's not a substitute for the ontology. While a PIM will contain many features (in the form of metadata and product models), the ontology is what translates the important elements across systems and provides knowledge relationships that are unlikely to be contained in the PIM. The PIM becomes more powerful because of ontological elements.

Ecommerce Depends on a Robust Collection of Attributes in the Ontology

The ontology might include products, product categories, campaigns, market segments, customer types, content types, channels, and suppliers. The ontology contains language variations through "equivalence relationships"—terms that represent the same concept but that may not be actual synonyms. For example, "opacity" and "transparency" could be equivalence terms because even though they have different meanings, they represent the same concept.

Other equivalence terms include terminology for use by the search engine: technical terms, acronyms, abbreviations, slang terms, and other non-preferred terminology. Ontologies contain references to resources that the user might not think of; they are like reference librarians that know what to suggest when the user enters an ambiguous query. They can also contain cross-sell, upsell, and other related product relationships, inherited from a PIM system or separately.

The ontology contains customer roles and their associated industries, interests, and problems. This information allows the search engine to return results in the correct context. Knowing the customer's industry, for example, allows for disambiguation of "mold stripping" in the example we described earlier.

Content is tagged with metadata from the ontology, which should be constructed to be the source of truth for all organizing principles in the enterprise. Product attributes are sourced from the ontology as well, and are ultimately applied to product records in the PIM system.

AI and machine learning technologies can aid in the process of applying the correct metadata to products by recognizing patterns and clustering and similar products so that an analyst can classify them. Text analytics machine learning programs can extract product data from source documents like

PDFs and engineering specifications. The ontology contains the reference data and gives the machine learning technology the correct lists from which to recognize attribute data. Conversely, these same tools can also begin to extract candidate terms and attributes from text to start or enrich the ontology. Figure 5-2 shows the start of a sample ontology.

Figure 5-2: Sample Elements of an Ecommerce Ontology

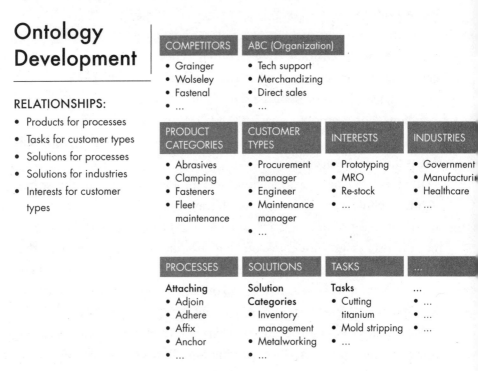

Ontology Development

RELATIONSHIPS:

- Products for processes
- Tasks for customer types
- Solutions for processes
- Solutions for industries
- Interests for customer types

COMPETITORS	ABC (Organization)
• Grainger	• Tech support
• Wolseley	• Merchandizing
• Fastenal	• Direct sales
• ...	• ...

PRODUCT CATEGORIES	CUSTOMER TYPES	INTERESTS	INDUSTRIES
• Abrasives	• Procurement manager	• Prototyping	• Government
• Clamping	• Engineer	• MRO	• Manufacturing
• Fasteners	• Maintenance manager	• Re-stock	• Healthcare
• Fleet maintenance	• ...	• ...	• ...

PROCESSES	SOLUTIONS	TASKS	...
Attaching	**Solution Categories**	**Tasks**	• ...
• Adjoin	• Inventory management	• Cutting titanium	• ...
• Adhere	• Metalworking	• Mold stripping	• ...
• Affix	• ...	• ...	
• Anchor			
• ...			

SPECIAL CONSIDERATIONS IN B2B COMPANIES

In business-to-business companies, especially, ecommerce is about more than product sales. Customers are choosing and purchasing services of all types; even in complex sales that typically require guidance and knowledge, they are conducting research online in advance of the sale. This is true for industries that have historically sold through personal relationships, including those in which sales have previously been dependent on human judgment and expertise.

In earlier times, paper catalogs contained product clues, or cues, that customers depended on. These wayfinding cues are different in the online world, because digital processes drastically increase the need for highly detailed information structures. When product data is missing, products drop from search results or do not display correctly in online comparisons. In other words, having the wrong product information design makes your products invisible.

Whether you are a retailer, a B2B enterprise, or a distributor, your ecommerce system performs a critical function in your customer journey by helping customers find and learn about your products. And if they can't find it, they can't buy it.

B2B ecommerce is less mature than B2C due to the complexity of the sales, the nature of large product catalogs, the unique needs of customers, and the traditional reliance on selling through human relationships. Industrial markets can be quite diverse and complex, which makes fine-tuning the online user experience more challenging. However, since B2B customers are also B2C customers in their non-work roles, they have become accustomed to high-quality web experiences. As websites have evolved, user expectations have increased. Digital natives—who have lived their entire lives with technology—expect to do everything through smartphones and to have easy access and "Google-like" search experiences.

As a result, B2B customers in all sectors are increasingly expecting a seamless, consistent experience. Organizations can compete based on how well they understand the types of problems their customers need to solve and how to best organize and present that information. Success in creating such an experience requires product taxonomies and data structured in a way that is intuitive to the customer.

The next chapter contains much more detail on the sales funnel, especially as it applies to B2B companies.

OVERLAPPING TOOLS AND ORGANIZATIONAL MATURITY

Complex ecommerce functionality includes elements of product information management, digital asset management, customer information management, content management, marketing and promotions management, email management, social media marketing, shopping cart functionality, payment and order management integration, data quality and governance, and more. Personalization mechanisms can and do span most of these functions. Many organizations have chosen a modular approach to building their platforms, with many best-of-breed applications being integrated with web services. This modular approach can optimize functionality with specialized approaches to niche problems, but it increases cost and complexity.

Ecommerce technology platforms can include a range of functions even as they integrate with other tools that provide specialized functionality. For example, some ecommerce tools include product information management (PIM) technology, but others leave that functionality to PIM vendors. Some PIM tools include digital asset management (to manage images, video, and other rich media). Specialized and customized tools make the environment more complex, adding cost and reducing agility.

How pervasive are these overlaps in function? Consider an exercise I conduct in workshops on information management strategy. I lead participants through the process of creating a content model for an invoice to be accessed in a content management environment. As I encourage participants ("What's missing? What else?"), they add details and more and more metadata. Then they suddenly realize that they have left the confines of content management and are actually designing an accounting system, not just a document structure. Details around line items and quantities, shipping addresses, pricing, and the like do not belong in the content management environment; they belong in the invoicing application.

Then they begin to ask themselves: What data did the customer actually need? What functionality? What tasks and problems are they trying to solve? And what is the most appropriate tool for the job? It is possible to design more detail in the PDF of the invoice, but why not just retrieve it from the accounting system?

This exercise illustrates the importance of "fitness to purpose": designing and configuring applications to have appropriate functionality rather than shoehorning in things that the package or platform was not designed for. You must choose technology in the full context of what is in place today and what will be needed in the future.

You should expect some overlap in the functionality of the various ecommerce systems, such as an ecommerce suite that includes some content management but that might also integrate with a content management system. The key is to define scenarios and use cases and to determine where those scenarios can be best handled with the greatest flexibility and least amount of complexity. Adding new code adds cost and complexity. While it is possible to build accounting functionality in a CMS, it would be costly and confusing to do so, since that is far from core functionality.

An ontology manages, translates, and integrates the inevitable design differences among customers, content, and product attributes. It helps speed development and integration by providing the reference terminology for each of the components of an ecommerce suite.

Maturity Assessment

One useful tool in evaluating ecommerce capability is the maturity model. Since ecommerce requires orchestration of information across multiple systems and processes, you must consider each of the major systems in relation to the critical functions that comprise the ecommerce technology stack. Orchestration is more than integration. It is the finely tuned digital machinery that manufactures the digital relationships with your customers.

The critical ecommerce functions include the following:

- **Product launch and item onboarding.** How long does it take to bring a new product online? Is this a fast, seamless automated process or one that takes many weeks and manual activities to accomplish?
- **Product information management.** How detailed is the product data model? Does it include the attributes that are important to target customers? Are solution and merchandising attributes and relationships defined? Can this data be sourced or distributed in a syndicated way? Specifically:
  - Are multiple taxonomies in use?
  - Do multiple taxonomies lead to an inconsistent user experience? (Different parts of a site sometimes use different taxonomies.)

- Does the information architecture use industry best practices?
- Does it leverage industry standards?
- Is content managed in a CMS?
- Is there a PIM system?
- Is the information architecture consistent across channels and devices?

- **Product configuration.** Is product information static, or does it allow for configuration and customization? Are there complex rules engines with configuration constraints? Does the system use an expert advisor bot for complex, custom-built-to-order products?
- **Analytics.** What is the level of sophistication of analysis of customers, segments, traffic, conversions, multivariant testing, and personalization metrics?
- **Commerce and order management.** What capabilities are available to customers? Does the system include conversational advisor order management, shopping-cart-level promotions, and segment personalization attribute triggers?
- **Payments and pricing.** Some less mature sites require users to make a call to obtain pricing information and do not have commerce capability. Others require registration or manual setup with a salesperson. More advanced capabilities include purchase workflow/approval, one-click ordering, automated replenishment with negotiated pricing, multidimensional personalization, and a seamless omnichannel experience.
- **Data quality.** For example, a PIM system can report on how completely product data is filled out using visualization tools, audit trails, data quality services, and compliance mechanisms. Ideally, this would link to business outcomes and automated exception reporting.

Table 5-1 describes maturity levels across each of these dimensions.

Maturity will likely be uneven, with some departments and processes being more advanced than others. It may not be necessary to fully optimize each activity. The process requirements, website capabilities, and engagement strategy may not require Stage 5 maturity.

Consider that the time required for a large enterprise to go from one maturity level to another is typically six months to one year. If the organization is at Stage 1 and the process requires Stage 4, but the timeline and budget requires attaining that maturity in six months, you will need additional resources. If budgets don't allow for that acceleration, you need to scale down the project.

Maturity Checklist for Ecommerce

To help you operationalize the maturity rubric I just described, Table 5-2 presents a useful checklist of ecommerce elements. The list is not meant to be exhaustive, but you can use it to place some functions along a continuum of complexity and maturity, with the staffer most likely to be able to help you assess maturity shown in parentheses. Create your own model based on the important elements, and grade where your current processes are versus the desired future state. That will provide some sense of the gap between the current state and the future.

Table 5-1: Example of B2B Ecommerce Maturity Levels

Capability \ Maturity	1-Unpredictable	2-Aware
Product Launch and Item Onboarding	Cycle times in weeks or months; manual processes	Multiple out-of-synch systems need to be updated and reconciled
Product Information Management	Poor data quality; manual validation; limited transformation	Category hierarchies and attributes identified; semi-automated data quality processes
Product Configuration	Basic static product selection without configuration	Base variant configuration
Analytics	No analytics on customer purchases	Basic customer segmentation and purchase analytics
Commerce and Order Management	No transaction capability	Basic commerce with persistent shopping cart; abandoned cart triggered promotions
Payments and Pricing	Call for pricing; no public pricing; no commerce capability	Pricing available with registration; manual setup with salesperson; basic catalog site
Data Quality	No data quality functionality	Limited data quality reporting

3-Competent	4-Synchronized	5-Choreographed
Multiple content streams triggered by product launch	Tuned taxonomies for channels; A/B testing for launches	Seamless cross-channel product launch; cycle times in days
business rules built into product data quality; manual hierarchy mapping to channels	Data quality feedback to vendors; consistent cross-channel mapping	Many-to-many vendor-to-channel cross-mapping; integration with domain analytics
Base variant and product customization capability	Complex configuration with rules engine and configuration constraints; business and design tool integration	Complex built-to-order integrator expert advisor bot; nested configurations; design and business tool integration
Reporting on-page traffic; popular products; conversion rates; orders and search terms	A/B testing with feedback adjustments; dashboards for UI; merchandizing; campaigns and product bundle performance testing	End-to-end KPIs linked to multi-variant testing and remediation; personalization optimization metrics
Cross-sell and upsell merchant configurable with shopping basket recommendations	Cross touchpoint promotion management; search-based merchandizing	Conversational advisor order management, including shopping cart level promotions; segment personalization attribute triggers
Basic personalization; purchase workflow/ approval; one-click ordering; bulk pricing	Automated replenishment with negotiated pricing; multi-currency; multi-language	Multidimensional personalization; seamless omnichannel experience
Integrated data quality metrics via PIM or PIM integration; attribute fill; completeness	Visualization tools; audit trails; integration with third-party data quality services; compliance mechanisms	Linkage to business outcomes; automated exception reporting; queue management and workflow; semi-automated fill

Table 5-2: Maturity Checklist for Ecommerce

Supplier Onboarding	• Have suppliers provided an inventory of available metadata? (sourcing manager) • Have product data models been validated against merchandizing requirements? (catalog manager, merchandiser) • Are data quality review processes and scorecards in place? (procurement, data quality manager) • Are supplier data curation responsibilities defined in a Master Services Agreement? (procurement) • Are data quality performance standards linked to procurement performance measures? (procurement)
Product Data Onboarding	• Are product managers getting needed content and data? (product data operations) • Is product data complete and consistent? (data quality manager) • Is product data appropriate for merchandising? (merchandiser) • Do product attributes help users make selections? (information architect) • Are technical specifications organized with product content? (product data operations) • Are images and rich media assets tagged with product data? (catalog manager)
Demand Generation Metrics	• Are social media campaigns assigned tracking codes? (marketing analyst, marketing manager) • Are promotions measured against baselines? (marketing analyst, marketing manager) • Are email engagement metrics monitored and acted upon by product marketers? (marketing analyst, marketing manager) • Are campaign effectiveness metrics benchmarked across categories? (marketing analyst, category manager) • Are engagement metrics aligned with customer lifecycle? (marketing analyst, category manager, information architect)

Table 5-2 (Continued)

Omnichannel Experience	• Are store promotions consistent with online promotions? (marketing analyst, marketing manager, regional manager) • Can customers find products in stock at stores? (marketing analyst, regional manager) • Can customers select products on mobile devices? (information architect) • Can customers begin transaction on device and complete in store? (merchandiser, ecommerce manager) • Are online preferences retained for personalized shopping? (ecommerce director, information architect)
Self-Service Metrics	• Is self-service content call deflection measured? (call center manager, knowledge base owner) • Is engineer knowledge base contribution measured? (knowledge base owner) • Is support content quality measured? (support manager, knowledge base owner) • Is user-generated content quality measured? (community manager, content manager)
Content Operations	• Is editorial content refresh workflow defined? (content manager) • Do expiration dates drive action? (editorial director, content manager) • Are asset rights managed and respected? (content manager) • Are current promotions lifecycles automated? (marketing manager, merchandiser) • Are category manager objectives communicated to content operations? (category manager, editorial director) • Is support content presented at point of need? (content manager, knowledge base owner) • Are user-generated content ingestion workflows defined? (community manager, content manager) • Is content tagging and association automated? (content manager, ecommerce director, merchandiser)

Table 5-2 (Continued)

Personalization Strategy	• Are buyer needs documented and user personas defined? (merchandiser, marketing manager, information architect) • Are tasks and objectives aligned with specific content? (content manager, information architect) • Are related content aggregation rules defined? (editorial manager, content manager, information architect, marketing analyst, merchandiser) • Are personalization rules developed for buyer segments? (information architect, marketing manager, marketing analyst, merchandiser) • Is content dynamically assembled based on user behavior? (information architect, marketing manager, marketing analyst, merchandiser)
Digital Assets	• Are spec sheets associated with product content? (product data operations) • Are engineering drawings available when appropriate? (merchandiser) • Are assets organized for retrieval and reuse? (information architect) • Are generic versus specific image requirements defined? (merchandiser) • Are marketing brochures organized appropriately? (information architect, marketing manager) • Are high-resolution images available as appropriate? (information architect, content manager)
Analytics	• Are content performance metrics monitored and embedded in governance processes? (information architect, marketing manager, marketing analyst, merchandiser) • Are user departure paths understood? (information architect, marketing analyst) • Is search effectiveness measured? (information architect, content manager) • Are conversion and purchase behaviors monitored across dimensions and factors? (marketing manager, marketing analyst, merchandiser)

Table 5-2 (Continued)

Content Architecture	• Are metadata models fully defined? (information architect, content manager)
	• Are controlled vocabularies harmonized? (information architect, content manager)
	• Does content architecture support customer experience—that is, do taxonomies and content models support customer tasks? (information architect, marketing manager, marketing analyst, merchandiser)
	• Are content and product data models and relationships aligned? (information architect, PIM system manager)
	• Does the content architecture support a dynamically generated experience: (information architect, marketing manager, marketing analyst, merchandiser)
	• Are all cross-sell opportunities supported with rich content? (merchandiser, content manager, editorial director)

The job of any ecommerce site is, ultimately, to sell. But sales requires specialized tools, as I'll describe in more detail in the next chapter.

TAKEAWAYS FROM CHAPTER 5

In this chapter, I've shown how AI has its broadest and most powerful application in ecommerce sites. But that's also where the product and customer data, design, and planning can go off the rails without appropriate attention to the ontology. These are the main points in this chapter:

- Ecommerce—even when it's not where the sale gets made—is where ontology-powered AI can have its biggest impact.
- In a modern site, search and site navigation have become a customized, dynamically updating conversation.
- Data is the foundation of modern ecommerce, and the quality of the experience depends on the quality of the data.

- Product taxonomies that reflect not just product features, but relationships, make sophisticated ecommerce possible.
- Standardized product taxonomies enable interoperability with the supply chain, but differentiated taxonomies can create competitive advantage.
- Customer classification begins with personas and mental models.
- Testing must include all types of potential customers and personas.
- Customer data platforms assemble all relevant customer data from multiple systems.
- Site customization starts with artisanal experiments but continues with improvements tested by neural networks.
- Ecommerce depends on a robust collection of attributes in the product ontology.
- Customer and product information systems inevitably overlap; efficiency requires straightening out their relationships with each other.
- You should assess the maturity of your customer systems to determine where improvements will have the biggest impact.

CHAPTER 6

SHARPENING THE SALES PROCESS

There once was a manufacturing organization—let's call it WidgetCo. WidgetCo's customers tended to do business by choosing parts from its thick printed catalogs and working with its helpful salespeople on the phone and in person. WidgetCo's mature and impressive salesforce had built and supported its reputation as a well-respected brand generating repeat sales to customers, in some cases serving the same customers for decades.

WidgetCo's biggest triumphs included "design wins," sales successes in which a manufacturing customer specified WidgetCo components for a product that would have a decades-long service life. A design win ensured a long and steady revenue stream, especially for products in highly regulated industries like aircraft manufacturing. With repeat orders rolling in on a regular basis from design wins, WidgetCo found it unnecessary to invest resources into moving any part of its well-established, high-touch sales process online. The company was much happier staying in its comfort zone. Everyone was content to carry on doing things as they had always been done, through trusty old paper catalogs, regular phone calls, and drinks with their buddies who had been buying from them for decades.

Why did the company embrace this old, analog workflow? Because both the buyers and WidgetCo's executives were old-school, with roots that long predated the web and smartphones. But older generations of business leaders did not recognize how technology was transforming their markets and their customers.

Unfortunately, while WidgetCo's existing customers knew its products and likely had had a well-worn copy of the WidgetCo catalog on their shelves for years, the next generation of engineers who are designing and choosing components for the products of today and tomorrow have lived with technology for their entire lives. To them, getting their information online is just the natural way they are used to working. Opening up a physical product catalog or picking up the phone to actually talk to another human being is not part of their worldview.

Eventually, WidgetCo realized that its paper catalogs and personal relationships needed an update. But because the company had not made any significant investments in ecommerce or modern systems, the change it needed to make was arduous and slow. WidgetCo became invisible to engineers working on new generations of designs that might have used its products. Its competitors' sales organizations used their web presences as a powerful selling tool when they met with prospects and customers, making it easy to research solutions, compare options, gather supporting data, and confidently recommend components to the customers' engineering, procurement, and manufacturing organizations. WidgetCo's salespeople were at a disadvantage. They missed several new generations of product categories where they had traditionally led in the market, and they rapidly lost market share, sliding from being an industry leader to fourth or fifth place in their flagship offerings. The company's stock declined by half and the CEO lost his job.

The lesson of WidgetCo is clear: The status quo is dangerous, and relationship-based selling is insufficient. Companies must invest in systems to support and surround their salespeople and optimize sales processes. And AI can help.

SALESPEOPLE RESIST BECAUSE THEY FEEL THEIR WORK CAN'T BE AUTOMATED

Salespeople, trained to nurture relationships, will tell you that machines can't help them. "Our business is based on personal relationships," they say. "We don't need to invest in ecommerce because our customers don't buy from us over the web. Technology support for our salespeople isn't the problem—they just need to work harder to connect with our customers." I hear this all the time, especially from B2B businesses and others whose sales are largely based on relationships and face-to-face pitch meetings.

This thinking is dangerously out of date. I'm not suggesting that the internet can replace salespeople. But smart companies can and must embrace AI, both for modernizing ecommerce and for optimizing every element of the sales process.

AI Helps Salespeople Deliver for Sophisticated Customers

Today's customers are better informed about solutions, pricing, competitors, and products because of the transparency that the web brings to business practices and complex solutions. You're only as visible to online customers as your ranking in search engines. Search ranking is based in part on the value and completeness of content and on data related to the search terms customers use to find vendors and research the marketplace.

Before a customer meets with you, they have used online resources to be more knowledgeable about your organization's offerings and options. This is true especially for the more complex sales that require human interaction. Consultative selling and complex, long-sales-cycle solutions require comprehensive supporting content and knowledge. That content and knowledge helps salespeople serve their targets and, properly designed, becomes an indispensable tool for accomplishing work.

Here's what you need to know: Future sales depend on a proper foundation of clear processes and curated data. Unless you understand the reinvention of those processes and how data enables the redefinition of the value chain, you're at risk of developing a short-sighted frame of reference and underinvesting in the foundational work that digital transformations require.

Because the entire value chain is defined by the movement of data from supplier to customer, any company's digital transformation is a data transformation. The value chain will be increasingly automated. Salespeople must adjust how they spend their time and interact. We must reduce their cognitive load, automate and augment routine and mundane tasks, and supply them with new tools for finding and reaching their targets.

In this chapter, I describe how AI is revolutionizing sales processes from end to end. This includes how companies collect and prioritize leads, how they qualify those leads, how they help salespeople conduct research, how they help customers configure and access price quotes, how they optimize the closing process, and how they execute contracts. AI, supported by appropriate information in an ontology, can make every element of the sales process more efficient. It doesn't replace salespeople; it just supercharges their abilities.

CHATBOTS HELP WITH LEAD CAPTURE

Salespeople always want the fresh leads (as dramatized in every salesperson's favorite movie, *Glengarry Glen Ross*), and marketing's job is to find those leads and hand them off to a business development or "inside sales" rep. These leads often come from a pool of contacts who download reports and white papers, register for webinars, sign up for newsletters, attend trade shows, or fill out a contact form on the company's website.

AI can help with lead generation. Some organizations are using chatbots to answer prospect questions and direct them to appropriate content. These types of systems require a deep understanding of the range of potential customer needs and the reasons for their site visit. "Conversational marketing" applications use natural language interactions to catalyze a conversation that can discover more details about specific customer needs. Tools like Drift use chatbots to converse with visitors and, once they are engaged, route the details of the interaction to specialists on a sales team, schedule demonstrations of the solution, and capture email addresses for follow-up.[1] These kinds of tools integrate with third- and first-party data sources to enrich the customer profile and compile enough details to determine whether the prospect is worth pursuing.

VIRTUAL ASSISTANTS HELP QUALIFY PROSPECTS

AI technologies can be used to research prospects to determine if they fit the criteria of targets. This qualification goes beyond industry, title, and size of organization; it takes into consideration more subtle marketplace signals that indicate that someone is in the market for the offering.

Many sales leaders qualify leads using BANTS criteria: budget, authority, need, timeline, and strategic fit. Are we engaging with someone who has the budget to buy? Are they the authority who can approve the purchase, or do we have a line of sight and an ability to communicate with that person? Is there a clear alignment of the prospect's need with our offering? Do they have a timeline that indicates it makes sense to focus resources, and is there a compelling event that is going to cause them to act? Are we strategically positioned to win?

Once a prospect meets two out of five BANTS criteria, the inside sales rep tags them as a marketing qualified lead (MQL). The MQL is handed off to sales, and sales moves them through the process and further qualifies them to three out of the five BANTS criteria, after which they become a sales qualified lead (SQL).

Educating prospects during their exploration of your products and services can help increase their readiness to buy once a salesperson becomes involved. Customers need to gain a level of comfort and familiarity with your approach or solution, especially if the need is complex or the choice involves many alternatives. An intelligent virtual assistant can lay the foundation for a salesperson by providing content and answering questions based on where the prospect is in the sales cycle: high level, overview, or background information for early stage investigation, followed by increasingly detailed content as the prospect gets closer to purchase. Where complex products and services are involved, basic client education can swallow up salespeople's time. Customers may not know the true nature of the problem they are trying to solve, or may not understand what is involved in solving that problem. Chatbots and virtual assistants can move prospects along the learning curve and prepare them for more effective interactions with a salesperson.

To prioritize leads and serve up the right content, AI harvests a variety of signals from systems that capture interactions. It then combines these signals to influence who the rep calls and what they say when they reach their prospect or customer, as shown in Table 6-1.

Table 6-1: Supporting Sales throughout the Process

Primary Signal	Source	Purpose	Role of AI	How it Supports Sales
Account details	CRM	Inform offers	Identifies similar targets based on latent attributes	Provides account list of prioritized targets for prospecting
Transaction history	ERP	Highlight potential gaps in product portfolio	Identifies missing products from portfolio based on shopping basket and prior purchase analysis	Makes specific product recommendations with supporting content and talking points
Web clickstream	CMS	Spot buying signals	Serves up personalized content based on stage and interests	Scores prospects buying propensity in near real time
Role of contact	CRM	Project individual needs	Provides tailored messaging based on similar prospects	Provides list of solutions designed to resonate with role
Product relationships	PIM	Configure solutions	Recommends complementary products and solutions	Suggests solution kits or packages for discussion with customer

For example, a large scientific supply company used these signals to help its salespeople determine who they should spend the most time with and what products and solutions they should recommend to their prospects and current customers. Because the landscape of scientific solutions, technologies, and methodologies is so vast, even specialists had a difficult time comprehending capabilities in detail. The digital marketing team worked with analytics specialists and the sales organization to identify and execute campaigns that would target customer segments with appropriate offers. They supported sales reps with an AI prediction algorithm that recommended content based on the customer history, industry, offer, and other sales predictors, presented to reps in a dashboard.

There is a trade-off between the speed at which a lead can be pursued and the level of depth for the engagement. The reps at this company could follow up quickly with a generic offer, or they could wait for analysis to help them more precisely understand the needs of a prospect and therefore engage more effectively.

AI MAKES LEAD-NURTURING MORE CONSISTENT

Any sales leader will tell you that the main challenge in using customer relationship management (CRM) technologies like salesforce.com lies in compliance: getting salespeople to use the system to track their outreach and interactions with prospects. If the data is not in the system, no AI program can help. Some salespeople like to "off-road" (some call these reps "free-range salespeople") rather than follow a process or a script. Even when the value proposition is compelling and the offer appropriate, it takes about ten touches to get through to a contact. But many salespeople do "hit and runs," sending an occasional email and sometimes following up with a call, sometimes not.

To nurture leads efficiently, initial calling and outreach should start with consistent communications using proven templates and messages. The best lead-nurturing programs are also consistent in cadence (the timing and frequency of communications) and messaging (varying the messages to touch on various value propositions that could resonate). These processes are often so consistent and repeatable that an automated program that sends customized messages to specific targets on a predetermined schedule can do the job.

A rules-based workflow system with preloaded email messaging can send appropriate messages to prospects. Another AI component can process the prospect's response with a natural language processing (NLP) engine that interprets "interest signals" to hand the live prospect off to a human. There are many ways someone could indicate interest: by responding, "Tell me more," "Let's talk," "Send me some info," "We can schedule a call," "I may be interested," or "Not right now but next month/quarter/year," for example. Text analytics of the response tells the bot when it's time to hand off to a human.

An example of this is a tool called Conversica, a virtual assistant that engages with prospects and determines through natural language processing whether they are holding their hand up to get more info, and then routes them to a human.

While this description makes it sound as if the whole conversation is automated, the reverse is actually true; only the cadence and routine communications are controlled by a machine, and that machine involves human sales staff when they can best move the conversation forward.

AI HELPS SALES STAFF SET PRIORITIES

What is the biggest differentiator between a highly effective, top-rank salesperson and the newbie who can't seem to make their numbers? While many factors are important—including salespeople's knowledge of solutions, interpersonal skills, core selling skills, understanding of the competitive landscape, and extent of their network—the number one consideration is how effectively they spend their time. Effective prospecting, the precursor to successful sales, is based on two factors: who you call and what you say. AI applications can help improve productivity by using aggregates of data from a range of sources to determine which prospects are most likely to be receptive to a call within a particular buying window.

One of the most valuable aspects of machine learning is its ability to find patterns or ascertain meaningful factors that would be difficult for a human to identify when analyzing large amounts of information. The AI analyzes a set of data that matches some criteria—a training set—and then the algorithm processes a new set of information using the patterns from that training set. While human analysts can identify explicit factors that seem to match their target market, such as industry, size of company, or region, machine learning can identify rarer, subtler, less easily discernible factors. These might include purchasing patterns; issuance of requests for proposals (RFPs); growth in particular sectors; new product releases; mergers; or any number of economic, demographic, and account characteristics.

Vendors such as EverString process lists of accounts that have met a success criteria that an organization deems important, analyze the accounts for subtle signals, and generate lists of similar target accounts for prospecting including ratings on the likelihood of success. This classic machine learning pattern identification taps sources of data that the vendor licenses from a network of information providers. EverString claims to process up to 20,000 data signals that are automatically and manually collected and collated from a range of public and private sources; it then uses its proprietary algorithms to process data sets.[2]

EverString collects data on organizations by spidering and linking through data relationships—similarly to how Facebook uses "friend of a friend" relationships to establish connections, like attending a common school, that may not be obvious. EverString reveals these relationships through a combination of human curation and machine learning on data from websites, job postings, news, funding, technology usage, and team profiles. They are known as "graph" data relationships, and their representation is specified in the ontology.

An approach such as this can help sales and marketing organizations devote scarce resources to the types of companies that will be most similar to promising past candidates. The challenge is always to determine which signals are most relevant. Something about the data set has to correlate with the characteristics and nature of the company's offering. Determining if such a service is effective requires experimenting with test data and training data. If you have 1,000 customers and prospects and you train the service on data showing the best among 500 of those, it should be able to identify the best customers in the remaining 500. Even if it does, you should then test it on a new prospect list that salespeople will reach out to.

Prospect Prioritization

AI and machine learning algorithms can score prospects based on buying signals and a propensity-to-buy model, allowing sales representatives to focus on the highest likelihood prospects. The best prospects can be bubbled to the top of the list when there is enough data to model buying cycles and identify cues that indicate a readiness to transact. Depending on the industry, nature of the purchase, type of buyer, and details of the sale cycle, different models and algorithms will predict purchase behavior with varying degrees of accuracy. Just as there may be subtle characteristics of companies who are similar to your best customers, there are subtle signals that indicate buying propensity.

Propensity models can influence messaging approaches and operate further up the funnel on earlier stage pipeline prospects. This functionality intersects with marketing automation and campaign management technologies, changing offers and messages depending on the behavior of the prospect.

Prospecting is never linear. It is difficult for marketers and sales management to determine the marketing vehicles and channels that generate a purchase decision. Salespeople use instinct and ingenuity to pursue prospects. I have known salespeople to apply many different approaches in doggedly pursuing prospects who they believe need their offering—including one person who sent a buyer a single glove with a message about getting the other glove if they could meet (I believe it was an apparel sale and was a very nice set of gloves). Clearly an approach like that should be used only on the most likely candidates, and a salesperson might make that prioritization based on knowing the needs of the client and on exhaustive research.

A propensity model will stand in for this firsthand knowledge and detailed research. It works by weighing factors and interaction patterns that similar customers have exhibited before their purchase and extrapolates to predict the buying behavior of a prospect who has never purchased. Propensity models require sufficient quality data, extensive tuning, and feedback loops that continually refine the algorithm. The more consistent the purchase behavior and sales cycle and the greater the quantity of supporting data, the more accurate the prediction will be. While many CRM systems include these types of algorithms, they also depend on integrating signals from a customer data platform that contains accurate representations of customer interactions. Poor quality or inconsistent data in any of the upstream systems can corrupt the program and degrade the predictive performance.

Tools that integrate with marketing platforms such as HubSpot or Marketo send sales offers and promotions at times when prospects are more ready to engage. One tool, Seventh Sense, claims to "send sales emails at the optimal time for maximum engagement." One way to determine engagement is by measuring email opens and responses to offers; however, these signals do not always translate into conversions. The only way to determine if an AI-powered sales technology can truly perform is by testing it on your content, offers, and targets.

Semantic Search: Prioritizing through Data Analysis

Semantic search helps collect and report on data and content relevant for sales. Semantic search applications can integrate structured and unstructured information in the context of a particular task, such as selling. They consolidate all of the content and data needed to understand the what (from structured data) and the why (from unstructured content).

This is valuable in sales because salespeople need to understand background information and history when calling on prospects. A search-based application can pull all records from interactions, prior purchases, and opportunities, as well as information about network contacts, industry news, and company-specific content.

Semantic search makes these associations through the ontology, using tools that automatically tag relevant data sources with customer or prospect identifiers, surfacing this information from multiple internal and external sources in a single interface. A semantic search approach also accounts for spelling variations and inconsistencies in terminology through the use of synonyms and thesaurus data. As with any other application, search-based applications must be developed by understanding detailed user requirements, and then tuned to the specific target market, sales process, and information sources appropriate for the organization. This process allows these applications to present the data in a way that is useful to your sales force and easy for managers and executives to track.

AUTOMATING THE CONFIGURE-PRICE-QUOTE (CPQ) PROCESS

A manufacturer of precast concrete products was upgrading their website for easier customer self-service. But, while precast concrete sounds decidedly low tech, orders can be highly complex, requiring an expert with knowledge of the industry, customer needs, manufacturing processes, and capabilities to guide selection of many variables and options. The orders must specify design elements of the most basic features of public infrastructure: the culverts, boxes, electrical vaults, and other items that must comply with a host of regulatory requirements, local ordinances, and architectural and utility designs.

The manufacturer found that it could offload the selection process from the sales reps using a technology that embedded the rules and relationships for product design into a configuration tool. This freed enormous amounts of time for the reps so they could do more actual selling and prospecting, rather than spending it on routine, repeatable, mundane tasks like picking the number and configuration of openings in a junction box.

We are familiar with online configuration tools that help with selection of products with diverse options—for example, when specifying and buying a new laptop computer. Any such purchase must specify processor power, amount of memory, hard-drive size, screen size, type of display, and other options. A configure-price-quote (CPQ) system behind the scenes automates the process by providing appropriate combinations of features and eliminating choices that don't make sense. CPQ combines elements of the customer journey (since we need to understand what they are looking for), content (which enables informed decisions), accurate and complete product data, and knowledge (of how the pieces fit together and how the solution needs to be configured to solve specific problems). Automating the process free sales professionals from activities that add no value.

An organization with a wide range of applications and diverse product portfolios can quickly overwhelm customers with all of the possible choices on a website. For example, consider Ingersoll Rand, which sells products for industrial and commercial markets related to air compressors, air handling, and pneumatic equipment. The buyers for these kinds of products have hundreds of application requirements, each with different variables related to product configurations and choices. The complexity of the purchasing process requires expertise across industries as diverse as aerospace, chemical processing, construction, electronics, food and beverages, liquified natural gas, marine, metal fabrication, mining, oil and gas, plastics, pharmaceuticals, power generation, shipbuilding, snowmaking, tankers, textiles, and wood products. Compressors are so ubiquitous that one is likely required any time that materials, air, solids, or liquids need to be manufactured, transported, or processed; they range from small handheld devices to enormous machines within chemical facilities, power plants, and paper mills.

Selling these endlessly varied machines and myriad of solutions demands engineering expertise; market knowledge; and an in-depth understanding of customer applications, problems, and solutions. Much of this knowledge is scattered throughout systems, knowledge bases, libraries, technical documents, engineering specifications, and the tacit expertise of specialists who work in the field. Surfacing the correct configuration to customers without overwhelming them with choices demands a blend of expert rules-based systems, document processing, product information, knowledge engineering, and customer analytics.

This problem demands a more intelligent CPQ engine. CPQ models can emulate how a human solves a problem by asking a series of structured questions that start by methodically deconstructing the customer's perspective and problem. The CPQ model then combines solution components and configuration selections to construct the product that most effectively addresses the scenario.

Customer-focused CPQ helps buyers solve problems and build solutions rather than simply selecting products. It also helps generate leads and track lead conversion. It must encompass the entire value chain of surrounding third-party products such as hardware, software, services, and financing. It also requires greater levels of collaboration between systems, internal personnel, and external partners such as vendors and distributors. As CPQ systems becomes more sophisticated, customers and multitier channel partners will want CPQ versions customized with their own branding, views, additional products or services, pricing, and routing.

CPQ is helpful in the back office as well. Back-office-focused CPQ connects with engineering, ERP, and manufacturing, ensuring that a product can be manufactured, and with CRM and sales operations, ensuring that an order be entered into CRM correctly.

Deploying CPQ can be challenging because of the complexity of the cross-department functions it touches, often resulting in a lack of clear organizational ownership. Since it is at the intersection of sales, marketing, knowledge processes, engineering, and production, CPQ requires cross-functional, cross-process integration and collaboration. It demands a technology solution that is managed by IT but is business-driven. Sophisticated CPQ functionality also requires rules engines to match capability maturity and the short- and long-term business requirements. Subject matter experts must build, deploy, and maintain rules and dependencies. Complex configurations require data models with complicated component relationships driven by engineering constraints. Design decisions for CPQ systems can have a significant downstream impact, and adoption can be challenging. Automation requires cross-process collaboration and coordination of logistics and engineering.

Table 6-2 is a checklist for planning, selecting, and deploying a CPQ system.

AUTOMATING PROPOSALS AND CONTRACTS

Developing statements of work, proposals, and contracts (or "inking" the deal) once a sales opportunity is ready to close can be extremely complex and time consuming. In my firm, a recent services engagement agreement went through 19 revisions of scope, deliverables, and milestones. I have also worked with a telecom company that designs, manufactures, and installs first-responder and emergency-management technology, where proposal documents ran hundreds of pages and required input from multiple departments and specialists. The documents also had to go through rigorous review from engineering, field service, operations, financial, and legal departments. This process can take weeks and cost tens of thousands of dollars. AI—more specifically text analytics, a branch

Table 6-2: CPQ Checklist

Define CPQ Business Objectives	• What are the objectives for each impacted functional area: sales, sales operations, marketing, product management, engineering, IT, legal, and finance? • Who are the target users? Sales representatives, customer self-service, channel partners, engineers? • What is the level of configuration options versus solution customization? • Are solutions repeatable, rules driven, and well defined, as opposed to requiring human judgment and expertise? • What is the nature of ad hoc exceptions to configuration options? • For edge cases, what knowledge can be captured and embedded in systems versus requiring escalation to subject matter experts?
Define User Profile	• Internal use versus multitier channel use versus self-service • Customization: dynamic customization of branding, pricing, and products as well as additional products/services • Internationalization/localization
Determine Architecture	• Platform independent versus ERP/CRM dependent • Degree of coding required for update (change management)
Set Configuration	• Advisement versus simple selection • Solution based versus product based • Rules engines: code versus codeless • Ability to address complementary products and services
Specify Pricing	• Geographic pricing, tiered partner pricing • Contract pricing • Promotion management, discounting, and margin analysis • Rules-based pricing/discount/margin management

Table 6-2 (continued)

Specify Quoting	<ul><li>Document export types and formats</li><li>Proposal/contract routing and management</li></ul>
Analyze Integration	<ul><li>Internal/external systems, including pricing engines, CRM, ERP, websites, partner management systems</li><li>Ability to leverage emerging technologies (conversational commerce, chatbots, administrative bots, knowledge bots)</li></ul>
Build Business Case and Budget	<ul><li>Efficiency KPIs, process metrics, and justification</li><li>Licensing cost: user, volume, flat fee</li><li>TCO (total cost of ownership): similar costs to ERP/CRM—(for every $1 spent on software $3–4 is spent on customization)</li><li>Maintenance: content and rules maintenance</li><li>Continuous user experience testing</li><li>Change management: support agile and rapid changes identified in user experience testing</li></ul>
Build Strategy for Change Management and Socialization	<ul><li>Is there a formal change management and communication plan in place?</li><li>Has the organization succeeded at adoption in prior efforts?</li><li>Are stakeholders fatigued?</li><li>Is an overarching governance structure in place for related functions?</li><li>Are functional executives truly on board for required decision-making and resource allocation?</li><li>Does leadership understand the commitment required for success?</li></ul>
Understand Data Challenges	<ul><li>Master data from multiple sources: customer, product, pricing, contract</li><li>Pricing complexity (tiered, channel partners, promotions, discounts) that presents integration challenges</li><li>System owners with different data quality objectives and challenges that impact other stakeholders</li><li>Customer data housed in systems with inconsistent formats, definitions and/or structures</li></ul>

of machine learning—and knowledge engineering approaches can significantly improve this process.

Similarly to CPQ applications, contract and proposal generation tools assemble and reuse content and components. These applications depend on a configuration bot that asks successive questions about the project parameters. It then assembles and routes the document to the appropriate parties and departments and identifies contract details that are potentially contradictory or that contain language that requires human review.

Dates and milestones in contracts are another challenge. Since contracts and agreements can vary in terms of structure, format, and language, renewal and review dates require additional manual checking. AI-assisted proposal and contract development can reduce errors and increase efficiency, speeding the time to proposal and allowing sales staff to spend their time more productively on engaging with prospects and customers.

SEARCHING FOR PATTERNS THAT CAN OPTIMIZE SALES CONVERSATIONS

In this chapter, I have analyzed how AI and automation can improve the efficiency of every element of the sales process, starting with the generation of leads, moving through the nurturing and prioritization of prospects, continuing with the configurators, and concluding with contracts.

But AI can do more than streamline processes. It can observe patterns in those processes and the people who participate in them. AI can process sales interactions and identify patterns that can be applied to scaling, refining, and targeting sales activities for maximum impact. In essence, AI can determine which techniques and people have the best track records and surface their techniques to improve the whole sales organization.

Walmart is among the organizations using AI to learn how the best salespeople interact with humans. Walmart's personal shopping service is building cognitive sales-assistant models that will augment, and one day may take the place of, human sales agents. While this project is still in the early stages of development, the data being gathered through human chat interactions will become the training data for sales bots that will better understand customer preferences and be able to interact in a more natural way.

Many call centers record all customer interactions; these recordings can be converted to text for analysis of patterns. For complex selling scenarios, AI analysts use the output from a range of human training applications, including extraction of best practices, win/loss analysis, script development, refinement of offerings, and message testing. They can analyze the nuances of dialog with prospects to distinguish the characteristics of a successful engagement from conversations where the engagement is less successful. Is there variation across the dialogs of the best performing salespeople? Or are there common elements that can be extracted? What portion of the time is spent listening versus presenting, and how does that change depending on variables such as where the prospect is in the sales cycle, the size of the organization, industry, type of solution, and other account and prospect characteristics? For scenarios that lend themselves to bots and automated sales tools, developers can use this data to build cognitive sales agents.

Using Simulations for Custom Sales Training

AI-powered training tools can improve the speed to competency for new sales hires by simulating selling situations, or more specifically, simulating scenarios tailored to the learning style and skill gaps of the individual. We already do this with human trainers using a technique called "nesting," in which a trainee is placed in a supervised environment while handling real customer calls. At the end of the call, the supervisor provides feedback and coaching. This approach has been successfully applied using training bots that listen to interactions and provide recommendations. AI tools can also monitor interactions and prompt the sales agent with suggested responses to objections or questions. This includes analysis of tone and sentiment to determine whether the customer is frustrated or not fully engaged, and recommendations for actions to get the conversation back on track or to escalate to another agent.

Identifying Profiles of High-Performing Salespeople

Sales demands a particular temperament and work style that can vary from industry to industry and between types of sales process. But assessing your best-performing salespeople using a talent, workstyle, and personality inventory tool can produce a benchmark by which you can assess other candidates. This approach uses predictive analytics and asks questions that are seemingly unrelated to work environments or the sales process but that reveal thinking styles and emotional characteristics that correlate to successful candidates in a particular role. AI technologies can go a step further than traditional personality inventory tools and can determine if a candidate has other, less clearly identifiable attributes that will predict whether or not they will be successful in a job, whether there are skill or knowledge gaps, and whether those gaps are inherent thinking styles or are remediable through training and skill development.

THE CRM ONTOLOGY POWERS ALL THESE ADVANCES

At the heart of all sales-related AI is an ontology—one that's intimately connected to the enterprise's CRM application. The CRM ontology includes customer descriptors that enable targeting, selection of appropriate offers, bundles, messaging, and channel strategy. At first glance, customer descriptors seem straightforward, but they actually require a thoughtful understanding of the customer, marketplace, and buyer needs.

On a website, for example, the list of values for a vertical industry could be short and simple. At one telecom manufacturer, the values included communications, finance and insurance, government, professional services, real estate, retail trade, transportation, and wholesale trade. However, in the CRM system, the value "government" was divided into multiple categories and subcategories, as shown in Table 6-3.

Why does the concept of government have different representations in these different systems? The reason is that, on the website, customers would self-select into "government" to view solutions that spanned the various government subsectors. Content was not significantly differentiated between solutions for state versus local government, for example. In the CRM system, content was more finely targeted in campaigns that operated through different channel partners, government publications,

Table 6-3: Sample Government Categories

Executive and Legislative	Justice and Public Safety	National Security and International Affairs
• Federal • State • Local	• Courts • Police • Correctional institutions • Fire • Emergency medical services • Disaster response	• Military • Embassies • Immigration • Border patrol

conferences, and other paths to market. To track the performance of marketing spending and more carefully tailor messaging and outreach, the CRM system used more detailed categories.

The practical upshot of this sort of variation in the presentation of a variable is that CRM classifications are dependent upon business development, marketing, and sales strategies rather than pure information management principles.

Consider the categories for "geography" or "region," for example. In one class exercise, I have groups of students define the taxonomy of terms to represent specific values for a professional services firm. The results of this exercise reveal an incredible divergence of thinking around what appears at first glance to be a straightforward idea. Table 6-4 shows some of the suggestions people come up with:

Table 6-4: Possible Categories for Geography or Region

• Country • State • City	• Northeast • Southeast • Northwest • Midwest	• North America • Euroope, Middle East, and Africa • Latin America • Asia-Pacific	• Africa • Asia • Eastern Europe • North America • South America

What if a salesperson were assigned Mid-Atlantic, New England, and New York for a region? Alternatively, territories could be assigned by county or by zip code. What determines the correct taxonomy for the concepts of region or geography?

The point here is that even such simple variables as vertical industry and geography are not actually simple at all. The ontology must relate all use cases of such variables in different corporate systems and document the rational and relevant connections among them. Only then can the AI-based sales systems in this chapter be successfully implemented.

Sales efficiency gets a lot of attention because it has the potential to generate higher revenues. Customer service, on the other hand, is a cost center. Or is it? As you'll see in the next chapter, customer service augmented by AI has the potential to generate higher-quality interactions at lower costs, turning the customer service group into a source of loyalty and improved revenue.

SURVIVAL OF THE FITTEST ALGORITHM

The systems I've described in this chapter are at the heart of what will be our next generation of intelligent virtual assistants or configuration/specification bots, like the imagined GraingerBot that I described in the first chapter. One day, every organization will capture and embody human judgment, knowledge, and engineering expertise in these tools. This shift is already happening in the world of microprocessor design, where algorithms are designing microcircuits that have billions of design elements that no human could keep in mind at once. The same change will happen across every industry as complexity outpaces our abilities to process vast numbers of factors in solution design. The organizations that do not develop these agents will not be able to compete with those who do. It will be a case of the survival of the fittest algorithm, data model, and knowledge base, all driven by a corporate ontology, the core source of value in the knowledge architecture.

TAKEAWAYS FROM CHAPTER 6

AI technologies can improve every part of the sales process by freeing sales staff from routine tasks and making them more efficient. As more parts of the process are incrementally improved and augmented, organizations that embrace advanced approaches to managing sales activities and resources will significantly outperform their competitors who do not make these investments. Those who fail to adopt AI will be hobbled by slower response times, less-effective sales teams, and higher-cost manual processes. They may as well be operating off of paper catalogs. These are the main points in this chapter:

- Use AI-powered chatbots to identify customer problems, connect them to appropriate content, and score their potential as leads.
- Connect AI to systems including CRM, ERP, content management (web), and PIM systems to make its interactions with customers and salespeople more intelligent.
- An AI-based system can send customized responses at the most productive cadence to leads and prospects, and then interpret the text-based responses and route ready prospects to human sales staff.
- Use machine learning to train an AI system to identify the most promising prospects, test it, and then implement it within your sales processes to determine which leads deserve the greatest proportion of salespeople's time and attention.
- A propensity model can enhance sales outreach by identifying not just the best prospects but the best times to engage with them.
- Use semantic search to analyze text information from internal and external sources and recommend the most productive approaches to leads based on events in the world and content in your databases.

- A configure-price-quote (CPQ) tool connects to multiple information sources and can be challenging to build, but it can free salespeople from massive amounts of drudgery so they can focus on human connections.
- While proposals and contracts are often complex and can require multiple rounds of reviews, an appropriately configured AI contract system can assemble components and focus staff on only the portions that require additional review.
- Machine learning, applied to patterns in sales conversations and sales staff efficiency ratings, can help select and train sales personnel for maximum efficiency.
- Behind all these advances is a CRM ontology; the more effort you put into refining it, the better all these AI tools will function.

CHAPTER 7

CUSTOMER SERVICE: DELIVERING HIGHER QUALITY AT A LOWER COST

W hen Mike Barton took over as president of Allstate Business Insurance in 2012, the company needed help. Although it was profitable, it wasn't growing. Barton's job was to find a way to get things moving again, and that meant rethinking the way the company worked. "It was a bit of a business teardown, as opposed to just a remodel," he says.

For Allstate, the business insurance market lacks the relative simplicity and consistency of its other products and markets. A life insurance policy is a life insurance policy. Cars are cars and homes are homes, and for the most part, insuring them isn't a task of brain-crushing complexity. But the small and medium-sized businesses that Allstate would like to insure are diverse. The customer might be a landscaper with six employees, a consulting firm with a dozen brainy workers flying all over the country, or a trucking company with hundreds of employees doing business across eight states—all of which have different risks, different insurance needs, and different prices for products.

One of Allstate's biggest assets, along with its sterling and well-advertised brand, is its sales channel. Ten thousand small insurance agencies spread across the country do a great job selling Allstate home and auto insurance policies. They're also happy to sell insurance to businesspeople who drop in, but they need help understanding how all the ins and outs apply to individual businesses. As a result, sales agents were inundating Allstate's business insurance call center with questions about policy underwriting.

Barton quickly identified the call center as the critical factor determining Allstate's costs and success rates in selling business insurance. The job of the call center employees is hard enough since they must master the complexities of every possible type of business insurance. In fact, each new rep needed 16 weeks of training to get up to speed. But like most call centers, Allstate's operation was plagued with high turnover; about one-third of the staff left every year. Because of the long training period, the turnover was particularly challenging to the group's productivity.

Another problem was consistency. Reps needed to find the right answer in the company's knowledge base and deliver it, on demand, to the local agent working with a particular client. With so many new reps, the answers weren't always consistent, which led to a secondary problem: answer shopping. Agents who didn't get the answer they wanted would sometimes call back, hoping to get a better answer on the next call. Sometimes they did. Answer shopping increased call volume even as it generated uncertainty about getting the right policies at the right price for each client.

Complexity, consistency, structured information—these are components that artificial intelligence excels at. Could AI solve the call center problems at Allstate Business Insurance?

Barton resolved to build a system called ABIE—the Allstate Business Insurance Expert—and make it available to agents selling business insurance all around the country. This approach would unburden the call center and allow agents to become better informed and more able to assist prospective customers. In principle, an agent could go online, see the ABIE avatar, type in a question in plain English, and get an answer—in text, as a PDF, or even in a video. But what would it take to build ABIE?

Allstate had to begin by developing a deep understanding of its own business. Business insurance has many components. ABIE had to learn information about types of clients: for example, that banks are financial institutions but landscapers aren't—and neither are financial advisors. It had to learn about different types of products—asset coverage, property coverage, liability coverage—with details on everything from losses due to computer viruses to liabilities of hair salons. It had to learn about packaging, pricing, and regional variations by state and county. In each of these spaces, some things had the same meaning, like "clients" and "customers"; some things were in the same class, like legal risks and physical damage risks; and some things had more complex connections, like those among the employees, managers, owners, investors, and customers of a business.

All of that information was buried in documents and policies at Allstate. A 25-page PDF of policy rules was not going to be the right answer for an agent who just wanted to know if flood damage to equipment was covered.

That's where my team came in. We helped Allstate Business Insurance to break down everything the company knew into pieces, and to organize those pieces into classifications of information—taxonomies. Those classifications were then brought together to form an ontology, which became the heart of the Allstate Business Insurance knowledge base. That tiered structuring made it possible for ABIE to understand business insurance. And that understanding in turn allowed ABIE to answer questions from the human agents that had proved difficult or impossible for the call center reps to handle.

It took a year to launch the first version of ABIE, but once it arrived on the scene it made an incredible difference. Allstate did a soft launch, letting agents know that ABIE was available but not pushing it. The more people used it, however, the more they found it helpful. Call center volume went down about 10% as agents realized they could serve themselves.

Then something happened that Barton didn't expect. ABIE, designed to help the agents, became an essential resource for the call center as well. It delivered concise, consistent answers, which in turn enabled the call center reps to be consistent in their conversations when agents did need to speak with them. The reps became less dependent on canned scripts, and answer shopping by agents became obsolete.

The results were dramatic. Caller satisfaction went way up. Callbacks plummeted because people were getting the right answer on the first call.

Productivity went up because training got shorter. Reps using the new system became productive—ready to help insurance agents—in just 12 weeks instead of 16.

Allstate's business is now growing, and the ABIE project is on version six. "We look at ABIE as a gigantic success factor for Allstate Business," Barton says. And by now, the level of effort required to maintain ABIE has become very low.

Since this started, years ago, Allstate has realized it could take the next step—allowing actual business owners, the end customers of Allstate Business Insurance, to talk to ABIE, the conversational agent on its website, allstate.com. "We optimized it for plain English and it answers thousands of the most commonly asked questions," Barton explains. And that's why ABIE should fuel Allstate Business Insurance for years to come.

CUSTOMER SERVICE IS MORE THAN A COST CENTER

Customer service organizations like Allstate have two primary objectives that often conflict. On the one hand, they would like to have the smartest, most effective answers for the questions people ask, to keep the customers happy. On the other hand, they would also like to reduce costs. Smarter reps who take more time to answer questions provide better service but cost more. Entry-level staffers are less expensive—especially if they're working in offshore call-center outsourcers in such countries as India or the Philippines—but they may have more difficulty understanding questions, finding answers, and communicating. This is a perpetual problem for any company with complex products, whether it's a telecom operator offering high-speed internet service, a printer manufacturer untangling hardware and software issues, or an insurance company writing policies.

The costs are significant. Customer service is an enormous part of the economy, with almost 2.9 million people working in the sector in the United States.[1] Though most organizations consider customer service to be a cost center, numerous studies have shown that investments in improving customer service lead to increased revenue and better bottom line results.[2]

Providing excellent customer service is a challenge. The causes range from disconnected systems and processes to high rates of turnover to a failure to understand the customer's perspective and needs at a detailed level. Misaligned incentives and metrics and lack of ownership or accountability get in the way of delivering better service for the greater good of the organization.

During my time working with customer service organizations, I have been surprised that many do not use knowledge bases to curate the information that service reps use. It seems to be a no-brainer—organize the things that people need to know in a logical, easily retrievable manner and watch the productivity improve. One challenge call centers face is that they are moving too fast to document and organize information that reps need. They have FAQs and troubleshooting guides, but those guides often represent too many sources of poorly organized or curated information.

But now the tide is shifting. Organizing and curating information doesn't just increase the productivity of call center reps. It makes it possible for organizations to deliver better service, faster, and more cheaply with a machine: a virtual assistant. ABIE is not a one-off—virtual assistants are the future of customer service.

A STRATEGIC PERSPECTIVE ON BOTS

Questions and answers in a fixed domain—whether that's insurance underwriting, hardware debugging, or getting you the exact right mobile data plan—are ripe for transformation by artificial intelligence. AI machines aren't smarter than humans. They're only faster. To be effective tools for customer service, computers need to know what the humans know. That's where the knowledge engineering comes in. Building a structured model of the domain in which the customer service takes place requires considerable effort and skill, but once that model is operational, the AI system can use its smarts to supply the exact piece of information a customer or a call center worker needs to answer a question. It can help both customers and customer service representatives.

BUILDING AN INTELLIGENT VIRTUAL ASSISTANT FOR CUSTOMER SERVICE

What is an intelligent virtual assistant?

"Virtual" means that the assistant lives in the machine rather than in the physical world. "Assistant" means that it's helping people—whether sales reps, call center agents, or customers—to solve problems. And what makes these virtual assistants intelligent? It's because they have knowledge of the business along with an ability to learn and get smarter.

Another name for virtual assistant is "chatbot." As you can imagine, a chatbot is simply an automated system that responds to requests in voice or text. An intelligent chatbot is just another name for an intelligent virtual assistant—it answers questions you have by drawing from a base of knowledge it has access to.

According to Adam Cheyer, the chief technology officer of the company that originally developed Apple's virtual assistant, Siri, the number of situations in which people ask a mobile device a question is relatively small. He identified 17 different possibilities.[3] Typically, people are searching for something—it might be tickets to an event, places to eat, or directions to a destination. Once the context of the search is defined, it is easier for the system to provide help, because voice recognition becomes simpler when the context is known.

The same holds for an intelligent virtual assistant. When the job and task context is definable, it is more feasible to design an application that achieves the goal. The context for ABIE was to help an agent and a customer—often a repeat customer from another line of business—to get business insurance. For example, when a customer who was a contractor came in to renew their homeowner's insurance, the agent could talk with the contractor about commercial auto insurance or insuring their tools within a business owner's policy. ABIE's knowledge of context helped it fill out complex underwriting forms. This virtual assistant's ability to vary its state in response to different situations and past experience is one of the trademarks of an intelligent system.

Chatbots and Virtual Assistants as Information Retrieval Mechanisms

Like search, chatbots and virtual assistants are ways to retrieve information. The key is to organize the information that these systems need to answer questions. To develop the information architecture for a virtual assistant, it is essential to define the range of problems it will handle in detail as well as all of the contexts in which those problem will be approached.

In the case of ABIE, Allstate defined a number of use cases, domain models for the different types of terms it dealt with, and a detailed ontology for the various contexts of the agent and the information they were seeking. Content models were available for different types of information, including frequently asked questions, reference materials, procedures, and manuals that covered everything the agents needed to know about business insurance products.

The next step was to break that information into pieces and contextualize it. That way, when the agents hit the help key in the application that they were using to write a policy or a quote or to issue a business insurance policy, the context was clear, their identity was known, and the right information was available. The project defined a total of 270 contexts in the workflow, so that when ABIE delivered a piece of granular information it was just right for that context.

The solution at Allstate was based on a well-understood problem, and it primarily used conventional and well-understood technology. The task was clear: build a search-based application with structured content. This made the outcome manageable and successful. When a question exceeds the limits of the virtual agent, the agent redirects the question to an actual person who can answer more complicated questions.

The approach used to build ABIE included continuously curated content that enables learning to take place through both manual and automated processes. The system starts with core content that supports specific user tasks and expands that knowledge through continuous examination of browse paths and search history, identifying successful and unsuccessful responses. Using system-generated metrics, humans curate content, refine search context, and update terminology to create the best results. Their work includes updating and adding terms to the taxonomy and adjusting query processing. The same metrics used to manually tune the system can then be applied to automated techniques such as automatically flagging challenging use cases and content issues.

Over time, a question-and-answer system grows to include very specific inquiries. All of the information that was gathered in the implementation of ABIE—including chat logs, search logs, and other sources—became training sets for the system. These manual, curated, and architected approaches may not seem like the magic that many virtual assistant vendors are claiming; however, that is the point—there is no magic. The foundation for these tools requires curation, well-structured content, and information architecture.

Virtual assistants are easier to understand once you realize that they belong to a class of applications that leverage advanced techniques around query processing and task contextualization. Search is the most familiar of these applications. To understand better where virtual agents fit in, let's look at the continuum of four possible information retrieval mechanisms (see Table 7-1):

Table 7-1: A Comparison of Information Retrieval Mechanisms

	Increasing Functionality →			
DESIGN CONSIDERATIONS	**BASIC SEARCH ENGINE**	**KNOWLEDGE PORTAL**	**VIRTUAL AGENT**	**INTELLIGENT ASSISTANT**
KNOWLEDGE BASE	Any text; multiple sources	Multiple sources; separate taxonomies and schemas	Domain specific ontologies; highly curated sources	Dynamic; info enrichment improves with interaction
SEARCH INTERACTION	Keyword or full-text query	Full-text query or faceted exploration	Query, explore facets; offers related info	Implicit query; recommends based on user's history
INFORMATION ARCHITECTURE	None necessary, but improves with metadata	Taxonomies; clustering; classification	Ontologies; clustering; classification; natural language processing (NLP)	Ontologies; clustering; classification; NLP; personalization
USER EXPERIENCE	Search box, documents list	Role-based	Conversational	Conversational; retains context; personalized
ENABLING TECHNOLOGY	Search	Search; classification; databases	NLP; search; classification; process engines	NLP; search; classification; machine learning

- **Basic search.** The data for basic search comes from a web crawler with access to data from many text sources. The search interactions are typically keywords, so the interaction is through a search box. The information architecture is often the Wild West, with little explicit design. Information architecture, metadata, and well-formed content are all signals used in search, so every investment made in those areas improves the quality of retrieval.

- **Knowledge portal.** A knowledge portal has multiple sources and more knowledge about the user context, so it can more fully leverage schemas and ontologies. Additional capabilities such as facets or browsing make it possible to surface the content and exploit the underlying information architecture. The knowledge portal would also be aware of roles; these provide context that helps to surface content that is more relevant to the users. Many employee portals and intranets exploit knowledge portal approaches.

- **Virtual agent.** The virtual agent is domain specific, task-oriented, and contextualized, with highly curated content sources for user tasks. Its information architecture is a very structured set of knowledge representations and classifications, equipped with natural language algorithms to interpret variations in terms and phrases. Interactions are structured with styles tailored to content types and more granular contexts. The virtual agent should know enough about what the user is trying to do to present the information in actionable form—for example, movie times and information on how to buy tickets.

- **Intelligent virtual assistant.** The most sophisticated information retrieval mechanism is the intelligent assistant. This mechanism is characterized by dynamic interactions and the ability to learn from interactions to improve the knowledge base. The assistant might also make proactive recommendations that amount to responding to implicit queries, drawing from data in contextual cues. The intelligent assistant draws on rules in an inference engine to derive responses that were not explicitly programmed, resulting in interaction that may be quite conversational. The user might get an answer and then refine the question in an exchange process far more natural than that associated with a search. The information architecture at this stage reflects very rich, well-defined content along with personalization. It might draw from big data sources, aggregate various feeds, and integrate with rich enterprise data sources. These data sources are essential to providing the levels of precision and proactive recommendation that characterize intelligent assistants.

The Role of Humans in Preparing Information

Both humans and computers have roles in the development of intelligent virtual assistants. People excel at identifying the best use cases, defining the meaningful interactions with the data, and creating the initial context and examples, also known as the "seed data." Machines can leverage this seed data in a phase of supervised learning and can automatically classify new data. Machines can also mine analytics and incorporate new knowledge to improve their accuracy.

Analysts agree that advances in bots and virtual assistants will require a thoughtful view of content and proficiency in other facets of the technology, such as an expertly developed content architecture, domain model, ontology, and knowledge base representing the information. Intelligent virtual assistants need to be focused within a narrow context, and they therefore benefit from clearly defined use cases and codified human expertise. The technology is cutting edge; however, it leverages foundational principles of content and structure. The first step is to define the problem to be solved, the information needed to solve that problem, and the elements of the process.

Some AI approaches use a large data set and statistical approaches to model interactions. Just as machine language translation gets better when trained on more examples of translations, an intelligent virtual assistant can ingest conversation dialogs and "translate" questions to answers. But this automated process does not always yield accurate answers, and when it comes to customer service, a good guess is not good enough. An AI agent that misquotes an insurance policy—or worse yet, appears to make promises that its masters can't keep—is dangerous. The missing elements in such a scenario are training and knowledge engineering.

To make an AI application successful, you must understand the structure of the knowledge it seeks. You must deliver that knowledge in a format that it understands. Only then can the speed and versatility of AI deliver the seemingly magical results that a customer service operation seeks.

KNOWLEDGE ENGINEERING IS THE KEY TO MAKING A VIRTUAL ASSISTANT SMART

For AI to work on a body of knowledge, that knowledge must contain a model that allows a computer to understand its structure. The science of revealing that structure is knowledge engineering. Knowledge engineering is a means of capturing and structuring information so that people can act on it in a particular context. For example, in the case of ABIE, the AI application needed to contain a representation of what a policy is and what varying forms it can take. It must "know" about different types of business and different kinds of coverage, plus anything else that a call center staffer might need to know.

How do you classify and organize this knowledge? Must an army of knowledge engineers review every document that Allstate uses? Not necessarily. For example, when documents are clearly structured, such as a description of liability insurance for a given industry, an automated system can extract consistent elements. It might start with a definition of the industry, continue with a list of risks, and finish with a list of recommended elements for each policy. Automated tools can read the document, identify new and existing terminology, provide the elements to build taxonomies, break documents apart, tag bits of content, and load them into an information system. Human judgment is often required as well, but the technology can make the process faster and more efficient. With the right tools, you can extract the key bits of knowledge from any consistently structured document by identifying what each part of the document represents. Once you've trained the system to interpret that document, it can process a whole slew of similar documents using what it has learned about how they're structured.[4]

Of course, many documents are not well structured, so they require more work to break apart and abstract key information. The key concept here is that the content and knowledge need to come from somewhere and must be organized across multiple dimensions (taxonomies from the ontology) for retrieval in the correct context. At Allstate Business Insurance, that process took about six months and three-quarters of a million dollars to complete. A team of knowledge engineers was assigned to oversee and review the outputs and to identify errors and inconsistencies. Over time, the ontology was continually refined and it became the standard way to process the corpus of knowledge that the call centers used, which in turn became the reference structure that the AI system could use.

Competency in knowledge engineering is essential, as is visibility into how a chatbot or virtual agent processes training content. Don't depend on the turn-key/black box vendors that are proliferating in the AI industry, because you'll be locked into those vendors' standards and rigid classifications that may not reflect the nuances in your data. You want to make sure you can own your own knowledge and the core processes that differentiate your organization.

Knowledge engineering makes call center agents more productive by structuring content for easier retrieval—whether by the support agent, through customer self-service, or by a bot that is trained to know what a question means and to find exactly the right answer.

In case you're wondering, this is how IBM's Watson got smart enough to be a *Jeopardy* champion. A host of knowledge engineers prepared the AI platform with a structured collection of knowledge—song lyrics, historical facts, even puns—and similarly classified the types of questions it might encounter. That took years. But once it was loaded up with that structured knowledge, Watson was able to answer *Jeopardy* questions in microseconds and famously beat its human competition. The problem is that specialized knowledge is not transferable to other applications. The challenge of training Watson on new content is one of the largest obstacles to its adoption.[5]

Knowledge engineering pays off in corporate virtual assistant projects. By quickly connecting people with questions to the answers they need, the systems increase customer satisfaction and close rates, even as they decrease call center costs. That's how companies can provide higher-quality service without increasing expense.

For example, NCR's Teradata division makes huge data warehouses that retailers use. The stored information is complex, and so are the questions that the retailers' customers have. But by using a knowledge base that structured and organized the information to make it findable by a computer, NCR was able to cut in half the time it typically took a customer to get an answer. Since NCR was handling 25,000 calls per month, this change made a dramatic difference in customer satisfaction.

MAKING THE BUSINESS CASE

First Investors Financial Services Group (FIFSG) is a pioneer in the subprime auto loan sector. In fact, many in the industry credit FIFSG with creating this industry and building it in a way that was helpful, rather than exploitative, for consumers rebuilding their credit. As part of the efforts to modernize operations Ryan Miller was brought in as FIFSG's chief digital officer (CDO). "The organization needed to update processes and digital capabilities to serve our customers—both the dealerships that we work with and the consumers whose car loans we service," says Miller.

As part of his investigation of new potential efficiencies, Miller looked into virtual assistants to lighten the load of the call center agents. The problem was two-fold: the conservative FIFSG organization was not convinced that customers would use an automated system for making payments, while the company's infrastructure required a number of costly changes to support these new technologies. One estimate for the cost exceeded $1 million, which looked like it could be too risky for the leadership's appetite.

Miller was in a good position to advocate for the system. He had built credibility with a number of successful projects, including a website redesign and revamps of internal processes for handling customer interactions. Rather than purchasing costly off-the-shelf solutions, he found ways to analyze processes for new efficiencies that also paved the way for future use of advanced technologies. These included automating email campaigns and text interactions as well as improving heavily regulated processes such as voluntary repossessions. Added together, the savings from over a dozen projects were equivalent to the cost of 18 full-time employees.

Consistent with his past successes, Miller used a lower-cost, lower-risk incremental approach to automation. Through this approach, the organization is developing a knowledge architecture that will serve existing call center agents and collection agents as well as future intelligent virtual agents. Implementing this resource will reduce risk, improve agent productivity, and enable better customer self-service. A well-architected knowledge base will speed time to value for agents by providing in-context help via either helper bots or semantic search. This low-risk, high-return project approach is a great way to start experimenting with bots and intelligent virtual agents: beginning with a narrow set of use cases, it builds a business case that justifies and enables development of other capabilities.

FIFSG is deploying virtual assistants across the organization in collections, loan originations, customer service, and at the help desk. The plan is to build a well-architected knowledge base that will support internal staff and that can be extended for access through helper bots and eventually self-service customer-facing bots. The helper bot is less sophisticated (and easier to build) than a customer-facing virtual assistant; FIFSG can train internal users to use it rather than designing it to handle the random variations in queries that might come from a customer. But the helper bot is still better than search because it is tolerant of variations in semantics and misspellings and is designed to answer questions rather than produce a list of documents that the customer service agent would have to read through.

Building a knowledge base with a bot application in mind helps to focus the designer on specific tasks and use cases and encourages them to be more concise with how answers are structured. The benefits will include faster time to productivity in the call center since new agents will have a knowledgeable helper to ask questions of. Helper bots are infinitely scalable, and building capabilities over time increases their value and utility. Their consistency and accuracy reduce compliance risks. Once bot accuracy is sufficiently dependable, FIFSG can potentially open them up to customers to allow them to get access to answers after regular business hours.

Steps in a Staged Approach, Starting with Agents

P.V. Kannan, who has rolled out many customer service chatbot applications through his company [24]7.ai, recommends a staged approach to introducing the technology to skeptical organizations. As he says in his book *The Age of Intent*, "[Y]our best chance of success remains moving slowly towards virtual agent implementation. . . . A rollout in a single region or with a single product or a limited percentage of customers makes sense. . . . [Y]ou'll need time for those executives who are still uncomfortable with the rollout to get used to it."[6]

Using chatbots for direct customer service isn't the easiest way to apply virtual agent technology, and it shouldn't be the first application you try.[7] Building bots to support call center agents, who then service the customers, as FIFSG is doing, is a good way to begin the transition. This way, the agents can be taught how to use the bot (for example, learning which use cases they are best for). Their use makes the agents more productive even as it improves the bots' performance.

Here are some steps for rolling out chatbots to call center agents, as illustrated in Figure 7-1:

- Identify processes that follow predictive patterns. These are the unambiguous outcomes that have a clear solution and can be described with a series of steps. This analysis also uses search logs and existing chat or customer service transcripts.
- Design dialogs by using the outputs of process analysis and mapping them to critical points in the journey where customers ask typical questions. Capture question phrase variations and classify according to intent.
- Identify content to support the task or process (training guides, FAQs, troubleshooting charts, etc.) and define metadata, content models, and vocabularies (the specific elements of the ontology) that will be used to structure the information.
- Componentize content sources by breaking them into specific answers to questions and identifying granular pieces of information that users need to solve their problems.
- Use crowdsourcing to gather phrase variations and refine ontology elements including intents, entities, and vocabularies. Crowdsourcing is a great way to learn how utterances can vary for a given intent.

Figure 7-1: Workstreams to Prepare a Bot for Functionality

PROCESS ANALYSIS
- Speech to text conversion
- Text mining/analytics on call logs/support content
- Search analytics
- Sceneries and use cases
- Identification of repeatable, unambiguous processes

DIALOGUE DESIGN & INTENT CLASSIFICATION
- Deconstruction of user journeys into dialogue components
- Precoordinated intent design
- Disambiguation models
- Intent entity extraction
- Dialogue context tagging model

CONTENT ANALYSIS, DOMAIN MODELING & ONTOLOGY DESIGN
- Content type and variable definitions
- Classification schema design
- Feature engineering
- Vocabulary development
- Associative relationship mapping

COMPONENTIZATION OF KNOWLEDGE CONTENT
- Deconstruction and componentization of FAQs, troubleshooting guides, reference materials, elearning modules, etc.
- Content refactoring and component tagging
- Integration of component models with user experience

TRAINING DATA CORPUS DEVELOPMENT
- Crowdsourcing of phrase variations for intent triggers (utterances)
- Classification of intent using customer issue and query data
- Entity extraction training and tuning

HYBRID LEARNING & CONTINUOUS IMPROVEMENT MODEL CREATION
- Escalation and handoff model
- Feedback workflow design: utterance, intent, and knowledge
- Success metric design
- Governance and accountability model

- Create hybrid learning workflows, including escalation mechanisms where humans monitor and correct bot performance. Integrate these into governance and to monitor for continuous improvement based on metrics (including success metrics, failure points, and current process baselines).

For now, human beings are still part of the equation. Even if you use a virtual assistant to support call center reps, you're going to have to hire, pay, and train those reps.

AI CAN HELP YOU MAKE SENSE OF CUSTOMER FEEDBACK

So far in this chapter, I've concentrated on how to improve the customer service function with AI. But when it comes to the service experience, AI is also valuable for a different kind of task: making sense of the feedback that customers provide.

The information about where things are going wrong is in the system: customers are telling you about problems with their comments about your products and services. Customers can provide feedback through any number of channels, starting with simple feedback on telephone surveys ("press 1 if you were satisfied, press 2 if you were not satisfied") and continuing with online support ticket submissions through a website, feedback to call center agents, emails, comments on discussion boards and forums, and social media posts. The volume of feedback is so extensive that humans can do little more than sample it, but text mining and text analytics can make sense of the masses of unstructured text in these channels. AI algorithms can classify the contents based on keywords, terms, concepts, product names, and sentiment, and these AI algorithms operate more effectively when they are coordinated with the ontology.

Text also provides hints about the context and process. Comments and complaints can be classified according to the nature of the issue: "Waited on hold too long, had to leave a message and was never called back" versus "Rep was rude and curt, still can't track my application" versus "My bill is very confusing and disputed charges were not removed," for example.

Through text mining, these complaints might be classified according to internal process: "Call center," "Underwriting," or "Billing." By then linking an internal process metric (such as call volume or loans processed) to customer feedback (number of complaints related to the process), the organization can make a change and track the impact on these metrics.

Surveys with either open-ended or structured questions can further tease out the important operational issues that influence whether or not someone would recommend a company to their friends. While simple and common likelihood-to-recommend metrics like Net Promoter Score are crude, they are revealing when used as part of a larger data-gathering framework.

Feedback attributes could include the product or service elements (are specific features useful?), price considerations (are fee structures clear?), brand (do consumers know and trust the company?), or service experience (did the reps have the knowledge required to solve a problem?). You can classify comments and feedback as positive or negative contributors in these areas. These classifications become categories in a "domain model," including taxonomies. AI text analytics tools can then use those taxonomies to classify voice-of-the-customer data sources to make sense of the customer experience.

Customer analytics programs require organizations to understand customer behaviors and link those behaviors to internal systems that are serving the customers throughout their lifecycle. Customers interact throughout a range of states based on where they are in their progressive interactions with the company. Each interaction leaves the customer with an impression, and each interaction is an opportunity to strengthen or weaken the relationship—to sell new products or services, to solve problems, or to fail in the process of doing so.

Systems can harvest data across processes and link it to customer feedback, generating a scorecard around process health. This approach helps organizations allocate resources and measure the impact of their customer experience improvements.

Customer service is not the only area where AI can make workers more productive and companies smarter. AI serves all sorts of productivity goals. That's the topic of the next chapter.

TAKEAWAYS FROM CHAPTER 7

Customer service is not just a cost center; done well, it can generate increased customer retention, renewal, and upselling as well. Bots can help. But building customer service bots, whether they interact with customers or just bolster existing contact center workers, is successful only if you undertake a deliberate knowledge engineering process to acquire, categorize, and manage the knowledge the bot must understand to do its work. These are the main points in this chapter:

- AI can improve the customer service experience, turning it into a revenue center, not just a cost center.
- Intelligent virtual assistants can retrieve structured information and present it as needed to contact center workers, and eventually to customers as well.
- Virtual assistants depend on knowledge curated in a knowledge architecture.
- People are still an essential element for preparing data for AI and for dealing with customers—AI simply makes them faster and smarter.
- You can justify the virtual agent investment with improvements in limited domains that allow service to deliver better answers more quickly and reduce call center staff turnover.
- AI can also help parse unstructured text to make sense of masses of customer feedback in various channels.

CHAPTER 8

ACCELERATING EMPLOYEE PRODUCTIVITY

PCL Construction builds big things. Founded in 1906, it is a $7 billion employee-owned family of construction businesses working across the United States, Canada, and Australia that builds hotels, sports facilities, bridges, office towers, chemical factories, water treatment plants, and anything else big and complicated.

PCL Construction's ability to solve challenging engineering and construction problems in extreme environments depends on knowledge and expertise captured, organized, and transmitted across the organization and shared across disciplines. That knowledge was shared through training classes, certifications, workshops, and a range of written communications organized in the company intranet, PCL Connects. The system housed checklists, business guides, policies, district news, project pages, building codes, technical reports, system manuals, safety information, company publications for specific audiences, health and wellness content, and just about anything else PCL employees needed to know. PCL people could even find knowledgeable engineers through its search function.

That sounds great. But in practice, the navigation within PCL Connects was poorly organized, topic areas were unclear or ambiguous, content was not properly labeled or tagged, and search operated so poorly that some people referred to it as a "random document generator" because the same search entered at different times could produce different results. One day, the search sections that generated the most useful information failed. It appeared to the company that all of its information was lost, until its IT organization found a way to restore it two weeks later. This disaster led to panic on the part of managers and department heads. When the system was finally brought back, it was clear that things had to change.

Executive leadership realized that this critical system was barely functioning and needed a major overhaul. For a company that understood the value of physical engineering for buildings and construction projects, it was not a big leap to understand the analogous construct in the virtual world: knowledge engineering. In the revamp of PCL Connects, all aspects of the business and its core knowledge were developed from the foundation up. The blueprints for the new development began with ontologies and a knowledge architecture.

The resulting overhaul led to increases in user satisfaction (from 20% to 80% approval), greater trust in the system, a 50% reduction in the amount of out-of-date and low-value content, and improved efficiency across multiple processes. The new PCL Connects, now part of the foundation of the knowledge sharing and learning culture at PCL, has become a major contributor to the company's continued success and longevity.

UNLESS KNOWLEDGE FLOWS FREELY WITHIN AN ORGANIZATION, THE ORGANISM BECOMES SCLEROTIC

In chapter 1, I explained how companies are like organisms. The flows of information within those companies are like the blood circulating throughout the organism. When the information flows freely and effectively, the organism is healthy. When those flows are slow and inefficient, the organism lurches along and minor setbacks become major points of failure, much like the failure of the search pages at PCL Construction.

Organizations' ability to compete is based on their knowledge of their customer's needs and their efficiencies in meeting those needs. By improving internal information flows, those internal efficiencies produce a competitive advantage in the marketplace. When information is organized for faster, easier retrieval, internal efficiency improves.

How Information Flows Became Central to Organizational Success

It's only in the last few decades that corporations have networked their internal systems together, with "knowledge workers" collaborating increasingly through technology. Before then, people met, produced paper reports, and sent them through the organization via interoffice mail. Documents, expense reports, meeting minutes, and anything else that had to be communicated from department to department went into reusable brown envelopes that were closed with a tie string and that contained dozens of spaces for the recipients' names and departments. When you received such an envelope, you crossed off the name of the previous recipient, slipped in your new document, and added the name of the next person to receive it in the next open space.

The idea of personal computers in the workplace was still relatively new in the mid-'80s, and email systems were not yet widespread. (I came across a stack of old business cards recently and realized they looked very odd— because there was no email or website address!) I recall meeting technology leaders at the time who described their issues as "We need to get more information online" and "What we really need is an email system."

Now the problem is in the other direction. We went from "We need to get more information online" to "We are drowning in information and don't know how to deal with it" in the course of a few years.

Connecting employees with collaboration and knowledge management "groupware" like Lotus Notes became all the rage for corporate information departments in the '90s. By eliminating paper processes and allowing workers to reuse each other's output, organizations hoped they would see enormous improvements in productivity and an increased return on investment in technology. Companies expected to save money by reducing production and shipping costs for rapidly outdated policy and procedure manuals.

But these proposed solutions created their own problems. Technology companies designed these collaboration tools so that nontechnical business users could create knowledge bases without any technical expertise and without adhering to application development practices. I recall teaching a class in application development where one of the attendees was the administrative assistant to the CEO of a Fortune 1000 company. He was sent to the class with no prior development experience because a vendor's salesperson had said that anyone could develop an application. He was tasked with learning to create applications that would become one of the critical means by which the CEO would share information with his executive team. (As I recall, that didn't end well. An application designed by an inexperienced amateur is not one that should be used in a critical process.)

The great thing about these technologies was that it was easy for nearly anyone to create applications without any need to involve the company's IT organization. The downside, of course, was that it was easy for nearly anyone to create applications without any need for the IT organization. The resulting explosion in undisciplined applications created as many problems as it attempted to solve.

Did we learn from that debacle? Well, consider the challenge of an employee today trying to find information to do a job. Like customers, employees have problems to solve and must wade through multiple options and systems to solve them. How do the people in *your* organization find the information they need to do their jobs? How do they learn about company initiatives? How do they know how to schedule a vacation, or what their health plan covers? How do they learn about new product features, or how they should (and shouldn't) talk about the company in the community when a PR crisis hits? And where the hell are the new expense forms? Which of these do you use?

- A wiki or intranet
- Shared files and directories
- Email updates, newsletters, company magazines
- Skype, Slack, Twilio, or other messaging apps
- Online meetings and webinars

- Phone calls and conference calls
- Posters in public areas or bulletin boards in the break room
- Team meetings and town halls
- Training sessions and workshops
- The water cooler, or "Ask Nancy—she knows everything."

This information environment full of poorly designed, fragmented, overlapping, disconnected systems continues to be a problem. Just as with marketing applications, these tools that are "easy to deploy" and meant to improve productivity have the unintended consequences of fragmenting knowledge and information, reducing productivity as the environment becomes more chaotic.

Chaos versus Control

In the 1960s spy spoof TV series *Get Smart*, the two factions that struggled for power were Kaos and Control. The '60s are long gone, but the struggle between chaos and control continues.

There is always a balance between controlled planning and design on the one hand and chaotic deployment and experimentation on the other. If we overplan and design all of the details of any environment, then by the time it is deployed, the problem we were trying to solve will have changed and the solution will no longer fit. But if we approach it with insufficient planning and design, the result will not meet the broader organizational demands.

Proliferating internal communications systems are patchy, disconnected, and highly prone to spreading poor quality or obsolete information, or to not spreading information at all. Poorly designed or personal naming conventions—"Bob's documents," "Important"—and inconsistent folder structures lead to incorrect, duplicate, or out-of-date content. Posting critical content in multiple locations to improve access leads to less findable content and version inconsistency.

Employees develop all sorts of rogue workarounds to get access to and share the resources and information that they need. Organizations waste effort recreating documents rather than reusing what has already been developed. When information is not organized in a meaningful way, employees lose faith in the accuracy of the information sources and no longer trust that they have the most up-to-date or accurate information. They will therefore double-check the sources, recreate reports, and duplicate efforts rather than trust what they find in the company's information systems. When knowledge workers complain about "information overload," they are really talking about "filter failure." They want only the *right* information. Without appropriate context, information loses relevancy and meaning. Because knowledge is transmitted through language and language can be ambiguous and subjective, capturing knowledge for reuse and processing by technology is especially challenging.

Inconsistency and the lack of processes for cleanup and curation lead to bad knowledge hygiene. This inexorably saps productivity and steadily increases costs in ways that are imperceptible at first but that bog the organization down by gumming up the circulation of information. The result is analogous to clogged arteries from a poor diet and lack of exercise. And just as with a healthy diet and regular exercise, good information hygiene requires discipline and hard work.

That said, knowledge is invariably messy and collaboration is chaotic. People solve problems through inefficient means and accomplish their work in haphazard ways—running into a colleague in a hall, having an impromptu meeting, sending email to teams, and engaging in dialogs through chat.

This sorry state of information management and the resulting inefficiency in most organizations is accepted as the norm; it is due to poor knowledge hygiene and a lack of intentional organizing principles. It doesn't just get in the way of getting normal work done, it also impedes the organization's ability to respond rapidly to a changing environment.

KNOWLEDGE MANAGEMENT CURES INFORMATION OVERLOAD

There is a better way to manage internal information: an integrated knowledge management system. The right knowledge system supports employee job functions and workforce management; reduces the need for training, onboarding, and human resources functions; improves efficiency; and reduces employee turnover. The overall system includes subsystems designed to address usability principles and take advantage of emerging technologies. It maximizes productivity by speeding up the information metabolism of every department.

We can think of these applications in the context of the lifecycle of an employee—from recruiting, screening, and hiring through training and skill development and ongoing day-to-day knowledge work. There are no clear dividing lines between these stages, as there is overlap of functionality, workflow, and technology. But this "employee lifecycle" is a good way to think through ways to improve productivity.

This system includes the elements shown in Table 8-1.

HOW TO OVERHAUL YOUR INTERNAL KNOWLEDGE SYSTEMS

To embark upon this overhaul, you need to understand all the types of knowledge that flow through your organization and the ways that knowledge is created, processed, and consumed. The challenge lies in understanding and measuring knowledge flows throughout the organization as well as the idiosyncrasies of human communications, collaboration, and creativity.

Let's look at three scales on which knowledge varies: by structure, by value, and by context.

Structured versus Unstructured Knowledge

Figure 8-1 shows the continuum of processes that create structured knowledge versus those that create unstructured knowledge. On the left is unstructured knowledge, created in chaotic, opportunistic, creative, collaborative spaces. On the right is knowledge structured for reuse, organized in a format to make it easier for workers to gain access to and use that knowledge.

Table 8-1: Elements of a Knowledge Management System

Recruiting, Screening, and Hiring	Training and Skill Development	Day-to-Day Knowledge Work
• Applicant screening through résumé processes as well as skill and capabilities assessments, identification of knowledge gaps, reskilling opportunities, experience reapplication, intellectual proclivity, and temperament alignment. • Statistical models of educational, emotional, and psychological makeup aligned with job profiles and models of successful applicants. • Workforce management using machine learning to predict customer support volumes based on factors like vacations, needed skills, seasonal variations, impact from the weather, and changes in demand due to promotions.	• Personalized eLearning that adapts to user thinking and learning styles. • Knowledge remediation and training through customized, personalized, real-time eLearning that can rapidly retrain people for new job roles. • Just-in-time training aids that provide context-appropriate information. • Augmented reality overlay applications that provide virtual reference for physical tasks. • Performance reviews with data-driven validation to reduce subjective judgment and improve career success and personal development.	• Collaboration spaces that support curation workflows and automated tagging. • Semantic search to improve information access (including search-based applications that integrate structured and unstructured information sources, and question-answering systems that identify employee intents with machine learning. • Helper, configuration, and transaction bots to enable retrieval of unstructured information, guide users through complex product and equipment set up, and perform routine queries of structured data sources.

When organizations cannot locate information, they may complain that it is scattered among collaboration sites and repositories, but the problem is that they are applying the wrong tool to the problem. A collaboration site is like a meeting room where people are working and solving problems or coming up with a plan. There may be printouts of documents, notes on the table, flip charts, diagrams on the white board, and so on.

This information is not structured for access; you would not barge into the room and start rifling through piles of paper in front of people and start asking for last quarter's strategic marketing plan. The people working would tell you to get out of there and leave them alone. Once they completed their work, they would discard their notes and put a finished copy of the report in a place where others could locate it: in the old days

Figure 8-1: Structured and Unstructured Knowledge Processes

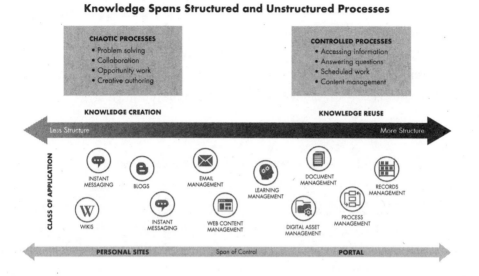

of paper, an actual library or records room; now, some sort of document repository.

Like this notional workroom, a collaboration site is a place to accomplish work rather than a place to access and reuse that work. Once the output is complete, those who produce it promote it to a repository and refine, review, tag, and structure it for the various channels and audiences that will consume it.

The tools and technologies must be appropriate for the purpose of the content and process. One would not try to collaborate with a team in a records management system—the structure is too rigid. At the same time, a wiki, which has a loosely controlled, ad hoc structure (wiki comes from the Hawaiian "wiki wiki," which means "very quick"), would not be the place to manage corporate records and legal documents.

High- versus Low-Value Knowledge

Value determines a second knowledge continuum (see Figure 8-2). Unfiltered, uncurated, and unstructured content is easier to create, but it is less valuable. Naturally, since such content is not a definitive answer to any question, it should be less findable than high-value content that has been vetted and curated for a particular purpose and audience. Consider a consulting firm that uses standard approaches in their engagements: an example of a deliverable may have some value, but an approved methodology to produce deliverables is of greater value. The cost to produce that approved content is higher since it requires more intensive review and refinement to make it more generally applicable. Some of this curated information ends up visible to customers, not just employees.

Figure 8-2: High- and Low-Value Knowledge

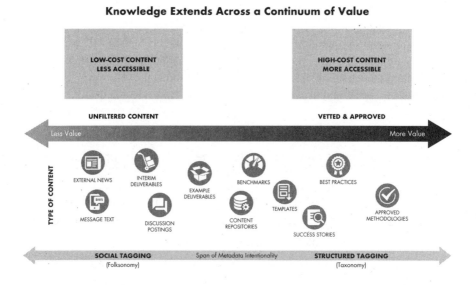

Website information that supports customers often begins as internal content. When a new product is launched, the internal content development and curation process needs to be efficient and synchronized with other launch activities and processes. This way, the support content is up to date, accurate, and available at the same time and across the same channels when the product goes live.

The upstream processes for creation, enrichment, and approval can include regulatory and legal review, marketing message alignment, and search optimization. Highly technical content that helps customers address complex problems originates upstream in engineering and product development organizations. Frequently, critical knowledge is locked in those upstream processes and in unstructured documents. It takes work to refine and organize that content to make it findable on websites and available to customers.

Separating low-value from high-value content allows people to locate what they need when they need it and reduces information overload.

Specific Task versus Enterprise-Wide Task Context

The third knowledge continuum to study is the continuum of task context: what sort of tasks the content is appropriate for (see Figure 8-3). When content and knowledge are put in the right task context, audiences can locate appropriately granular content. This context considers a range of information based on audience needs: highly detailed information that supports solutions to very specific problems versus broadly applicable information that concerns the wider enterprise.

Figure 8-3: Knowledge Organized by Task Contex

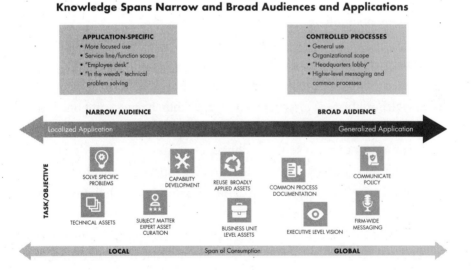

Engineering troubleshooting guides are specific to a narrow audience and are exhaustive and detailed. Organizational strategy and executive vision statements are high level, broad, and all encompassing. The span of control for the former is very narrow, and it requires subject matter expertise to review, tag, and vet content. The latter requires approval at the most senior level since it is communicated across the enterprise and outward to the marketplace.

One way to think of this difference is to consider an employee's desk (for those who still have desks) in contrast to the corporate lobby. You can have photos of your kids on your desk, and you might also have checklists or reference materials that are specific to your job. The lobby of the organization may have posted corporate values, photos of products or factories, and strategic messaging or vision statements. You can control what is on your desk, but a higher authority determines what graces the corporate lobby walls.

AI IMPROVES THE ACCESSIBILITY OF KEY CONTENT

Explicit and deliberate tagging makes it easier for people to find the structured, high-value content in document repositories. But there is still value in the unstructured content used in the process of explicitly creating these lower value documents. This is where AI can help.

Text analytics was one of the first forms of machine learning used to identify patterns in textual content. This process uses example documents to train an auto-classifier so it can apply tags to masses of documents without human intervention. Rather than having someone look at a piece of content and decide what it is about, the auto-classifier system creates models to represent the concepts contained in the documents, references an ontology, and applies the appropriate terms to the document. The ontology helps organize the information so that it is easier to locate and retrieve.

Much of machine learning concerns pattern recognition and the identification of what are called "features," which are ways of describing the information. Expressed in the terminology I discussed in chapter 2, this is the "is-ness" and the "about-ness" of the information. Machines can identify very subtle features that humans would not recognize or necessarily understand.

Explicit versus Tacit Knowledge and Expertise

Knowledge can be tacit (based on experience) or explicit (captured and written down). A procedure is explicit, whereas an experience is tacit.

For example, I was having my office remodeled a couple of years back and the plasterers worked effortlessly on special stilts strapped to their legs, using efficient, deft strokes of their trowels to remove plaster from their "hawk" (the mortarboard) and smooth it onto the walls and ceilings. If you write down the steps to plaster a room, they're pretty simple: place the dry mortar in a drum with water, mix it up until it is the correct consistency, strap on your stilts, and, with the hawk in one hand and the trowel in the other, smooth the plaster onto the surface. That is the explicit procedural knowledge about plastering a room.

When I asked the foreman how long it took to become proficient at plastering, he said about five years working at it full time. That experience becomes the tacit knowledge about plastering. Of course, judgment and expertise are tacit knowledge; people know more than they say and say more than they can write down. Many times, an expert will not even be able to explain how they do a particular job. Capturing experiential knowledge for reuse is extremely difficult. Human judgment and creativity are difficult to codify, capture, or emulate. They are uniquely human.

Tacit knowledge sometimes does not make it out of the heads of engineers and into a form that is consumable by downstream systems. Sometimes this disconnect impacts product quality, support costs, and ultimately, customer satisfaction. Sales engineers and presales support experts also gather solutions to problems over their years of experience. When no one captures this knowledge, the result is inefficiencies, duplicate effort, and wasted time.

So how does tacit knowledge get into the knowledge base? It is documented in the form of training, process documentation, quality control materials, and maintenance manuals. It is embedded in the unstructured documents indexed by text analytics. Or, often, it just doesn't get into the knowledge base at all. It remains in the heads of workers. But a well-designed knowledge system, like the one at PCL Construction, can refer people to those workers who have the knowledge in their heads, not just to knowledge that's written down in documents.

Automation and Knowledge Bases

AI is emerging that can remove some of the overhead and manual work involved in developing and curating knowledge bases. The ontology contains reference data pertaining to the knowledge architecture—the "is-ness" and "about-ness" of information. While humans' ability to keep concepts in mind maxes out at a relatively small number of items, AI tools can remember much more; they can remove some of the manual, tedious, boring work of tagging content with metadata.

Text analytics can operate in a number of different ways. Rules-based tagging has an if/then type of structure. If the document or page contains a term or phrase from a defined set of terms, then the system can classify it using that concept and term. For example, when documents contain the organization's legal name, the term "contract," and the name of a customer (from a list of customers in the ontology), the system then applies the tag "Customer contract." Knowledge management professionals can define other descriptors, along with rules to more accurately classify documents.

In large collections, a statistical classification approach can be effective. This requires examples (a training set) for each node in a classification structure. If tagging across multiple dimensions is necessary, a training set has to be created that spans those dimensions. In the early days of machine learning classifiers, up to 1,000 documents could be needed per node. Even if your taxonomy had only 100 nodes, that would be a lot of labeled training data (100,000 documents). Improvements in technology mean that data sets can now span multiple dimensions. What if you have a smaller set of content? It is possible to use a pre-trained algorithm (trained on a different but similar body of content) that will not require as much work.

In a type of machine learning called transfer learning, the algorithm is trained on a large data set to solve a problem. It is then applied to a related or similar problem that may have less training data. The larger set provides the framework for the solution and the smaller set can then be used to tune the algorithm to the new, related problem, to make the process of adjusting to new content less difficult. Once the algorithms and rules are tuned, the algorithm can solve the new, similar problem (in this case, tagging, routing, and posting documents automatically to a knowledge base).

This technique is very important when training virtual assistants in a hybrid human/bot environment. A pretrained algorithm for understanding the customer's intent will not always accurately estimate the intent of your particular customers. When the human corrects the bot, the machine can learn more about the front-end interpretation of the customer (the intent) or the back-end response (the knowledge base). A workflow approval process can automatically enable the ontology to capture new intents or new classifications.

Ontology Provides Consistency

The ontology is the source of predefined terminology. It helps improve data quality and consistency; it is the source of truth that developers, merchandisers, users, and systems can look to for the most up-to-date reference data and lexicons. It also contains term variations; intents (for virtual agents); utterances; dialog snippets; and entities such as customer names, product classifications, and customer types. The ontology is the source of all of the information architecture elements that comprise content models.

IMPROVING CONTENT QUALITY

Knowledge bases need ongoing maintenance, management, curation, and cleansing. What content is most useful? What is not useful? What causes users to give up and recreate a document or call a support line? What parts of the knowledge base are dead ends? While most knowledge applications contain feedback mechanisms, web analytics can provide additional data to back up assumptions or refute hypotheses about the value of knowledge in the knowledge base.

An analysis of actual user behavior provides information for knowledge sources just as it does for information about products. If someone exits a page, what do they do next? Do they continue on their task or pick up the phone to call a colleague or support center? Analyzing these behaviors can be effective, provided the system is designed to capture this information and that insights are acted upon. It is important to look at the end-to-end process. Perhaps the employee should not be accessing the knowledge base in the first place—they may be using the wrong process or beginning with the incorrect application.

Considered in full detail, this means that you need to analyze employee behavior just as you would customer behavior. Employee journeys can be classified and tracked just as customer journeys can be. Few companies analyze employee experience at this level of detail, but this type of analysis can contribute greatly to improving the usability of knowledge systems.

Redundant, Out-of-Date, and Trivial Content (ROT)

Though some parts of the process for keeping knowledge bases clean and up to date require human intervention, other parts can be automated. One organization that favored automation put expiration dates on its content, and since all the content was loaded on the same day and set to be reviewed in three months, content owners were inundated with reminders at the three-month anniversary, which they promptly ignored or deleted. Automation of content review and cleaning needs to be thoughtful, with clearly established ownership of content and staggered review dates. Not all documents require the same level of review; if a document does not have a lot of value and does not change often, perhaps it should be reviewed once per year, absent a triggering or regulatory event. Records can be archived automatically, depending on document class and the retention policy of the organization.

Text analytics can help here. It can analyze documents for sensitive information, personally identifiable information, intellectual property, or other flags that would trigger different content preservation and review rules.

AI Can Help Surface High-Value Content

With so much of the world's knowledge hidden away in unstructured content, a number of companies are using AI and machine learning to identify higher value content and to surface lost history or IP. AI can flag documents for a range of use cases. There are specialist tools to handle contract expirations and renewals, rights management for copyright protected content, e-discovery in complex trials where almost all communications are electronic, and retrieval and extraction of data contained in PDFs and unstructured content. This type of content ranges from company performance and analysis in financial reports to product specification details in engineering content. These applications are saving countless worker hours that would otherwise be low-level drudgery, thus freeing knowledge workers up for more challenging and creative tasks.

HOW THE KNOWLEDGE BASE SUPPORTS THE BUSINESS

The availability of knowledge within the enterprise directly affects the customer experience. That's why it matters.

Employees can't serve customers effectively without access to the organization's knowledge about customers' challenges and the solutions that are available. Each stage of the customer journey corresponds with internal processes and departments. Those processes and departments require enabling systems with the capability to surface the right information to their employees. When employees' time is wasted on "random document generators"—like the one that originally operated at PCL Construction—that is time they cannot spend satisfying customers and creating value for the organization.

Figure 8-4 shows the connections between the external customer journey and the internal accountabilities and corresponding processes. The employees that are responsible for these processes have to create information outputs from some other department's information input. The harder it is for them to locate exactly what they need or the harder it is for them to make sense of that information, the slower and less efficient their contribution to the overall value chain of the organization will be. The friction in an employee's journey and supporting processes slows down the customer's journey.

Employees solving problems must often wade through multiple options and systems to solve them. AI that powers systems for employees has the potential to improve their productivity, which in turn improves their ability to serve customers.

Figure 8-4: Processes, Accountabilities, and Systems Map to Customer Journeys

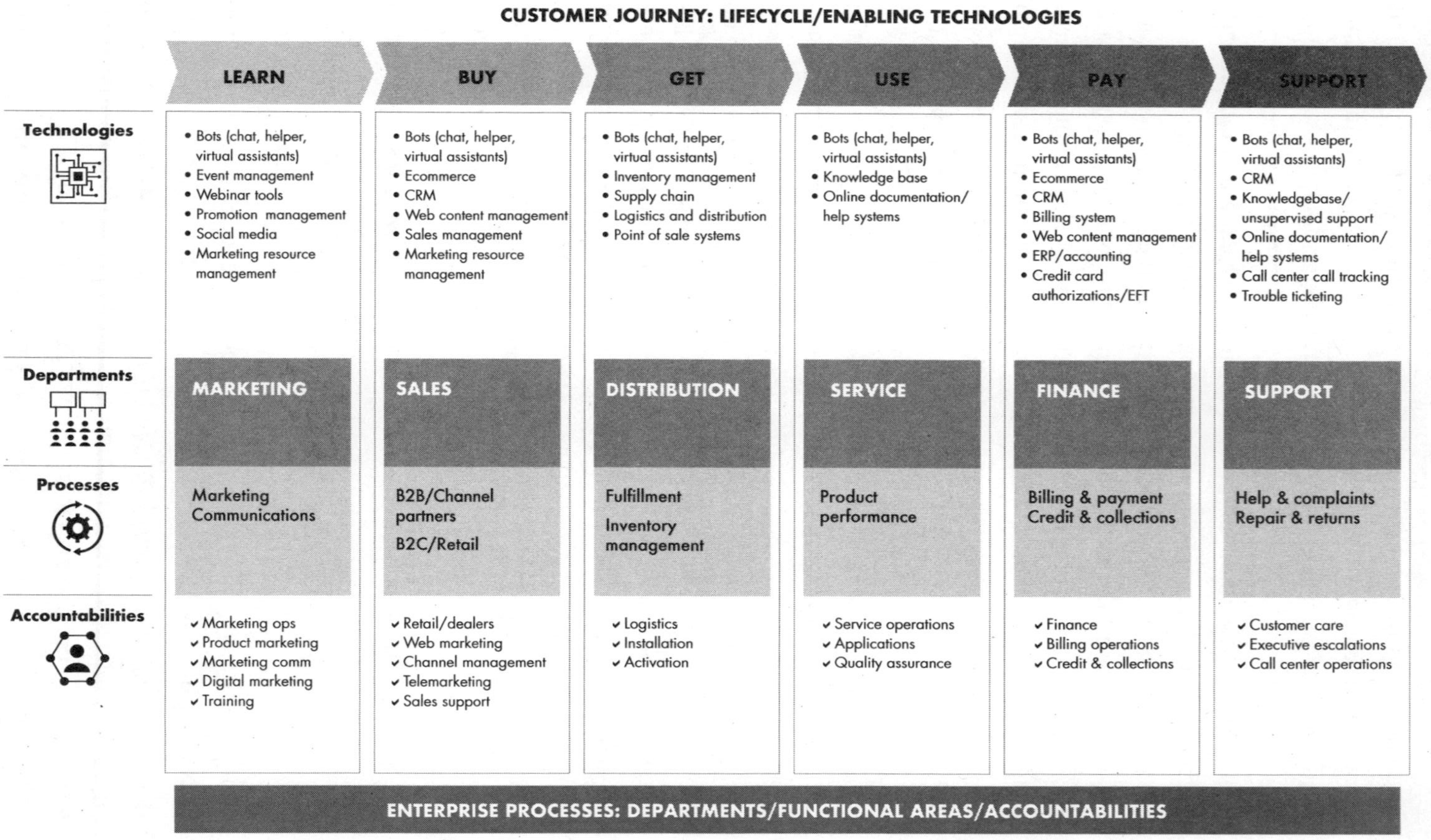

CUSTOMER JOURNEY: LIFECYCLE/ENABLING TECHNOLOGIES

	LEARN	BUY	GET	USE	PAY	SUPPORT
Technologies	• Bots (chat, helper, virtual assistants) • Event management • Webinar tools • Promotion management • Social media • Marketing resource management	• Bots (chat, helper, virtual assistants) • Ecommerce • CRM • Web content management • Sales management • Marketing resource management	• Bots (chat, helper, virtual assistants) • Inventory management • Supply chain • Logistics and distribution • Point of sale systems	• Bots (chat, helper, virtual assistants) • Knowledge base • Online documentation/help systems	• Bots (chat, helper, virtual assistants) • Ecommerce • CRM • Billing system • Web content management • Online documentation/help systems • ERP/accounting • Credit card authorizations/EFT	• Bots (chat, helper, virtual assistants) • CRM • Knowledgebase/unsupervised support • Online documentation/help systems • Call center call tracking • Trouble ticketing
Departments	MARKETING	SALES	DISTRIBUTION	SERVICE	FINANCE	SUPPORT
Processes	Marketing Communications	B2B/Channel partners B2C/Retail	Fulfillment Inventory management	Product performance	Billing & payment Credit & collections	Help & complaints Repair & returns
Accountabilities	✓ Marketing ops ✓ Product marketing ✓ Marketing comm ✓ Digital marketing ✓ Training	✓ Retail/dealers ✓ Web marketing ✓ Channel management ✓ Telemarketing ✓ Sales support	✓ Logistics ✓ Installation ✓ Activation	✓ Service operations ✓ Applications ✓ Quality assurance	✓ Finance ✓ Billing operations ✓ Credit & collections	✓ Customer care ✓ Executive escalations ✓ Call center operations

ENTERPRISE PROCESSES: DEPARTMENTS/FUNCTIONAL AREAS/ACCOUNTABILITIES

This is the secret behind customer experience: When customers experience some kind of interaction with an organization, they are often interacting with information and processes that are enabled by people somewhere upstream. For example, consider the Learn, Buy, Get, Use, Pay, Support lifecycle typical of a telecom provider. People "learn" about the product or service through activities of the marketing organization, such as advertising campaigns, digital marketing programs, public relations efforts, and so on. They "buy" from the sales function. They "get" the product from the distribution and logistics operation or "use" the services of the service organization, they "pay" through finance, and they receive "support" from, well, customer support.

This pattern is consistent, with some variations, in every industry. If the internal process has a bottleneck or inefficiency, that will impact the customer's experience. Each of the internal processes are supported by multiple systems and applications that can sometimes have incomplete, inconsistent, or incorrect information. Or information may have to be reentered from one system into another.

Many organizations resort to "acts of heroics" to enable these processes, with employees, reacting to a series of crises, working late nights or weekends to accomplish their work. But acts of heroics do not scale. Inevitably the process breaks down and comes crashing to a halt with an even bigger crisis that people need to respond to.

In the case of less structured processes that have exceptions or require judgment to execute, those functions are enabled by knowledge workers who use the inputs of other knowledge workers to be productive.

An interesting analytics approach is to compare the measurement of an internal process efficiency with an external measurement of the same process from the customer's perspective. Cases where a call center resolves their support calls on the first contact can be compared with the measure of how often customers report that their problem was resolved on their first call. Those measures should align, although in many cases they don't. The alignment of internal metrics and external experiences provides more fuel for knowledge management approaches to make workers more productive.

Context: Understanding Users, Tasks, and Use Cases

No matter the circumstance—whether a customer is trying to find a product or an answer to a question on your website, or an employee is trying to solve a problem—the fundamental principle is one of context. That is why context is central to the success of any system collecting and delivering knowledge.

Putting something into context is centering it in a framework of understanding. Language is ambiguous, and terms have many different meanings. "Making information easier to find" means reducing the cognitive load on the user—not forcing them to think harder. Organizing information for easy access requires a structure that is aligned with the nature of the problem the user is trying to solve—or at least with the way they think about the problem.

Since different users have different ways of thinking about their issues and problems, applications have to be contextualized for various audiences. For a financial services firm attempting to serve investors saving for retirement, the context is (broadly) retirement. Investors with different goals—say, saving for college—will have a different context, as will the employees serving those investors. Of course, "retirement" is an ambiguous concept that requires further contextualizing. We approach the problem by imagining the different ways people might have actual conversations about retirement. Our real-world interactions are constantly providing a stream of contextualizing clues and cues to help make sense of a question that might start a discussion.

The virtual world misses many signals that we might receive if someone says, "Tell me about retirement." In the real world, responses would vary based on the physical context. Are you speaking to another person standing at the coffee station during a break at a financial conference? Is the conversation at a lunch for people approaching retirement? Is it in your office with another financial professional? Other cues include how the people you are speaking with are dressed and how they present themselves, their tone of voice and body posture, whether they make eye contact, and so on.

In the virtual world, of course, we miss those cues and need to make up for them with other contextual signals.

How Context Fits into the Ontology

When an ontology is developed, it needs to be applied to many different systems and data sources. These applications will require a range of contexts, as defined by respective scenarios and use cases. Who are the actors that will be using the system? What tasks and analyses will they be trying to perform?

The ontology contains not just concepts but representations of how those concepts relate to one another. These relationships can act like a help desk person who knows which system needs to be used for a particular transaction. In fact, ontologies can contain relationships that allow retrieval tools like conversational search and virtual assistants to know where to look for specialized information. If you are searching for a particular transaction, the ontology can contain information about the appropriate compliance and tax issues for the transaction.

The key to building the ontology appropriately is to start with a narrow focus on the most important issues, questions, and problems. This ensures that the ontology will be practical. It then expands over time to cover more use cases, actors, and scenarios. Driven by these, the ontology ties together internal systems and processes so that the user experience (whether internal or external) is seamless. There is no technological limit to how many use cases an ontology can catalog. Ontologies can support hundreds of use cases that over time will grow to thousands and even tens of thousands. For example, the Allstate Business Insurance Expert virtual assistant we described in the previous chapter spanned several hundred use cases.

Measuring the Effectiveness of a Knowledge System

The key to successfully improving internal efficiencies of knowledge work is mapping the flow of knowledge and information in support of processes aligned with specific business outcomes. Projects to manage knowledge have been notoriously prone to failure and have suffered from unrealistic expectations on the part of end users who want the system to "know what they want" and anticipate their needs and supply information from a variety of sources. Even as the information ecosystem of the organization has grown more complex, workers expect that information access should be easier, more intuitive, and "user friendly." (My answer to that is "User friendly? Why didn't I think of that? I thought you wanted it to be incomprehensible.")

Users believe that corporate information systems should retrieve any information desired, "like Google." The problem is that this imperative is abstract and not aligned with specific, measurable outcomes. Ambiguous requirements like "allowing users to find the information they need" are not actionable. Knowledge programs can suffer from being too abstract and too far removed from the front lines of business. If a project to improve the flow of information does not impact a customer or directly improve the efficiency of a process in a specific measurable way, it will be difficult to show the project's value and gain support for it.

We can measure efficiency and effectiveness using approaches that include compiling a detailed view of data quality and completeness, measuring process performance, and assessing outcomes according to business imperatives. Ideally you can map data to processes, outcomes, and business strategy (see Figure 8-5).

Figure 8-5: Mapping Data to Processes, Outcomes, and Strategy

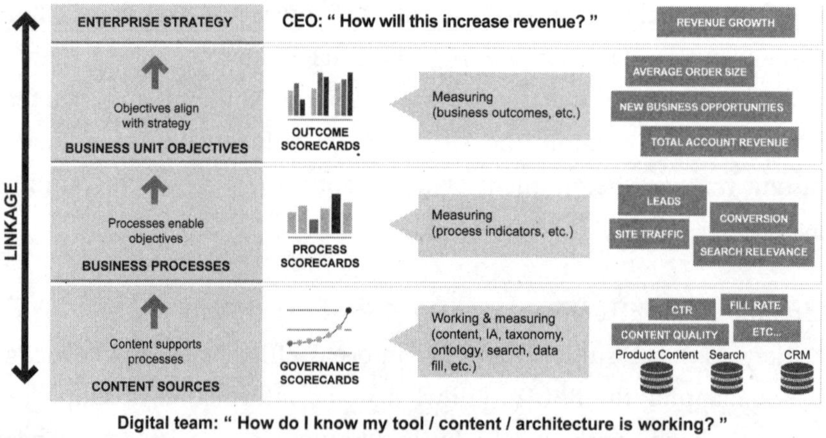

To make these metrics effective, the key is to measure each of these levels of detail with scorecards. From "in the weeds" data and content quality measures to process measures and business outcome measures, every level of detail needs a score. Once we understand the knowledge flows and

processes, when measurements fall outside of projected or expected ranges we can apply an action or intervention and measure the impact of the change. This allows for a feedback loop that can eventually be automated. (For more details on how metrics enable governance, see chapter 10.)

Content and knowledge remain the lifeblood of organizations, but in most organizations simple, uncurated search is still how people find things. However, beginning the process of adding structure will improve organizational maturity and move the enterprise toward AI-powered access to information. Structured, curated information in the form of metadata tags, componentization, information architecture, and ontologies will then be a must-have rather than a nice-to-have. The key to establishing value from tracking these knowledge flows is to link them to a measurable outcome. Find the corporate pain point that can be quantified and begin with that.

So far in this chapter, we've discussed how employees gather and use knowledge. But how does the organization find employees that fit its needs? That's the problem that TeleTech needed to solve, and AI was a big part of the solution.[1]

HOW TELETECH USED AI TO REVOLUTIONIZE CALL CENTER STAFFING

Henry Truong is an engineer who started his career working on computer-aided design tools. He likes to solve problems and make things efficient. So when the founder of TeleTech, the fourth-largest contact center company in the world, reached out to him, he began thinking about how an engineering mind like his could help.

TeleTech supports a diverse set of companies in fields like telecom, hospitality, and retail auto sales. If you need to create or manage a call center, TeleTech is the company you call. The company manages 100,000 people answering phone calls—many of whom are employees of other companies. Truong decided to join TeleTech for one reason: to see if he could bring the same principles of efficiency he had applied in computer-aided design to the messy, people-intensive world of call centers.

For a company like TeleTech, speed is crucial. For example, IBM and some other companies wanted TeleTech to set up a call center for Spanish-speaking customers. For a project like that, the economic drivers suggest that the call center be located in Argentina or Mexico. But you can't just instantly create a call center with hundreds of reps in a foreign country. For one thing, sifting through the applicants is a monumental task. Of every 100 people applying for a call center position in Argentina or Mexico, only one gets hired. Interviewing is a massive time sink, slowing down the process of getting the call center online.

But institutional knowledge is available for use in the hiring process, in the same way it helps with any other process. In this case, TeleTech had knowledge about what makes an applicant's résumé worth another look, as well as what makes an applicant successful in an interview. So Truong set out to build an applicant-screening machine.

He trained the machine by feeding it thousands of résumés of successful hires from the past. The machine could now identify the characteristics of a résumé worth passing on. Similarly, it heard voice transcripts of interviews with successful candidates. Knowledge engineers helped train the machine to recognize the characteristics of those interviews that identified candidates worth keeping. This knowledge—the key elements of résumés and interviews that lead to success—became the center of an AI candidate-screening process.

Let's examine how Truong's hiring system, powered with this knowledge, sorts through 100 applicants to find the one worth keeping.

Truong's system first narrows the applicant group by screening résumés, which kicks out 50 of the 100 applicants. Then it actually conducts a telephone interview using an interactive voice-response system. It reviews the answers and kicks out another 45 applicants. That leaves five. The machine then ranks these remaining candidates, using its knowledge of successful applicant answers. Finally, HR staffers review the five applicants and pick any that meet the company's hiring standards.

Truong's approach cuts time and expense. A process that used to cost $100 per hire now costs only $10.

Next comes training for the call center employees. Here again, Truong took a structured approach, breaking down the knowledge that the call center employees need into atomic pieces. Those pieces became modules for online learning.

New hires use the modules to rehearse the situations they will encounter in the field. They form small groups and quiz each other. And because the machine monitors what they are learning—and where they're having trouble—it can use the information to select content that the employees most need to see. This capability speeds up the learning process.

This new approach reduced TeleTech's training time and cost by two-thirds. And because of the more efficient screening process that feeds people into this program, 95% of the candidates complete the training and become productive call center workers.

When knowledge in a company is deployed appropriately—including through AI—efficiency improves. That's what happened at TeleTech. And that's what ought to happen when any company makes the right kinds of investments in managing the information flows that make the company successful.

This chapter has explained how knowledge management can make people more effective at their jobs. But the world of business is not just about people—it's also about things. That's the topic of the next chapter.

TAKEAWAYS FROM CHAPTER 8

AI and efficient knowledge retrieval systems can enhance productivity across a range of human knowledge worker tasks, including hiring. These are the main points in this chapter:

- Information overload—or more properly, filter failure—keeps people from getting their work done effectively.
- The challenge is to balance chaos (the creation of information in an ad hoc way) with control (managed information in its final, useful form).
- Knowledge management is the key to helping people be efficient. This includes screening and hiring the correct people,

training them effectively, and providing them with access to the correct, contextualized information in their day-to-day work processes.

- To overhaul your internal knowledge systems, manage information based on whether it is unstructured versus structured, low versus high value, and in the context of an application versus global context.
- Use text analytics—AI supported by an ontology—to classify unstructured information and tag it appropriately.
- Organizations need processes to improve content quality and eliminate ROT (redundant, out-of-date, or trivial content).
- Knowledge bases support the processes that impact every step in the customer lifecycle.
- Knowledge management can improve every type of process, including hiring.

CHAPTER 9

PHYSICAL MEETS DIGITAL: MANUFACTURING, SUPPLY CHAIN, AND LOGISTICS

As chief digital information officer at the Cleveland Museum of Art, Jane Alexander is responsible for helping to create some of the most innovative digital projects in US museums today.[1] As she told me, "Hardware has a five-year lifecycle"—so you never know what sort of experiences will be possible next. And it's the experiences technology creates that are important to Alexander—she wants people to come away excited about the physical art objects, not the "wow" factor of the technology itself. To deliver those experiences consistently, what matters is not so much the hardware of the next project, but the back-end system that powers it.

Take the museum's ArtLens Wall. It's a 40-foot, interactive display of every object on view in the museum. Visitors can interact with anything they see and can learn more about how artworks are related across cultures and time periods. They can select any object in the museum and use their mobile phones to create tours that direct them to the physical artworks they're most interested in. The magic of ArtLens comes from its integrated data management system and the ontology behind it.

The story of that system began when the museum closed for renovations about a decade ago. During that time, as many objects as possible—nearly 80% of the museum's holdings—were digitally photographed and put into a digital asset management system while detailed metadata on each object went into a collections management system. Integrating these two systems ensured there was one source of truth for collection records—a central, constantly updating, flexible back-end.

Alexander says, "The life cycle of a museum object is complicated. It needs to be tracked." In explaining how this centralized back-end would help the museum run more smoothly, she told me, "I'm a lazy type A. I want everything to be running perfectly. This means putting work into the back-end beforehand. If you don't have a fully integrated back-end, if you're not managing your data consistently, the staff has to learn things over and over again and re-do work multiple times. If you don't have a way for information to flow and you try to do [an innovative new project], it won't work." Information mapping is necessary for any outward-facing interactive project to be scalable and sustainable.

As a result, Alexander has focused relentlessly on making sure the entire museum is involved with the processes that maintain the value of the data by keeping it up to date. In a typical museum setting, as she describes, "During design and development, everyone will fight over ownership of content. Once the project is launched, nobody has time to maintain it." Now these updates are based on the other workings of the museum.

Things change all the time. Artwork goes into conservation. Paintings move. The date changes. The name of the artist who created the object is discovered. A work goes out on loan. That's all additional data. When a curator or registrar updates these factors for their own records, the integrated system immediately pushes them out to all front-facing projects.

One result of keeping data up to date is that the museum has expanded its reach outside the walls of the building. By exposing its data in application programming interfaces (APIs), the Cleveland Museum of Art has enabled the world—from corporations like Microsoft to individuals on social media platforms—to create and innovate using this data. Projects ranging from Microsoft's HoloLens augmented reality application to Twitter bots are making even more people aware of the value of the museum's collections.

This focus on a clean and flexible back-end proved prescient when the museum decided to reach out to "digital natives" and give them new ways to interact with the art. The result was the ARTLENS Gallery, an interactive space and companion app. In addition to the ArtLens Wall, this project includes an emotion-sensing interactive application that uses AI to read viewers' reactions to artworks and then allows them to save the results to their phones. Another application tracks where people's eyes go while they view artwork, after which it uses that data to illuminate how artists compose images. A feature of the ArtLens app scans visual cues in artworks and then overlays informative augmented reality filters using visitors' smartphone cameras.

Now the art museum, where the average age of visitors was once over 55, reaches many more people in their teens, twenties, and thirties. The Cleveland Museum of Art has created relevance, a tough challenge for a category that's often perceived as stuffy and resistant to change.

More important is the future. Though no one can predict what new technology might open up in the years to come, Jane Alexander is sure the museum will be ready for whatever develops, because it will run off the back-end systems and ontology that she's worked so diligently to keep ready. Her systems will connect the newest technology seamlessly to the physical world of the museum and its collection of objects so that visitors can connect with the art.

REALITY AND THE DIGITAL WORLD

The most fascinating thing about Jane Alexander's visionary improvements at the Cleveland Museum of Art is how they have connected the physical reality of paintings and museum visitors to the virtual world of data and knowledge. For any company that makes physical products;

ships things; or maintains physical spaces like stores, schools, hospitals, or hotels, the connections between data and the physical world is a crucial part of how AI can advance the enterprise.

Much of what I have discussed so far in this book lives in the purely digital realm. The crucial elements of customer experiences and customer journeys are enabled and supported by digital information on our devices. That's where information flows happen, and it is where the data and the ontology live. To someone from the 1950s, a conversation about these information concepts would be completely foreign and confusing. They might understand bills and invoices, plans and timesheets, designs, assembly instructions, machine settings, and lists of material, but for them, most of those would be on paper. Except in specialized scientific or large-scale mainframe systems, the virtual world largely did not exist 60 years ago.

It would be very difficult to explain to someone from that era how anyone could spend all day "working with information." Even 20 years ago, when people predicted our information economy, few could understand its scope, and how it could generate enormously successful and profitable companies that did not produce anything physical. Today, that trend has been turned on its head. Thousands of digital products and processes have so fully supplanted their physical progenitors that we can hardly remember the forms they once took.

Despite this massive shift, much of modern-day business remains anchored in the physical realm. So let's revisit the material world and reflect on our virtual representations of physical goods. Let's examine the design, intelligence, problem solving, and creativity that goes into those goods. And let's look at how AI technologies will ultimate accelerate these processes, improve efficiencies, and make new types of products possible.

We'll start with a closer look at manufacturing.

MANIPULATION OF MATTER IS MANIPULATION OF INFORMATION

Manufacturing is the application of knowledge to the material world. A product is the application of knowledge to matter through approaches and methods that have been developed and refined over time.

The entire manufacturing world is about the manipulation of atoms and molecules with knowledge and information. After all, even a product as sophisticated as a smartphone is just sand, oil, and metal, all very cleverly arranged. The accumulated knowledge and expertise from centuries of cross-discipline applications of science, mathematics, and engineering have enabled our modern, technologically-driven existence and created unimaginable wealth. Even the poorest consumers have access to material goods and technologies superior to sophisticated goods from long ago.

Engineering is the application of knowledge—science, mathematics, and empirical evidence—to the innovation, design, construction, operation, and maintenance of everything. Engineering, whether civil, mechanical, structural, electrical, or chemical, is about the knowledge. It's about the data. It's about the information.

Product Innovation Now Comes from Data

Product innovation is data innovation. It is human creativity combined with expertise, analytics, and know-how from across fields and industries. Many products in the industrial world form inputs to other products, and information is a crucial part of these transactions. The modern manufacturer is a manufacturer of data and information as much as it is a manufacturer of physical goods.

These information streams require numerous systems and applications that become the vehicles for human collaboration and problem solving. Ontologies allow for systems and applications to communicate with one another; to pass data up and down the information supply chain and get answers quickly; to move design changes throughout the organization; and to ensure that the correct information, in the correct context, is brought to the attention of the people who need it.

When the knowledge and product architecture of the enterprise is disconnected, haphazard, or in disarray, information flows slow down and product development takes longer and is less efficient. The ontology and related information hygiene principles, including consistent terminology and data structures across applications, speed the information metabolism of all manufacturing and distribution processes.

Digital Twins in Design, Prototyping, Manufacturing, and Testing

As information technology has evolved in the manufacturing sector, computer-aided design/computer-aided manufacturing (CAD/CAM) has grown more capable and sophisticated. This chapter is not meant to provide a comprehensive survey of the state of the art; instead, it frames the role of ontologies, information architecture principles, and AI applications in this context.

One challenge in designing complex products is the numerous variables that can be adjusted for any given requirement. In the days before sophisticated technology, product developers would design items, mold makers and tool-and-die craftspeople would prototype them, manufacturers would make them, and developers would iteratively test them using physical prototypes. When a design did not meet the physical requirements of the application, product developers would repeat the process by creating, testing, adapting, and tweaking new molds and prototypes.

As computer design and modeling tools became more capable, a designer could design a product and its constituent components in virtual space and test it using mathematical and engineering model-based simulations. Such a product now has a "digital twin"—a virtual representation of the product or process with its simulated performance and behaviors. This designer can test and refine the twin alongside—or sometimes without—a physical version of the product.

Product developers use digital twins to simulate, predict, and optimize the product and the production system before investing in physical prototypes and assets.[2] Numerous interrelated variables characterize modern products; one manufacturer of semiconductor wafers reported that their AI algorithms to optimize manufacturing had millions of variables. As a result of this complexity, machine learning and AI algorithms are indispensable for modeling and predicting the performance of digital twins of products from design phases through manufacturing and performance testing over the products' lives. AI can model and predict the performance of a product even before the product is physically prototyped and manufactured. AI technologies can process multiple complex variables and fast-moving streams of performance data and operating parameters through all testing processes: load testing, stress testing, failure testing, and modeling the impact of chemical, physical, and (in the case of medical devices) biological variables. Digital twins are also used to predict maintenance needs, potential failure points, and problems that might impact other systems and processes.

Although models are approximations of reality, product designers can combine multiple algorithms to represent dynamic systems and provide new levels of insight for product design and manufacture. Product developers use digital twins in the design stages of the product lifecycle to simulate performance as they change design parameters, in the production stage to simulate and optimize manufacturing operations, and in field performance of products to understand how they are being used and how real-world operating conditions are aligning with performance models. Sensors in the products, in product assemblies, and in the systems in which they function can provide real-time feedback and closed-loop learning to further refine and improve designs.

AI in Robotic Manufacturing

In early generations of industrial robots, the equipment was inherently dangerous, lacking the safety sensors and shutoffs that would stop an operation if a human got in the way. Powerful high-speed robots worked behind safety shields and away from humans. But now, next-generation robots with embedded AI technologies are increasingly working side by side with humans. Humans train robotic processes to manipulate goods and parts by moving the robotic arms, manipulators, and actuators through the process, allowing the robot to learn by replicating human motions. The robot assists with repetitive tasks and is flexible enough to work from impromptu changes in steps, tasks, or motions taught by the human partner.

AI can also guide humans in complex assembly or maintenance tasks. The human is more dextrous and able to better deal with ambiguous situations, while the AI is able to troubleshoot and provide detailed engineering overlays using augmented or virtual reality to show exactly what needs to happen to effect the change or maintenance task. These "cobots" (collaborative bots) make use of the best capabilities of humans and robots and are able to offload from workers the repetitive, dangerous, or physically demanding tasks. This reduces fatigue, increases safety, reduces turnover, and provides a more satisfying partnership between technology and production workers.

Data Hygiene Is Crucial

Proper data hygiene enables effective human–bot collaboration. Knowledge bases need to capture lessons learned, and test results need to be captured and communicated back to design engineers.

In manufacturing, it is easy to become quickly overloaded by large amounts of information or to lose track of the most recent and up-to-date versions of designs and supporting materials. For example, at one food manufacturer, the label and recipe process was so complex, with many workstreams coming together, that on a regular basis there would be a mismatch between a product recipe and the label. It might be a minor change in a nearly identical ingredient, but that mismatch meant that millions of dollars of products were out of labeling compliance, which was only discovered once the products were in the field. That led to millions of dollars of products having to be destroyed.

A text analytics algorithm was applied to check for inconsistencies throughout large and varied product runs to ensure that there was no mismatch due to changes being made. While that simple approach is not terribly exciting, it had tremendous value for the manufacturer.

Quality Control

Manufacturers can monitor product defects after the fact, measuring compliance with specifications and searching for the root cause of problems by sampling outputs and analyzing products that have to be scrapped or reworked. When making changes or justifying production trade-offs, manufacturers hoping to anticipate quality issues analyze risks from manufacturing processes and combine that knowledge with human expertise.

One study by two Texas Tech researchers considered the faults that might be introduced when manufacturing a high-precision electric motor: the rotor could be out of balance; winding connections might not be properly conducting; there might be magnetic field variations; and there could be failures of commutators, bearings, or loose parts.[3] By analyzing "spectral features" of vibrations produced when testing the motor (in one case, 16 different features were identified), each of the specific types of faults could be diagnosed. The differences in the signatures of these signals were so subtle that a machine learning algorithm was required to identify these faults.

AI Can Make New Molecules Possible

When I went to college, I studied biology and chemistry. At the time, I loved the science and math, but I was terrible in lab. I was the worst. My labmates would produce beautiful crystalline substances in the organic synthesis lab, and I would end up with brown gunk. We would use the state-of-the-art equipment at the time—nuclear magnetic resonance—to identify the target compound; the grad student running the instrument would say, "Well, it could be in there," since the signal had so much noise from my test tube of brown gunk.

Had I graduated with a chemistry degree today, I would have been steeped in a world of data and computer science. Chemistry, biochemistry, genomics, and proteomics are all conducted with sensitive computerized instrumentation that uses advanced probes, sensors, antibodies, and reagents to do the difficult analysis work. Modern science is data science.

The sequencing of the human genome has opened up enormous opportunities for the advancement of biological and life sciences, from personalized medicine to drug discovery to gene therapy. The biggest challenge is dealing with the massive amounts of data from laboratory instrumentation. LIMS—laboratory information management systems—are the class of technology that collect and manage the deluge of research data; AI and machine learning algorithms are the only way to process, interpret, and act on these enormous data sets.

Organizations like Thermo Fisher Scientific are increasingly providing data management and analysis services to research labs, pharmaceutical companies, hospitals, environmental science organizations, manufacturers of all types, and universities. Integrating and managing the data from many different systems, processes, applications, protocols, and standards is an enormous challenge. But that integration is a prerequisite to leveraging AI in the analysis of infinitesimally minuscule-scale research on molecular processes and entities.

In science, the tinier the phenomenon, the larger and more sophisticated the equipment and more massive the scale of the data. Genomic and proteomic experiments, along with new gene editing tools such as CRISPR and Cas9, allow unimagined precision for intervention in genetic conditions that were previously considered untreatable, incurable, and inevitably fatal. Genomic and proteomic analysis creates 25 petabytes per year—enough data to fill a stack of 4-gigabyte DVDs a half-mile high, and this is expected to grow to between 2 and 40 exabytes.[4] An exabyte is 1,000 petabytes—quite a stack of DVDs.

The complexity of analysis and volume of data that is generated in trying to understand our biological and physical nature (as data-driven beings for all practical purposes) is beyond comprehension. AI and machine learning tools are the only way to make sense of this vast ocean of data and to derive theories and draw conclusions that can solve human diseases. It is a monumental task.

HOW AI APPLIES THROUGHOUT THE PRODUCT LIFECYCLE

We can analyze the product lifecycle just as we previously analyzed the customer lifecycle (see chapter 3). Product developers conceive products based on a need in the marketplace. They design them, sometimes beginning with sketches, and then move them to computer design tools. They must adjust and adapt the designs to tune functionality and address problems with manufacturing, cost, complexity, features, reliability, or integration with other products or systems. They need to fashion prototypes and then test the products in labs, in the field, and eventually with customers. Finally, they need a way to feed back information on performance to the designers and integrate it into the design process iteratively.

These activities are collaborative, and they entail feedback mechanisms and data collection along each step of the process. In fact, many product lifecycle management technologies are collaboration and knowledge-sharing technologies; the same functionality that supports aspects of the customer lifecycle also supports the product lifecycle.

Where do AI technologies and ontologies fit into the process? With numerous systems and large amounts of structured and unstructured information at each step of the process, product development shares the same data and information hygiene, management, organization, and access problems as marketing.

Here are some ways that AI can be leveraged at each stage of a product lifecycle:

- **Sketch.** Typically, designers start sketches with design programs. When designs are properly catalogued (using terminology and a content model from the ontology), they can be compared to other conceptual sketches. Rather than starting with a clean sheet of paper, a designer can be inspired by prior efforts. Visual recognition programs can classify and retrieve designs by various characteristics and locate alternatives that an engineer may not have firsthand knowledge of.

- **Models.** Models are a step in the design process to identify manufacturing issues and costs that may not be apparent when the design is still on paper. Rather than building physical models (clay prototypes or custom fabrications made of specified materials), designers create them virtually. Model-based design is a 3-D virtual representation of a physical object's design that can be tested through a "multiphysics" simulation—what I described earlier in this chapter as a "digital twin."[5] This approach reduces time to design and can introduce performance parameters earlier in the process to constrain design choices.

- **Rework decisions.** During manufacturing operations, it is sometimes cheaper to acknowledge a defect on the production line and repair it after the part or assembly is completed. Stopping the line, troubleshooting, making repairs, and restarting the line can be very costly; depending on the frequency and severity of the defect, along with the cost of repairs and the length of the manufacturing run, it might make more sense to put labor into the process after the fact. This is an optimization problem with numerous inputs and variables as well as unknown values. AI simulations can help predict the cost of each alternative and model best-, worst-, and likely-case scenarios to allow for a more informed decision.

- **As-built records.** In many manufacturing situations, an exact record of the details of manufacture can be challenging to track over time. This is an information management and preservation problem, but using AI to interpret manufacturing histories can identify subtle issues related to product quality, performance, and hidden cost factors. The correct management of manufacturing history with highly instrumented machinery, model-based design, and downstream ongoing capture of lifetime performance metrics provides a benefit: a very rich view of how materials, methods, and design interact in the long run.

- **Product ideation.** Some organizations have been using AI to create design variations given input parameters and expected performance. Generative design programs can develop numerous design concepts to achieve a given set of functions within constraints on manufacturing, cost, weight, or materials. According to Brian Mathews, vice president of platform engineering at Autodesk, "With generative design, you can effectively rent 50,000 computers [in the cloud] for an hour," at an approximate cost of $20,000. "That means you can do things you never could have done before: You can do 50,000 days of engineering in one day."[6]

Product Lifecycle Intelligence

Product lifecycle management has been supplanted by product lifecycle intelligence (PLI), which is the use of advanced analytics across every step and stage of the product lifecycle to improve the results of innovation.

According to senior managers Jordan Reynolds and Ryan Whittle at Kalypso, a global innovation consulting firm, the digital trail associated with products from aircraft to smartphones tells a story of how those products came to be.[7] The concept of PLI is to capture, review, and analyze that data to make new predictions for, and improve innovation around, future versions of products.

In principle, PLI enables the exploration of product development performance, affording an understanding of root causes of performance, an identification of trends, an extrapolation of current parameters to future performance, an ability to recommend changes to approaches to avoid issues or improve results, and an automation of actions such as process and workflow updates.

Kalypso describes the following scenario:

- **Exploration:** What is the current picture of team performance based on historical data? What are the benchmarks for new product development, change frequency, and cycle time? Are we getting products to market quickly enough? Data from PLI would be able to measure overall performance and contributing factors to that performance.

- **Explanation:** What are the causes of excessive cycle time and large numbers of design changes? What other conditions impact products with long development times? PLI would take into account process approval changes and the assignment of tasks to resources. It could reveal correlations between long development timelines and specific task and approval roles.

- **Prediction:** The algorithms and data sources can perform what-if analysis and provide time estimates for new product development and management process changes. A better understanding of factors and influencers allows for improved performance prediction.

- **Prescription:** PLI can make specific recommendations to optimize a range of parameters and circumstances—for example, suggesting ways to improve quality without impacting cycle times or regulatory compliance.

- **Automation:** For routine changes to processes, PLI can automate changes to optimize resources and goals. Human intervention should provide a sanity check until there is enough trust in the system from a track record of correct predictions.

Reynolds and Whittle cite the example of analyzing vibrations from a drive shaft in a passenger car. In this context, algorithms can mine manufacturing data, determine patterns that correlate to field performance, identify anomalies in the data, suggest areas for exploration, define tasks that need to be completed in verifying or eliminating a hypothesis, estimate the time needed to complete the tasks, provide a suggested resource list (human experts) that need to be enlisted in each area of exploration, and sequence tasks for completion with verification steps. Doing this analysis manually would require many person-weeks of effort. A product lifecycle intelligence application can complete these steps in a matter of minutes or hours.

This assumes that the data is accessible, of sufficient quality, and complete. It presumes that the various contributory factors are understood and that there is data from past product designs and field performance that can be compared to the current problem. It is a matter not of "ingesting all of the data" but of intelligently identifying causative factors and variables and creating a hypothesis about the root cause. That cannot be done by an algorithm alone; it requires human judgment and creativity.

The prerequisites for this scenario are a product lifecycle management system, historical data that can be located and integrated for analysis, and a high-level understanding of analytics and machine learning algorithm assumptions and principles. Product and manufacturing engineers do not need to understand the advanced mathematics of machine learning and AI technologies, but they do need to understand the data inputs, assumptions about the patterns and outputs they are interested in, and how the algorithm arrives at an answer.

AI Analysis of Manufacturing

There are some forms of algorithm (such as neural networks) that experts say no human can understand. That statement is misleading. Though the ways that neural networks are configured to solve a specific problem may be beyond human (even expert human) understanding, the basic problem-solving assumptions and the answer that the program is trying to produce should be clear and understandable.

A machine learning program that identifies factors contributing to product performance should have clear inputs and a hypothesis for an output. An example is a process like injection molding, as described in a paper by four researchers from the Polytechnic University of Bari, Italy:

Injection moulding processes are characterized by dynamic characteristics since process input variables are the melting temperatures, the velocity of the cylinder, [and] the holding, the pressure that produces the polymer flow into the model cavity and they vary in a complex manner. The phenomena occurring in the process are very complex, time-varying, nonlinear and uncertain. This complexity makes it difficult to relate the input operating variables to the product quality such as geometry accuracy and geometry surface smoothness. These processes have been implemented and optimized with the use of artificial intelligence . . . .[8]

The important point here is that a production expert understands the factors that contribute to a manufactured product's quality. Those factors may be difficult to understand on a cause-and-effect basis because there are a large number of them and they interact in subtle and complex ways. Artificial intelligence algorithms like neural networks can take many inputs and find an optimized solution.

A very significant problem for manufacturers is the lack of skilled labor for operating machines that require judgment and real-time adjustments due to subtle variations in conditions such as the degree of wear of a cutting tool. An experienced machinist has developed a feel for how to change the feed rate of materials as the process conditions change, but they would be hard pressed to explain exactly how they do it. Artificial intelligence applications can learn from a skilled operator by monitoring various parameters and correlating them with changes in vibrations, temperature, and rotational speed. As described in the Texas Tech paper mentioned earlier, the program can then emulate how a human operator would perform under the same subtle variations in conditions.

HOW AI AND DATA IMPROVE SUPPLY CHAINS

Since enterprises are like organisms in an economic ecosystem, the principles that enable a healthy biological ecosystem are, from a physical, chemical, and informational perspective, identical to those that enable a healthy business ecosystem and that ensure the survival of members of that business ecosystem. Value is created by solving problems through the application of information and creativity. By speeding the information flows and reducing inefficiencies, we are equipping our part of the bigger picture to operate effectively, adapt quickly, and evolve to meet competitive threats and exploit opportunities in the environment.

As I mentioned in chapter 5, supply chains are a crucial and complex part of the information flowing in this ecosystem. They are an intricately structured and variable system that is highly sensitive, with many possible outcomes based on even minor changes in the initial conditions or components. Supply chains feature a large collection of interacting components that are difficult to understand or examine due to their design and operations. And they represent a system in process, changing and developing over time.[9]

It's critical to think holistically about the information ecosystem as you prepare the digital representation of various stages of product design and development. Even a product designed in isolation from other systems and groups—whether in a specialized department or in a separate contracting organization—is still part of an information ecosystem. Information that may be inconsequential to the group that is creating the product, such as an obscure material specification that has no immediate value, will likely have value either downstream (perhaps to a distributor or engineering group) or upstream (perhaps to a procurement manager or supply chain manager).

Too often, these unseen dependencies and information relationships are neglected, and the impact of this neglect can be significant. If a piece of data that will be needed when assembling or distributing a future product is not captured, is lost, or is incorrectly represented, the cost of remediation is orders of magnitude larger than that of addressing the data need at the source. (Think, for example, about Jane Alexander's foresight in preparing all the data in the Cleveland Museum of Art in an architecture that would be helpful for future projects that were unknowable at the time she prepared the data systems.)

Of course, it is difficult to know what will be important in the future without mapping out the information supply chain. Today's manufacturers and product designers do not simply design and manufacture physical goods. They design and manufacture data streams and data specifications that are as important as the good itself. But this requirement is not always well considered at the time of design. A marketer may need a piece of data that resides in engineering. Getting that data after design teams have moved on or personnel have shifted priorities is difficult and costly.

It is not feasible to capture every piece of data that could potentially be useful for an unknown downstream purpose. Instead, you need to map the data flows that correspond with the physical and manufacturing flow and collaborate with downstream consumers of the data to understand and anticipate needs. Then capture and manage that data provenance in the right structure and application and in compliance with data quality standards.

Design, manufacturing, and marketing groups need to be aware of downstream processes. Each department and group must understand how the data exhaust produced by their processes is going to inform both upstream and downstream systems. Your data exhaust is someone else's data fuel.

For example, in life sciences research, antibodies are manufactured through certain processes and the data associated with those processes is critical to end users. But even more important are the ways that fellow researchers use a particular antibody in experiments that have been written up in peer-reviewed journals. How do other researchers use the associated reagents? How well did they perform under certain protocols? What were the upstream manufacturing processes? What are the downstream applications? Where did they not perform?

For your enterprise, there are similar questions. How do your processes fit in with the larger business objectives, marketing strategy, customer education, and organizational processes? What information is important to customers, competitors, and suppliers? What are their roles in the information ecosystem? Mapping out and understanding these dependencies is critical to optimizing information flows beyond the immediate needs of the process at hand. Understanding and planning for these needs will help your organization differentiate based on a deeper understanding of the data. This is how your organization turns hidden data flows into a competitive advantage.

Distribution of Physical Goods Includes Distribution of Data

Once products are manufactured, they need to be distributed from the point of manufacture to the point of usage. For traditional retailers, goods are moved from manufacturer to a distribution center or warehouse and then to a retail store or directly to the consumer. For business-to-business manufacturers, the supply chain can be immensely complicated, with distributors and routes to market through other manufacturers, who in turn create their products using components sourced through other manufacturers and distributors within a highly complex web of relationships.

Large brands can have tens of thousands to hundreds of thousands of suppliers. Consider the manufacturer of a complex machine such as an aircraft. An Airbus A380 contains four million parts made by 1,500 companies.[10] The global supply chain is a complex system with many variables and influencing factors. Durable manufactured products can have decades-long lifespans, and companies need to stock replacement parts—or be prepared to manufacture them—throughout the product's usable life. This also means they need to manage the associated data throughout the product's life.

While technologies, manufacturing techniques, and the sophistication level of products have become more advanced, the desire for variation and customization has increased the cost and difficulty of managing a diversity of suppliers. Competitive pressures have shortened product cycle times and accelerated fulfillment logistics while reducing inventory levels to save carrying costs. There's an enormous flow of goods and items that are highly esoteric and specific to an industry or a process, but that flow has metadata and identifiers for everything in it. Every object in your house requires a chain of manufacturers who in turn depend on other manufacturers to provide tooling, parts, and materials to create their products.

Every one of these components has a metadata lifecycle that has flowed through the processes: from concept, through design and acquisition of raw materials, through manufacturing, and across multiple distribution and logistics channels. Every physical item has an associated information lifecycle that tracks how and where it originated, where it was distributed, and how it made it to the point where it is put to use.

Efficiencies in the physical movement of goods require efficiencies in the associated data flows. Tighter coordination of supplier logistics requires better integration of the data between suppliers. Organizations that want to improve the efficiencies of supply chains need to improve the efficacies of information exchange. But this also requires greater transparency and trust with trading partners. Many large organizations deal with new vendors on a weekly basis. According to one source, a food manufacturer dealt with 1,000 vendors for a single line of lasagna.[11] Combine this level of complexity and volume with a lack of transparency to upstream suppliers, and problems with safety, quality, and ethical sourcing become inevitable, generating PR disasters that can destroy brand trust and significantly impact the future of an organization.

In supply chains, AI can help locate interchangeable parts or substitute components, materials, alternate formulations, or ingredients. It can gather and consolidate supplier data from multiple diverse sources to ensure a holistic understanding of their practices. It can also analyze agreements, past purchases, and quality trends along with service-level agreements that would require costly, difficult-to-scale human analysis.

The key is once again to have an ontology that defines the correct data elements for vendor and supplier qualifications, services, terms and conditions, and historical performance. Without a single source of supplier truth, this type of trend analysis is not feasible.

In fact, many organizations with complex trading partner networks are building standards that enable transparency and traceability throughout the entire supply chain. One startup called EVRYTHNG aims to create a digital identity for every single one of the 4 trillion consumer products manufactured every year, based on international standards. EVRYTHNG identities will enable tracking of not just every *type* of product but every *individual item*. The platform creates what the company calls an "active digital identity" on the web that can be accessed through a QR code or near field communication tag on the item. This digital identity includes metadata describing the object and its whole journey from creation through distribution, eventual sale, and in some cases recycling—indicating where it is as well as who has interacted with it.

One immediate application of this technology is the tracking of products in supply chains. The resulting tracking data not only provides insight into where counterfeit products are being made, it also allows companies with thousands of suppliers to see which suppliers are productive and for which products they are excelling. Ralph Lauren is using this technology to track clothing and consumer goods; a large seafood company called Mowi uses it to track fish products from the fish farm to the supermarket or restaurant.

Consumers will also be able to interact with their own products, see where they came from, and access digital services linked to the products. As Niall Murphy, CEO of EVRYTHNG, explains, "Bringing large scale data science to manufacturing and supply chain traceability is transformative." And given this mass of real-world data, applying artificial intelligence is how companies will see the patterns and use them to improve efficiency and gain insights.

Supply chain data is at the core of transparency. The question is how to identify and prioritize the correct data elements for monitoring and management. This is done by assessing risks according to product category and severity of impact, and those classifications are controlled vocabularies that are managed in the ontology.

Procurement organizations need to understand and monitor the critical data elements and to include not just pricing, delivery logistics, quality measures, and specifications but also data standards as part of their service-level agreements with suppliers. Since procurement understands the broader landscape of suppliers, it is incumbent upon that department to enforce data standards that will be leveraged by multiple downstream users and processes. If data is not in the correct format or is missing elements or of poor quality, then penalties need to be assessed just as they would be for any other product deficiency. Educating procurement on the downstream impact of data issues is critical to the optimization of the supply chain.

If you are a manufacturer that works through a network of distributors, having your data supply chain aligned with the needs of downstream consumers is even more important. You are ingesting data from your suppliers and enriching it with additional merchandising or application data elements. You may be destroying data as you combine components into finished products, but you may also need to maintain traceability and provenance in the event of manufacturer defects and part recalls. Having traceability in the supply chain and understanding which elements can be lost or transformed is critical to demand prediction and management, source replenishment, and understanding how customers buy and use your components or assemblies of components.

ONTOLOGIES ENABLE STANDARDS

Ontologies are standards. They contain common terminology as well as data elements that allow for consistency in information structures across applications. That allows information to flow more smoothly and without manual translations, mapping, or manipulation when viewing or consolidating information from different systems.

GS1 is one well-known standards organization that works across sectors. GS1 includes multiple types of identifiers such as the ubiquitous bar codes that allow retail scanners to work, plus standards for locations, assets, documents, shipments, coupons, components, and parts. It also includes standards for information exchanges, including transactions, electronic data interchange, and product master data. (The digital identity that EVRYTHNG creates is based in part on the GS1 standard.)

Standards allow for the fast movement of items through supply chains and for organizations' quick and efficient tracking of inventory and transactions. These externally facing and public standards are critical to the efficient interchange of information, and they reduce the costs of transactions and data aggregation. But that does not mean that everything is made public. Internal standards can improve efficiencies even when they are not shared with other parties due to the proprietary nature of trade secrets. The organization will need to build internal standards that apply to processes, procedures, manufacturing techniques, formulas, and other differentiators.

Embracing a common language and shared mental model, including appropriate standards, is part of the culture and character of the organization. A cookie-cutter, off-the-shelf standard, or one appropriated from another organization, will not fit the work style and personality of teams that have formed deep and productive working relationships. Groups should own the detailed areas of knowledge and how that knowledge is organized while also following corporate practices and well-accepted approaches to building out effective taxonomies and ontologies. This becomes a collaborative exercise that increases employees' awareness of interdependencies and of the role and value of other parts of the organization.

B2B Distribution Transformation Requires Discipline

In distribution, any time you're moving things around you have to predict demand. In a complex system like this, variations in seemingly unrelated areas in the physical, political, and human world can have outsize impacts on supplies and market demands. Variations in weather patterns, trade issues, and manufacturers of esoteric ingredients or minor components can make it hard to know how much of anything you need at one time in any location.

Machine learning and AI applications can make sense of resource management inputs and parameters and can help to identify anomalies. This contributes to determining where to allocate resourcing and spare parts inventories, or how to hedge risks in critical supply elements. By anticipating and correlating seemingly unrelated factors to map replacement and substitute parts and ingredients, you can mitigate disruptions. Success here is dependent on historical data, human judgment, and an ontology that contains product, component, assembly, and other relationships that inform AI programs.

SMART OBJECTS

As more physical goods are sensor-enabled, dumb, standardized manufactured commodities can be imbued with differentiated value. How much value depends on how that data is leveraged. Consider the types of questions that smart objects in the supply chain can answer:

- What features are customers using?
- How many units of the product are being used in the marketplace?
- How is the product performing—what are the effects of wear, stresses, unusual or extreme conditions, failure rates, and efficiencies? (I explore this in more detail in the next section.)
- Where is the product in the downstream channel? (At the warehouse, at the distribution center, on the manufacturer factory floor, in the finished good, at the dealer, in transit, at the final destination?)
- In what products is the component being assembled?
- What application is it being used for?
- How is it performing in a system of other components?

Based on these data points, it will be possible to offer new services for smart devices. For example, you could guarantee performance based on field data, maximize uptime for devices using the component, optimize systems of components based on conditions, refine functionality based on user feedback, or enable control of devices by remote operators.

Preventative Maintenance Based on Failure Predictors

It is possible to create new business services and add new value propositions based on data from devices. For example, a manufacturer might not normally have a field service group but could offer to use performance monitoring to prevent maintenance outages. The device informs the home office that it is beginning to show wear patterns through various vibration and sound signatures. Rather than wait for a failure, the manufacturer or vendor upgrades the part—perhaps on a subscription basis.

For B2B manufacturers and distributors to offer these services, they need to understand their products' functionality at a data level and understand how their customers plan on using their products.

Smart Spaces

As the Cleveland Museum of Art learned, buildings are another place where the physical intersects with the virtual. We can optimize buildings for human interaction and collaboration, commerce, process efficiency, safety, and operating costs. We can get the best of all of these worlds with instrumented buildings equipped with sensors and mechanisms to track physical traffic.

Retailers are analyzing human behaviour and understanding how people move through a store and find what they need. This is done through video monitoring or through opt-in beacon technology that provides an incentive (coupons, discounts, or other loyalty awards) for shoppers, allowing the retailer to track their preferences. Purchase behaviors can be correlated with in-store traffic patterns and influencers. Retailers can assist wayfinding through public spaces and create interactive applications that lead individuals to exactly the shelf and product that they need.

Virtual Reality and the Internet of Things

Engineers are beginning to design advanced, connected features into products, including virtual reality integrated with maintenance, bots that provide instruction and answer questions, internet-connected sensors, monitoring, diagnosis, prediction, control, optimization, and autonomy. These features make a big difference.

For example, my home has a generator, and since it is a decade old, the company needs to send a technician out to check on its operation and service it. The newest models do not have that antiquated requirement. They simply call home with their operating parameters and tell the supplier when they need attention. This is what manufacturing executives and managers need to prepare for: the integration of self-diagnostic and reporting capabilities, but also the necessity of managing the deluge of data from their devices.

Ontologies and content componentization are especially important when developing content that feeds applications such as virtual reality instructional materials. It is now possible to overlay design specifications on the physical part that needs to be replaced, repaired, or adjusted. That requires a content model, or content architecture, that can be assigned with terminology and identifiers that match the product to the appropriate design guides and training materials. This means that an ontology has to contain the right values for parts and instructions. Machine vision systems must have the capability to visually identify the correct component in sometimes extremely complex and difficult to access physical environments.

Intelligence can also be embedded in machinery so that, for example, a sensor-enabled device could report back operating parameters and signatures for vibration, sound, and heat that could then be matched with reference data to indicate that the machinery is in need of maintenance or replacement. The machinery could even have the intelligence locally available to assist the technician in making repairs, based on documentation updated with the latest techniques, diagnostic software, and calibration from its remote connection to the factory.

When enough products have these features, entire industries can be transformed. For example, AI is even enabling autonomous operation of huge mining operations. These operations use systems of equipment that come from different manufacturers but that operate as a coordinated set of machines to monitor their shared operations, reduce human exposure to dangerous conditions, and reduce operating costs. The entire mining lifecycle leverages analytics, machine intelligence, and autonomous equipment to optimize operations and reduce human labor.

The insights that come from instrumenting and tracking physical objects enable companies to monitor and improve their strategies in real time—as I describe in the next chapter.

TAKEAWAYS FROM CHAPTER 9

The relationships between the physical world and the digital world will transform how companies operate, at scales ranging from the molecular to the massive operations of mining industries. AI can help to optimize and make sense of supply chain dynamics, work to differentiate commodity products, and use sensor data in a variety of ways that improve efficiencies. With the right ontology and data structures behind these initiatives, everything businesses do is trackable, and is therefore subject to improvement through AI techniques. This is the future of manufacturing, supply chains, and physical spaces—where everything is digitally enhanced. These are the main points in this chapter:

- If you do not have the product metadata, your products will become invisible in distribution.
- Products are now designed and created virtually in CAD/CAM systems, enabling them to carry trackable information and enabling product lifecycle intelligence.
- AI can correlate multiple variables to minimize manufacturing defects.
- Appropriate data can create efficiencies and transparency in supply chains, but that requires adherence to standards and cooperation among manufacturers and suppliers.
- Connected, instrumented components can enable new functions, such as predicting failure in the field.

CHAPTER 10

AI-POWERED STRATEGY AND GOVERNANCE

C an AI actually help you manage your business?

In theory, you could put all the information your organization is generating into a massive AI engine, which would chew through it and generate insights about where the business is working well and where it is failing. But that's in theory.

A technology vendor called Leaderscape, focused on business transformation, is attempting to put that theory into practice.

Here's how Alex Kormushoff, CEO of Leaderscape, explained it to me. In a business, there are ways to measure traditional activities, like products or services, strategy, processes, financial metrics, customer data, and execution. But as a business changes and focuses on transformation, the real metrics that matter are "soft" metrics, like people, leadership, culture, and communication. The Leaderscape platform, properly calibrated, can actually score those metrics and tell you where the business is failing to perform and where there are opportunities to improve.

The algorithms in the platform connect to a library of over 400 possible drivers of business value and another 400 sources of business risk. You can also customize it with your own factors to track. It identifies value and risk drivers using both metrics from traditional sources like ERP, CRM, and financial systems, and assessments from stakeholders such as employees, customers, suppliers, dealers, and distributors. The platform then provides business executives with analytics, critical gaps, and insights into disconnects between their business strategy and execution—and it continually improves based on the data it collects.

Here's an example. At a Fortune 100 global manufacturing company, one business unit was proving to be a stubborn problem. Everything looked good on the surface. But earnings were down, it wasn't clear what was wrong, and senior managers had run out of ideas to fix the problem.

Surveys and other data streams feeding into the Leaderscape platform revealed insights that weren't visible in any other form. There were culture problems: the organization lacked a defined culture and used a mix of contradictory leadership styles. The executive team weren't clear on common goals. Different groups of employees were following different influences, generating confusion and missed delivery dates. Manufacturing was siloed by function. And all of this inefficiency was generating a drag on earnings relative to the division's potential.

These were factors that the business had never recognized before. Now they are digging in and building a restructuring project around the data they've collected. And results are already improving.

With the insights from the Leaderscape algorithms, the subsidiary is on its way to realizing $300 million a year in annual cost savings, improvements in business process, alignment among leaders on objectives and methods, and a complete shift to a performance-based culture.

This story might sound like one you read in a business school case study—except for the part about the algorithms. In those case studies, high-priced management consultants appear, collect some spotty and inconsistent data, and make recommendations based on their experience and gut. Instead, businesses like this manufacturing subsidiary are making management changes based on data collection and algorithms instead of the advice of management consultants.

AI is going to be able to tell us what's wrong with a business and how to make it run better and faster than ever before. It's just a matter of applying the right technology, tools, and intelligence to the problem.

REINVENTING THE BUSINESS

Earlier chapters in this book were about how to use AI to do things better. But what about using AI to do better things?

Self-learning AI makes itself smarter as it goes about its tasks. Then it can report back to you to tell you what it has learned about your business so that you can make better business decisions about what to do next, where to focus your resources, and who to serve. This is AI-powered strategy, and Leaderscape's platform is an example.

We've already seen how AI improves processes. But it can also capture data that informs your R&D, product development, marketing, and supply chain decisions. You may learn that your core customer is not who you thought they were. You may discover needs and desires that you didn't know your customer had, and that discovery may lead you to retool your products or service offering. It may even lead you to rethink your entire value proposition.

AI-powered strategy combines human creativity with data insights and large-scale analysis, pattern identification, and prediction enabled by AI technologies. Humans still need to decide what is important to other humans; human judgment, knowledge, and experience are still critical. Human creativity, combined with the power of computer technology, continues to build more and more capabilities. Each successive generation builds on the achievements of millions of person-years of problem solving, imagination, ingenuity, perseverance, and mental work that creates vast digital machinery to connect humankind.

AI adds new types of computational machinery to this vast and varied digital landscape and creates new ways for knowledge and creativity to be applied to every problem that society encounters. By no means does this suggest that AI is the answer to all of society's problems, but AI supported by human knowledge helps find patterns in the data and information that flows through this digital machinery, just as Leaderscape's platform did at that manufacturing subsidiary.

Weak Signals, Optimization, and Predictions

AI and machine learning algorithms can improve the application of resources in a variety of scenarios, from the allocation of advertising budgets across channels to workforce demand management. These algorithms can predict an outcome based on a pattern of behaviors or signals—for example, banking customers who are about to move to another institution or machinery in the field that is going to fail. In each case, these signals come from multiple sources of data that are too complex or subtle for a human to interpret.

Some signals are difficult to perceive or interpret any other way. Traditional means of separating out "noise" may be insufficiently sensitive, or the resulting signals may be too subtle to make sense of. AI is ideal for picking up weak signals from diverse sources that machine learning identifies as historical precursors to a problem or a shift in the way the business is running.

AI will help organizations rethink business models and value chains in response to real-time feedback on how customers, markets, and competitors are responding to product and service offerings. Strong signals come in the form of sales results, market share, and stock performance. More subtle and nuanced signals come from not only the fine-grained details of how customers respond to messaging but also how they use individual · products and even the features of those products.

In addition to using text analytics on customer feedback as I described in chapter 7, AI can analyze customer reactions from online behaviors—for example, clickstream analysis is able to track when users are attempting to locate information or are interacting with specific web content. These signals can provide actionable data about how customers are reacting to each stage of engagement throughout their lifecycle.

Sensor Data Can Generate Insights That Were Previously Invisible

The internet of things (IoT) will enable companies to record, process, and analyze information from our environment and act upon it. Every product can now become intelligent and provide information about how it is being used and can also configure itself to users' preferences. With the right security and data architecture (captured in an ontology), devices can communicate with your preferences stored in the cloud and set the lighting, temperature, music, and even images on smart surfaces in your environment.

Product manufacturers can monitor how their products are performing and anticipate failures, breakdowns, and needed maintenance. They can also make changes to product features with real-time updates of functionality. The product becomes a container for software that the company can remotely update on the basis of a customer's usage and as new functionality is developed. My Tesla improves as its software is updated from time to time, providing me with new capabilities and advancements as it gets older. Most purely physical products and goods do not get better with age. Software enhancements to physical products can improve their usefulness over their lives.

As we saw in the last chapter, sensors in products and facilities can provide real-time usability data and allow adjustments based on user feedback and interactions. If new features reduce usage, then that signal can be deconstructed to determine the root cause.

Product companies can also provide analyses of field performance data as a service to the users of products, and these services can differentiate and add value to commodity products through subscription models. By monitoring performance in larger product ecosystems, manufacturers can optimize efficiencies through proactive maintenance and proactive replenishment of consumables.

Organizations need to think creatively about what they would do with data about their products, potentially even expanding to new businesses outside their core. Tesla, for example, has enormous amounts of real-time driving data that can allow it to more accurately assess driving risks and price insurance competitively—information that will be fundamental to the company's insurance offering announced in August 2019. Other insurers are offering apps that allow phones to monitor and feed the same data back to lower their premiums. There is a trade-off in privacy, but some will find the savings worth it.

HOW DISCIPLINED AI ENABLES COMPANIES TO DELIVER NEW VALUE-ADDED SERVICES

Companies' ability to track product distribution, usage, and performance through real-time customer feedback means that they can extend their value proposition. An organization can offer new services—such as guaranteed uptime; usage-based billing; or improved performance, preventive maintenance, and logistics and supply chain optimization.

Some organizations are helping customers improve how their products are performing in an ecosystem of other products, or helping their customers achieve broader goals by acting as an orchestration platform that optimizes and integrates other products and services. For example, Under Armour was traditionally a sportswear company, but after acquiring the fitness tracking app MyFitnessPal, it has broadened its offerings and value proposition by supporting a range of connected sports products through its digital platform. Customers are getting more value from products that are not sold by Under Armour via the company's ability to integrate and measure performance through other, noncompany devices.[1]

Similarly, farming equipment organizations like John Deere are enabling their equipment with sensors and intelligence that help farmers optimize the use of all of their machinery, not just those made by the company.[2] These extensions of the value proposition differentiate offerings from the competition and form the basis for new revenue streams and potential secondary revenue from the data exhaust of these ecosystems.

The GS1 Digital Link standard allows organizations to connect directly with each consumer on a product-by-product basis. That level of detail and granularity yields unprecedented insights into consumer behavior and product performance. Harvesting these insights helps the company better understand customer needs and extend services that ensure customers get the most value from the products. Real-time usability data tunes the user experience and allows for testing of new features and functions. Providers of control technologies, like Honeywell, increasingly sell building optimization as an outcome rather than technology to simply control the equipment.

The challenge in exploiting data from smart products and customer behavior lies in two specific areas. The first is managing and analyzing the vast amounts of data that a marketplace full of your products will be generating. The second is acting on that data by deriving meaningful insights and applying those insights to increase value to your customers. What are the boundaries of the core competence of the organization? Should you as a manufacturer of consumable scientific supplies offer laboratory data analysis and equipment optimization as Thermo Fisher Scientific does? Will that adjacency be too far from the core, or will customers reject it because it is not perceived to be core expertise? Does a manufacturer of machine bearings want to be in the preventative maintenance business? Discipline in assessing the value proposition itself; a detailed understanding of customer needs; and a realistic assessment of core expertise, infrastructure, and data management/machine learning maturity all need to be part of the strategic planning for extending new services. If the organization lacks the basic discipline to manage its internal data architecture and hygiene, it will be difficult for it to extend this into value-added services in the marketplace.

Taking advantage of all this data is possible only with a heightened level of data discipline. That discipline emerges from a governance framework. I'll explore how that governance works in the rest of this chapter, with a detailed analysis of how one publishing company took advantage of it strategically over a ten-year period.

DECISION-MAKING STRUCTURES AND GOVERNANCE FOR AN AI-POWERED ENTERPRISE

In the end, strategy has value only to the extent that there is discipline behind it. That is where metrics-driven governance comes in.

Governance holds new initiatives together by solidifying new habits, course-correcting, and measuring success. Metrics-driven governance allows for the measurement of detailed data (and data quality) indicators as well as metrics at the business process, strategic outcome level. This ensures that investments are aligned with the strategy of the organization and that executives can make decisions based on data.

Because different processes have dramatically different clock speeds, process drivers, and business outcomes, it's a tough sell to fix problems that require a change in how the organization broadly ingests and manages data. Both the costs and the benefits of data discipline are lumpy. The people who can fix the problem have little incentive to do so. If it's not their problem and they don't have the budget, they will not focus on data issues.

The solution is executive sponsorship of governance programs by leaders who have responsibility for end-to-end processes such as those in digital transformation programs. As I'll describe in the next chapter, digital transformations are data transformations. This means by definition that such programs have to look at the entire value chain holistically, from end to end.

How a Large Publishing Company Implemented Company-wide Governance

Years ago, a global publishing company came to us seeking a mechanism to pull together the information and value from more than 20 big-budget technology projects and more than 100 operating units. Many of the projects and programs had grown organically and were run independently of any kind of centralized standards for data, data architecture, methodology, or best practices. This led to wasted efforts, a lack of shared lessons learned, inconsistent user experiences across systems, poorly integrated technologies, and an inability to operationalize and deploy new tools.

Sound familiar? This is exactly what is taking place in the organizations trying to get value from emerging AI, cognitive, and machine learning technologies. We helped the company create a series of decision-making structures and procedures, along with a metrics framework that lasted far longer than we—or they—could possibly have expected.

In any enterprise, one thing needs to remain constant—a mechanism for allocating resources, solving problems, and ensuring a return on investments. What we created for this publisher enabled that mechanism, and it required the same foundation that your own organization will require as you move forward with your AI initiatives. It can be applied to any IT, data, content, knowledge, personalization, search, or customer experience program.

We expected our solution to be useful for 12 to 18 months. But five years after the project, I met someone from the company and mentioned that our governance framework had once been called "the bible" for technology programs and initiatives. They then told me, "We still call it the bible." I met up with another executive five years after that, fully ten years after we created the original "bible." He said, "We are still calling it the bible." A ten-year lifespan for any technology deliverable is unheard of—but as I will describe, the structure divided a number of larger programs and problems into smaller pieces and determined who should be responsible and accountable for all technology decision-making as well as suggested structures, lifespans, agendas, roles, and objectives—a robust structure that proved useful for an extended period. In the remainder of this chapter, I will explain how you can adapt this kind of structure for AI programs.

Long-Term Governance Structure and Operations

The publisher we worked with included numerous and diverse imprints (publishing brands). The governance project was born from the company's desire to manage and operationalize standards and new technologies for content assets across imprints and divisions and to align application programs and practices. To achieve this goal, the organization needed to establish an operational framework and an associated governance strategy.

In most organizations, the "G" word has negative connotations. It is perceived to be unwieldy, to slow things down, and to burden projects and programs. At the publisher, the constituent groups varied widely in terms of their maturity, their capabilities, the scope and nature of their technology objectives, their degree of integration into the larger organization, and their legacy processes and systems.

Although the process of establishing a governance framework might seem intimidating at first due to the size and complexity of this enterprise and the large number of programs and standards, the framework provided a predictable structure and mechanisms for effective governance. Once you establish a solid governance method, it can continue working with minimal changes for many years.

If this program were deployed today, it would be classified as an AI initiative. Why? Because the technologies contained AI and machine learning algorithms like text analytics, semantic search, personaliza-tion, entity extraction, and other techniques that are now recognized as artificial intelligence.

Evaluating the Existing Structures and Processes

At the publisher, we began by gathering information about existing struc-tures: types of governing bodies, project types, ongoing versus temporary efforts, sponsorships, charters, reporting, and specific problems and chal-lenges related to technology adoption and data and content processes. There were fast-changing technologies and many decentralized experi-ments, just as there are with AI today. Building on the structures that are already in place and working is the least disruptive approach. Our goal was to understand those structures and identify gaps. We also needed to understand the company's organizational structure, including geogra-phies, business units, and imprints.

The publisher had developed committees and councils to manage pro-grams and set policy and strategic direction around content technologies and standards development. The executive committee was a steering body for the overall program. The global council governed standards and repos-itory strategy and had oversight over workflow systems implementations (including metadata standards). The business council determined the business priorities for the program. Various task forces and project groups reported through these entities on strategic initiatives. There were more than 20 standards-related projects.

Gaps in Governance

We discovered that there was an organizational gap between the digital delivery groups who understood the technology and those who would be developing and implementing policy decisions. This is common when any organization develops new models and ways of doing business enabled by technology change. Our interviews also revealed these issues:

- A need for more granular work teams and working groups. Too much planning stayed at a high level and was not implemented because teams were not assigned to dig into the weeds.

- No integrated communications plan to manage messages to various stakeholders. As with today's AI projects, communication and change management are extremely important.
- Insufficient mechanisms to encourage sharing of best practices, new approaches, and creative ways around technical limitations. This is something we see every day in organizations deploying AI.
- A lack of use cases and usability studies to measure the impact of technologies being deployed. As with AI projects, enterprises need to establish use cases and metrics so that they can measure and adjust effectiveness.
- No clear project onboarding function. An enterprise needs to ensure that new projects are aware of standards and that those projects can leverage existing standards and practices and communicate variations from current standards. Similarly, as ontologies and data architecture standards are deployed to support AI, an approach for onboarding projects must determine whether the ontology needs to be refined or extended.
- The absence of a training function. Enterprises must bring users up to speed in aspects of usage and practices for operationalizing new tools.
- Few mechanisms for monitoring compliance for projects. Without compliance with ontology and architectural requirements, programs will go rogue, leading to siloes, disconnected tools, and friction throughout the process.

Developing a Framework

The company had engaged in content strategy development across operating companies and had begun development of a framework of common standards for metadata. The purpose of such a framework is to create an approach that will take into consideration all of the multiple technologies, audiences, and projects for a given target capability. We analyzed the organization's environment and derived "governance dimensions": the considerations that affect the creation of policies and procedures, including business units, imprints, functional roles, types of content, locations, subject areas like science or business, technologies, and business problems or imperatives.

AI programs will require similar governance dimensions and will need a strategic framework for a given capability. For example, a personalization strategy will define how various systems will use customer signals to orchestrate content, knowledge, and data throughout the customer journey. A factory optimization strategy will define the needed elements and inputs for optimization, data sources, owners, objectives, and instrumented machinery.

At the publisher, we worked with the current governance environment to extend and adjust it, continuing to capitalize on prior work, reporting mechanisms, project mobilization and tracking, and other processes that were in place and working reasonably well. We proposed a series of changes to:

- reach a broader constituency and aggregate best practices across the organization;
- drive standards adoption deeper into the fabric of the organization;
- establish a formal structure to allow for detailed action plans, accountability, responsibility, communication, and reporting;
- define clear communication plans; and
- establish two-way communications and mechanisms for collaboration between the standards committee and the businesses.

Entities and Their Purposes

To allocate resources, solve problems, and adopt new technologies across the organization, we outlined the lifespan and outputs of suggested entities as shown in Table 10-1, which details characteristics of types of bodies. Observe that this structure is technology agnostic. This is one reason why it endured for ten years and why it would apply pretty much as is to AI initiatives. The number of entities depends on the size of the organization and on the scope and interrelationships of initiatives.

Table 10-1: Entities and Their Purposes at a Publishing Organization

Entity Type	Description	Lifespan	Ouput	Reporting/ Communications
Council	A permanent advisory body of high-end experts supporting committees, resolving escalated issues, setting priorities	Ongoing	Policy development, resource allocation	Executive management
Steering Committee	A permanent body that exists to oversee, define vision, develop strategic direction, seek endorsement and funding, and coordinate with councils	Ongoing	Strategic recommendations	Council
Work Team/ Working Group	A temporary or permanent group that develops detailed deliverables	Temporary/ ongoing	Ongoing, detailed execution plans and decisions	Council or committee
Task Force	A cross-functional assembly of representatives of groups, established for the purpose of accomplishing a definite objective within a limited time frame, and that reports to a larger body such as a committee	Limited	Strategy and policy recommendations	Council or committee
Project	A defined area of investigation or prototyping with timeline and defined/expected outcome	Limited	Proof of concept, or specific findings and deliverables	Findings to stakeholders
Subject Matter Interest Group	A community with a particular interest in a specific topical area	Ongoing	Specific and collective program feedback	Two-way communications to teams/councils

The RACI Chart

Our analysis pointed to the need for more granular work teams and groups. To determine the appropriate roles for each of the groups, we completed a detailed RACI (responsible/accountable/consulted/informed) analysis. A RACI chart defines responsibilities of different governance bodies in relation to different types of standards and content-management-related projects that depend on these standards:

- **R** (responsible) identifies the team that performs the task. In most cases, only one body will be responsible for a project or standard.
- **A** (accountable) identifies the team to which the responsible team is reporting. That team initiates the project, reviews its progress, and has the authority to change its nature or to end it.
- **C** (consulted) identifies the team(s) whose input is sought and factored in prior to any decision.
- **I** (informed) identifies teams that need to be informed after decisions are made. They may be required to take action as a result of the decision or just to be aware of it and factor it in when making any related decisions.

An excerpt from the full RACI chart we prepared for the publisher is shown in Table 10-2. The column headings in the table show types of content management standards that needed to be developed and/or maintained within the company, and projects aimed at achieving particular business goals that had dependencies on these standards. The row headings include governance bodies as described above. The RACI chart was established to assign responsibility and collaboration within team working agendas.

A similar chart is appropriate for AI and machine learning programs and projects. Each initiative requires a combination of resources at both the strategic (policy and executive oversight) level and the tactical execution level. Many of the leading management consulting firms are recommending exactly this approach for AI projects (for example, a task force to evaluate multiple vendors for a particular capability or a working group to define integration requirements).

The publisher's focus was on leveraging the numerous internal and external standards that they needed to use in each of the projects, technologies, and business objectives. AI projects will also need to pay attention to standards—like the DITA standard used in Allstate's ABIE program and the GS1 standard that supports EVRYTHNG's internet-of-things program. Many AI standards are in development. For an enterprise, the ontology is the record of internal and external standards needed to drive enterprise deployment of AI and enable integration with partner ecosystems and external data sources.

Reporting, Tools, and Templates

Given the number of ongoing decision-making activities in the publishing operation, it was useful to adopt standardized reporting for artifacts like project charters and decision summaries. Although each operating company at the publisher had its own project management approach and templates, we proposed the adoption of standardized templates to establish corporate-wide data, analytics, and policy reporting mechanisms. This reduced the time required to get up to speed when reading and interpreting results, provided consistent methodology, and eliminated the duplication of work.

Resource Management

One recurring theme that arose during this project was the difficulty of ensuring that the right people were represented in decision-making forums and had adequate time to focus on projects they are assigned to. This ongoing challenge must be managed at the highest level in any organization. In the publishing company, the global council and business council owned the business objectives and managed competing priorities and projects. Any unresolved issues were escalated to the executive level.

It was also important to get the right constituents on each working group, task force, or project, and to include only people specifically required for a decision. Part of the framework was a running list of the participants needed to make and sign off on important decisions, and to avoid wasting their time on trivial matters. Senior-level team members reviewed significant recommendations specified in the RACI chart to ensure their alignment with larger objectives.

Table 10-2: A Portion of a RACI Chart for Governance

| Governance Entity | Standards | | | | | | | | | Reuse of science assets | Reuse of business assets |
| | Metadata | | | | | | Taxonomy | Markup | File construction | | |
	Identification	Discovery (topical)	Structural	Rights	Products	Metadata					
CM Exec Committee	I	I	I	I	I	I	I	I	I	I	I
Global Business Council							I	I	I	A	A
Rights Council				A			I	C	I	C	C
GCMC	A	I	A	A	A	A	A	A	A	C	C
Standards Committee	A	A	A	I	A	A	A	A	A	I	I
XML Working Group	C	I	C	I	I	C	I	R	R	C	C
ACAP Standards Task Force	I	I		C	C	I	I	I	I	I	I
PLUS Metadata Team	I	I	I	R	C	I	I	C	I	C	C
Topical Content Reuse		R	I	C	C		I	C	C	R	R
Metadata Team(s)	R	C	R	R	R	R	C	C	C	C	C
Workflow Management Teams	I		C	C	C		I	I	C	I	I
Content Modeling Task Force	C	C	R	I	C	C	C	R	R	C	C
Taxonomy Team(s)	C	C	C	C	C	C	R	C	C	I	I
Subject Matter Groups		C					I				

	Digital delivery	Custom publishing	Multi-channel delivery	Paperless prepress	Rights management	Internal search	External search	Interoperability
Project/Business Goal								
	I	I	I		I			I
	A	C	C	C	C	C	C	C
	I	C	C		A	I	I	C
	A	A	A	A	C	A	A	A
	C	C	I		C	I	C	R
	C	R	R	C	Y	C	C	R
	C	I	I		R		C	C
	C	C	C		R	I	I	C
	C	R	I		I	C	C	C
	C	C	C		R	R	C	C
	C	C	C	R	I			
	C	C	C	C	I	C	C	C
	I	I	I		I	R	R	C

Once the organizational structure is validated, the next stage is the implementation of governance processes. This is the point at which goals, objectives, roles, and responsibilities are assigned. At this point, meeting cadences and agendas are established, the escalation process is defined, and communication plans are formalized to ensure clear lines of authority.

Standards Committee

The standards committee at the publisher included people who either worked on a given program full-time or were actively engaged in policies and practices for content, data management, and text analytics within their business units. The organizational structure is shown in Figure 10-1.

Figure 10-1: Organizational Structure for Standards at a Publisher

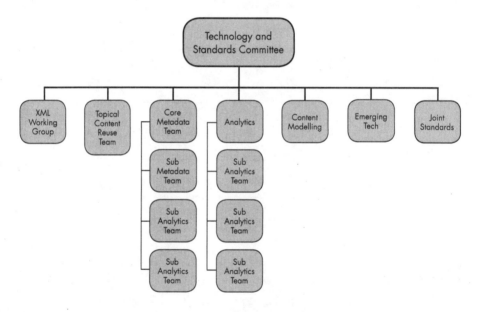

The committee chair was responsible for setting priorities, managing consensus and direction, assigning committee members' responsibilities, scheduling meetings, facilitating and supporting committee members' establishment of forums and training sessions, establishing and managing committee liaisons with external boards, and reporting progress toward goals and outcomes to the global council.

Committee members were responsible for monitoring the activities of standards-setting bodies, identifying issues that committee members need to be aware of and address, creating forums for discussion of proposed standards, coordinating input from their operating company, developing strategy and materials for training on new standards, and maintaining standard links and resources in a centralized location accessible to all employees. The membership of the standards committee should reflect all the key stakeholders and functional areas. These will vary depending on the industry. The publishing organization required that its committee include the following:

- at least one representative from each operating company;
- representation from XML (web formatting) working groups;
- a taxonomist, a metadata architect, and an information architect/ usability analyst;
- a technology tool expert;
- a search tool expert;
- a text analytics tool expert; and
- selected representatives from primary groups that need to leverage standards: photo and imaging, design and layout, XML, archiving, and the education/learning management system.

This list is typical of the composition of a steering committee for governance, in that it includes members of operational entities and those responsible for content management, text analytics, taxonomy, metadata, and search. At the more granular level, each group, such as the metadata team, taxonomy team, and analytics team, had a detailed list of responsibilities that identified their responsibilities as specified in the RACI chart: what they were responsible for, accountable for, consulted on, or informed about.

Technology

Key elements of a governance program like the publisher's deal with applications of technology from an organizational management perspective. Technology is an enabler for functions related to governance, such as content management, text analytics, machine learning, metadata analysis, and semantic search. Tools must comply with standards. The technology governance process should ensure that tools and systems are in alignment with other requirements relating to security, operating systems, technology platforms, and vendor details, for example. Metrics-driven enforcement mechanisms must be staged into production.

Training

To be effective, a governance program needs to be explained and socialized throughout the organization. The publisher, for example, created educational sessions customized for specific audiences: governance principles, the role of standards, enterprise architecture, and rights information management.

An internal training plan will need to consider many elements, such as whether training will take place online, in the classroom, through a train-the-trainer model, or some other modality. In the case of the publisher, the company needed to draft documentation to go along with the training. Different audiences may receive customized training. It is important to conduct a training needs assessment, define critical success factors, and ensure that instructors and participants are properly prepared.

What This Means for Your Organization

While governance is not exciting, sexy, or terribly interesting to many, it is the glue that holds programs together and ensures that projects get appropriate resources and deliver an acceptable return on investment. It is used to hold groups and teams accountable, and to monitor progress in areas that may be entirely new to the enterprise. As it is technology agnostic, it can be adapted to any industry.

This approach, combined with the metrics framework tied to the customer lifecycle (or other appropriate process lifecycles such as product or employee lifecycles), is the best mechanism an organization can adopt to ensure AI program success. The framework, when fully fleshed out and adapted to your company's initiatives and objectives, addresses all of the best practices in AI program management and will endure as a standard set of decision-making, risk management, feedback, and monitoring structures for your organization—perhaps even for as long as it has lasted in the global publisher.

In the next chapter, I pull all of my advice together and tell you what to plan for in the future.

TAKEAWAYS FROM CHAPTER 10

AI can have a dramatic effect on your business—once you adopt company-wide discipline about it. The key is to tap the power of standards-based AI insights to manage your business, and to put in place governance that ensures those insights are based on valid information and practices. These are the main points in this chapter:

- AI can capture data across the organization.
- AI can surface weak signals that aren't visible any other way, enabling measurements of the company's health, predictions about the business, and an early identification of trends.
- Sensor data can make new forms of intelligence visible.
- A disciplined AI program can make the delivery of new value-added services possible, even for product companies.
- An AI-powered enterprise needs decision-making structures, including a data standards bible and a framework for managing AI projects.
- Effective AI governance depends on tools that include governing bodies, decision-making procedures, feedback metrics, a RACI chart, reporting tools and templates, an oversight committee and working groups, and a training and change management program.

CHAPTER 11

LEADING INTO THE FUTURE

My consultancy once worked with a global industrial parts company that had 20,000 employees and $4.5 billion in annual revenue. The company, which manufactures antennas, cables, connectors, and power supplies for use in buildings and other large venues, needed to revamp its product data and overall website performance. The products it manufactures are complex and technical, and the company has a large global network of partners and distributors.

The company had attempted to bolt on AI technologies that purportedly improved personalization, with disappointing results. Unfortunately, its product data was incomplete, inaccurate, not kept up to date, badly organized, improperly tagged, and difficult to find. In the absence of good product data, the personalized product recommendations were poor, which resulted in weak online conversion rates. The company had plenty of data but few insights into what was going wrong, as there were no consistent measures of which products were performing well and why.

Success for this company would require a comprehensive, holistic approach to its data and initiatives.

We started by first evaluating website usability heuristics, analyzing the quality of product data, and defining user personas and associated evaluation and purchase scenarios. The goal was to clean up the product data and content hygiene and then test various approaches to personalizing content for site visitors.

We identified issues with product data quality and developed an action plan to redesign primary navigation, the full product hierarchy, attribute definition and normalization, and the product onboarding processes. The company needed to implement new approaches for decision-making that were more intentional and data driven and less based on opinions of merchandisers and managers. We developed a detailed playbook and set of recommendations so that the company could improve product structures, site navigation, and usability through a structured, data-driven governance process. This allowed for comparison of performance before and after any changes to navigation, user interfaces, or deployment of personalization technologies.

Google Analytics showed that 11% of product-seeking visitors to the website landed on the home page, 5% landed on product navigation pages, and a whopping 77% arrived at product landing pages. Based on this, we recommended improvements to the product taxonomy that would allow product pages to generate personalized recommendations to pages for related products. The company implemented a number of taxonomy governance policies, including enforcing style and labeling guidelines as well as notifying product marketing and product managers of all changes.

We pioneered an FAQ chat feature on pages that had high bounce rates. At first, a human agent monitored the pages, offering suggestions to users and engaging them in discussions. That approach evolved into a chatbot proactively serving up recommendations, tips, and decision-making criteria. Comparison and configuration bots were also possible for pages with high traffic and high bounce rates.

Since these changes were put in place, the company has seen an uplift in page views per visit, a reduction in bounce rates, and a positive impact on conversions.

But the real lasting improvement here was not from the destination but the journey. This company will never again focus on tweaking elements of its site nor on implementing shiny new technology features based on vendors' promises. It has learned not only the value of putting its data house in order but also how to build all future success on a foundation of data discipline, measurement, and structured decision-making. And this makes all the difference.

THE REAL VALUE OF MOONSHOTS

Why bother with all this work? It's not just because of what you get. It's because of who you become.

Consider NASA's Apollo program in the 1960s, which mobilized more than 400,000 people and cost nearly $100 billion.[1] The program required the collective knowledge and expertise of 20,000 companies and universities to succeed.[2] Its guidance computers included one of the first applications of integrated circuits, running at what seems now a meager 1 megahertz clock speed with 4,196 bytes of memory and about 32,000 bytes of storage.[3]

The term *moonshot* denotes a highly risky, expensive, game-changing project. There is no clearly defined path to the outcome, and the means to get there may have to be invented. The only thing that is clear is the vision for the outcome. The Apollo program led to revolutionary advances in every field as scientists and engineers solved the thousands of problems that space travel presented. According to one source, NASA programs are responsible for several thousand inventions.[4] Having a person on the moon in and of itself did not create a lot of value. Getting there certainly did.

Similarly, consider the value of the AI journey and of solving problems that will have lasting value as you conceive of your paradigm-changing moonshot. Like the Apollo program, your AI initiatives may have grand plans that stretch far into the future, but you will also reap many rewards along the way if you plan well.

AI WILL DETERMINE YOUR ENTERPRISE'S SUCCESS

The winners and losers of the next 15 years will be determined by who best harnesses AI for solving business problems for employees and customers.

This is about executing with the right resources and having the right supporting processes.

AI will bring profound change and opportunity to your business and society. One way to get there is through incremental changes that will have a cumulative transformational effect. Wholesale reinvention of the business and value chain is possible, but most legacy businesses will need to develop competencies in many areas to make this approach realistic.

There is an advantage to creating a vision unconstrained by the limitations of today's processes and systems and to using that vision as a catalyst for constrained planning. Establishing a vision can be energizing and exciting, but establishing a vision without a credible plan for achieving it, even if over a period of years, can cause management and employee cynicism and stakeholder fatigue. Many "digital transformation programs" suffer from ambiguous goals, inconsistent interpretation, insufficient funding, and poor alignment with tangible, measurable objectives. AI projects have suffered from the same challenges and have received a black eye from overpromised and overhyped expectations and unrealistic goals. Vision without execution is delusion. And delusion does not enhance one's career.

Manage Change or Get Run Over

Change is happening at a faster rate. Agile, born-digital competitors are threatening to upend longstanding business models, and digital capabilities increasingly depend less on the tools themselves and more on rethinking the business process and customer value proposition. When business leaders come to IT with an ask, the things they want are not always aligned with what they really need.

New applications can have intrinsic conceptual appeal, but novelty should not be confused with business value. Nevertheless, management may read an article about technologies that are not fully baked or that are not cost-effective at the present level of industry maturity and think, "We need this." Or they may be persuaded by a vendor pitch that, though not actually an outright lie, promotes "aspirational functionality" that is not realistic at present.

Many new products are coming into a marketplace that is continually evolving. New marketing and customer engagement technologies number in the thousands. Data integration, normalization, and management technologies are proliferating almost as quickly. New software-as-a-service stacks for every department and function are causing a further fragmentation of processes, content, and data. Some initiatives that are theoretically possible may not yet be practical. Much of the cognitive computing and virtual assistant technology offered by start-ups and large software vendors is still far from being cost-effective or scalable. But organizations do need to get outside their comfort zone and try some of these new things—sometimes knowing they are not yet baked and that conceptual proofs will be thrown away. The challenge is in separating initiatives that are ready and practical from those that are in the experimental, science project stage—and knowing what to do with each one.

In this chaotic environment, managers need to focus on what's real: laying a foundation with a solid ontology, measuring the maturity of their organization to identify what's actually possible, and then moving forward with a roadmap of AI priorities aligned with business goals.

Laying the Data Foundation for AI Isn't Fun, but It Is Essential

Basic data discipline is not fun or sexy. But neither were most of the problems that had to be solved to get to the moon.

Questioning and examining the basics does not get people excited. If the process for managing data is broken, the objective my clients often set for me is to "just fix it"—don't tell them why it's broken or how broken it is. I worked with a manufacturer of power sports equipment whose CEO hated the presentation we gave about solving their ecommerce issues. We explained what needed to happen, but he just wanted an answer to the question, "How much will it cost?" Had I just said $15 million, I am sure that would have been the end of my relationship with him. I needed to explore the nature of the problem with him and work toward a solution together. I would not be able to do it, even with $15 million, without a commitment from the organization. There is more to the problem than a number or bodies.

Digging deeper into underlying assumptions or core processes means potential disruption and a risk of impacting short-term profits. The true value of digital transformation—as I'll show in this chapter—is in questioning the obvious and looking for the real need, instead of becoming fascinated by the shiny new thing that is making headlines at the moment.

DIGITAL AGILITY AND THE DATA-DRIVEN BUSINESS MINDSET

Regardless of the level of maturity in your organization, one of the most significant challenges that technology and business leaders face is process complexity and the need for end-to-end data flows throughout those processes. New digital technologies—especially those related to the customer experience—require revamped or entirely new supporting processes. Integrated digital marketing requires a different skillset, mindset, and organizational design. Building toward a 360-degree understanding of the customer requires that data move through end-to-end digital value chains without the friction caused by brittle integrations or manual processes.

Digital transformations require a view of processes that may turn traditional value chains upside down—for instance, disrupting field service with predictive analytics that trigger preventive maintenance rather than having the service staff wait for a phone call. This process entails onboarding and managing new data streams, understanding how to interpret those streams, and instrumenting the appropriate analytics to monitor them.

Customer lifecycle management, for example, is cross-departmental and cross-functional. It entails processes, functional areas, departments, and applications that cut across every aspect of how the organization serves its customers. Dashboards need to tell the organization how to remediate an out-of-bounds indicator, such as a high bounce rate from an ecommerce site after a product launch or a large number of returns after a promotion.

By monitoring the effectiveness of each step of the customer journey, you can measure the health of upstream systems and supporting functions continually, triggering remediation when analytics reveal anomalies. While the IT organization can provide infrastructure and instrumentation, the business side needs to develop metrics and key performance indicators as well as a remediation playbook based on its knowledge of customer needs and how to optimize the delivery of the desired customer experience.

Who Is Responsible for Quality Data?

The ideal customer experience is dependent upon complete, consistent, high-quality data. While the CIO and the IT organization are seen as the providers of customer experience data, that is not actually where responsibility belongs. Just as the business owns its processes, it also has to be responsible for both the data that fuels those processes and the data that those processes generate.

Consider a sales organization that builds CRM databases of leads and designs sales campaigns. Would the sales leadership blame the IT organization if inside salespeople failed to enter information about the calls they made each day? Entering that information is part of the job of the sales representative. You can apply this line of thinking to many parts of the organization. Unless the IT group completely owns an end-to-end process, it can't be held responsible for the quality of data that is essential to that process.

IT needs to educate the business units about how to own their data. It should also provide the company with the correct initial design, tooling, instrumentation, and infrastructure. IT also needs to help develop the playbooks that allow business functions to optimize data-driven processes. But the business must own data quality, consistency, completeness, and provenance. This shift requires extensive cultural and process change and a significant investment to get off to the right start. (The business side will not have the skills or resources to design content and data architectures or to clean up a backlog of bad data from years of neglect and underinvestment.)

Thinking Digitally

In addition to the process challenges and technical issues it raises, getting the organization to develop a data-driven business mindset is also a significant cultural challenge. This mindset begins at the design and capability development phase. It requires framing digital capabilities in terms of end-to-end processes and experiences rather than focusing on point solutions. Once capabilities are developed, the business must "think digitally"—driving decisions with data; testing products, services, and offerings iteratively; quickly finding what does not work ("failing fast"); and rapidly evolving the customer experience.

Most organizations are weighed down by legacy tools and applications that were designed and deployed without long-term integration, management, governance, and adaptability in mind. Those who created them were considering problems spanning a limited group of processes owned by a siloed function. Multiple cycles of development based on this line of thinking incurred significant technical debt and spawned incompatible architectures and inconsistent data structures. Rapid and agile deployment is the rationale for incurring technical debt. The paradox is that the approach impedes future agility. Rapid, agile, iterative evolution of offerings, products, and processes under these circumstances is not possible. Adding new capabilities requires significant time and cost.

All of this adds up to a lumbering, complex ecosystem of tools, technologies, and processes that is difficult to modify, leading to an inability of the organization to respond to customer and market changes in a timely fashion.

But wait—there's hope.

It is possible to remediate some of these challenges without a massive, risky, "rip and replace" approach. Data virtualization, ontology-driven integration layers, semantic search/unified information access tools, and back-end robotic process automation (RPA) are all viable approaches to help organizations make up for their past digital sins. A good starting point is to inventory data sources, develop ownership policies, establish quality measures, map trust dependencies, and create consistent reference architectures. Because clean, consistent, quality data is the fuel for the organization's applications, adding the role of chief data officer may prove to be a valuable catalyst for effecting needed process and culture change.

Leaders and business owners need to be aware of emerging technologies and their potential, but they also need to understand the foundational elements that are required to achieve this potential. They must not let their stakeholders get distracted by slick vendor demos. Leaders also need to help the business understand its own role in owning the data that enables the advanced capabilities to serve customers. The business must foster a mindset that is focused on coordinated action rather than decisions made in isolation. Getting that buy-in can go a long way toward improving business/IT partnerships.

You can't get started properly on the problem until you know where your organization stands. You need an AI roadmap and a clear idea of the maturity of your organization.

BUILDING THE AI ROADMAP

An AI roadmap is an approach to defining and managing the transformations that will accompany AI efforts. It provides a structured way to move through the many programs needed to realize success.

The roadmap begins with an assessment of the maturity of the business across multiple dimensions today and moves on to a definition of a future vision. Once the assessment and vision are completed, it becomes possible to identify the systemic gaps that need to be filled. Then those steps can be built into the roadmap.

Orchestration is about maximizing organizational efficiency and achieving scalability for the new digital business model. It requires a complete understanding of internal information flows that are the source of value. Understanding workflows and data flows leads to better operational integration. Mining the data for business intelligence leads to more productive knowledge workers and better business decision-making.

The maturity models around content operations, customer experience, product information, and knowledge engineering describe characteristics that support each of these functions, as I'll describe in the next section. Data and governance are part of all of these processes. A contextualized information architecture is critically important for structuring data and content while tagging them with the appropriate metadata for defining relationships between classes of information.

The information architecture, embodied in elements of the ontology, reflects the landscape of your organization. It requires close collaboration between the business stakeholders in your organization and the IT practitioners that will build an infrastructure to deliver business value. Business value comes in the form of personalized customer experiences and marketing programs that increase engagement and ultimately revenue, accurate business insights to inform resource allocation, and more efficient business processes to reduce costs.

Internal enterprise information and customer-facing content has to be accurate, findable by your audience, and contextualized—that is, appropriate to the problem the audience is trying to solve. Context helps determine how information is organized. This evaluation needs to be done across all digital assets so that product information is organized contextually to reflect buyer preferences. Enterprise search and external site search are optimized to make the most relevant content findable. Data governance processes will ensure data quality and accuracy to feed any kind of AI or machine learning program.

SETTING THE RIGHT OBJECTIVES ON THE BASIS OF ORGANIZATIONAL MATURITY

Executives developing a long-term roadmap for AI and cognitive technology have the challenge of balancing short-term wins with longer-term payoff and capability development. Organizations are measured on a quarterly basis, but journeys to new capabilities take years. Leadership changes. Businesses are reorganized. Stakeholders become fatigued. For digital transformations that encompass multiple functions, that span business units at global scale, and that require tens or hundreds of millions of dollars of investment, leadership needs to be confident in the ability to execute. It must also have the commitment to get through disruptive change that, by demanding significant changes to processes, business models, technologies, and skill sets, will impact short-term profits.

The journey requires resilience and endurance. It's a marathon, not a sprint. Just as none of us could run a marathon without training, it is not possible to deploy advanced capabilities and technologies in a sustainable, cost-effective way without certain prerequisites. Applications and tools may work in pilot, but scaling and deploying into production across the enterprise requires a level of maturity in supporting processes. Only then can the organization rapidly iterate, adapt, learn, and evolve through ongoing experiments and incremental deployment.

The key to success on the journey is to define what is needed to support a future state, to benchmark where you stand today, and to measure the level of maturity using "heuristics": rules of thumb, standards, and descriptions of supporting processes and tools. You can measure maturity, or level of proficiency, across various dimensions—information architecture, content management, digital marketing capabilities, data and analytics, customer data, and more—according to a five-stage model. The five stages are Unpredictable, Aware, Competent, Synchronized, and Choreographed. Level 5 can be considered aspirational in many organizations, and not every process and dimension needs to be at this level.

This scale is used in the planning process when estimating the timelines and resources needed to develop a target capability. If the target capability requires advanced content management and the organization is immature in that capability, then the organization needs a way to fill that gap. Advanced functionality—like personalization at scale—requires multiple sets of capabilities of sufficient maturity that can come together to orchestrate the multiple data and content sources needed to act on the digital body language of the customer.

Assessment of Maturity Levels Is Fundamental to Digital Transformation

Organizations need to understand maturity levels in core capabilities so that they can build an AI-powered enterprise on top of a flexible infrastructure rather than on immature capabilities. If the infrastructure is flawed, does this mean that the organization halts the digital transformation? No, it doesn't. What it does mean is that the organization needs to allocate resources and prioritize the efforts that typically don't interest executives. We've touched on many elements throughout the book, but now let's sum up what needs to happen.

Every organization deals with customers. The value AI can bring is in anticipating their needs and offering them the products they want when they want them. AI-powered personalization and recommendation engines can only work if you have a deep understanding of the customer and can represent that understanding in models that both AI and traditional technologies can interpret and act upon.

As a result, one goal of your digital transformation must be maturity in understanding and serving the customer throughout their journey. What does it take to serve up that information once you understand what they want? That requires that your product data be well defined with the correct attributes that represent the features and details that are important to

the customer. This in turn requires maturity in product data and supporting processes and technologies.

You also need to provide the answers and content your customers
want—whether in the presales/marketing stage or during their buying
journey. This requires that content operations are well tuned and on par
with the other elements. You need to harvest insights and understanding
from throughout the organization about ways your products solve problems. You need meaningful messaging, manufacturing methods, quality
procedures, and service and support through mature knowledge processes, including collaboration and knowledge management.

Keeping each of these capabilities at the levels of maturity needed will
require ongoing efforts and resources since your market is in continual
flux. Governance that is grounded in data and performance in each area
ensures that the organization is getting value from investments.

Assessing the current state of maturity in each of these areas in the context of a future vision of streamlined internal and external processes will
reveal significant gaps throughout the enterprise. Most managers don't feel
it is a realistic expectation to have the right information in the right person's
hands at any given moment. They feel the organization is too encumbered
by legacy systems, processes, and mindsets. If that is the case, then start
planning for the eventual "vaporization" of your organization, as author and
digital veteran Robert Tercek describes it.[5] Your organization must adapt to
new realities of the digital landscape and build agility as the foundation for
an adaptable business model. Ontologies are part of that flexibility, as they
will form the framework for each of the information capabilities. There are
realities of budgets, time frames, and the marketplace, but the critical piece
is the organizational will and discipline to commit to the journey.

Benchmarking Capabilities Using Maturity Models

Every organization is at a different level of capability in its application and
operationalization of digital technologies. It is difficult to predict business conditions, the competitive landscape, customer needs, and of course technology over the long time frames that transformation requires. However, there
are fundamental principles that endure and that need to be developed with
a long-term planning horizon in mind, as shown in Tables 11-1 through 11-5.

Table 11-1: Maturity Model for Content Optimization

Capability \ Maturity	1-Unpredictable	2-Aware
Content Operations	Information sprawl; chaotic, inconsistent, and unguided	Stable and labor-intensive rudimentary lifecycle; siloed activities with department-level incentives; one-off experiments; low reuse
Information Architecture	Static, monolithic documents; tool- and device-specific content structures	Templates and copies with burde some tagging requirements
Technology Integration	Multiple tools with inconsistent architecture	Partially harmonized infrastructu manual reuse; significant overla ping functionality
User Proficiency & Content Practices	Poor or minimal usage; lack of awareness of capabilities or content practices	Early adopters and power users using out-of-box features; little control of content
Governance	Information sprawl; lack of vision; no intentional decision-making	Awareness of challenges; activity is monitored but not constrained

3-Competent	4-Synchronized	5-Choreographed
omprehensive content fecycle; rudimentary haring; broad audience egmentation	Adaptive content repurposed across applications and channels; content effectiveness reporting	Automation-supported production enables meaningful personalization; accountability for content effectiveness
ase-driven component euse; rules-based tagging, mited customization	Multidimensional modeling of content in selected channels for few defined customer groups	High-fidelity multidimensional content model across multiple content asset types and channels
emi-automated content euse across systems with armonized metadata hroughout customer lifecycle	Programmatic content reuse and component assembly using signals from upstream and downstream applications	Omnichannel, integrated, harmonized, personalized content from headless CMS feeding all downstream systems
epartmental collaboration ith basic content control	Cross-team project-oriented collaboration with information lifecycle management	Automated workflows and reporting for compliance with enterprise content standards
ssigned responsibilities; versight and communications infrastructure in place	Intentional decision-making; resource allocation; change controls in effect	Agenda-driven business leadership and stakeholder engagement to effect continuous process improvement

Table 11-2: Maturity Model for Customer Information

Capability \ Maturity	1-Unpredictable	2-Aware
Sources/Application	Identity hard to determine; unknowable data quality; data stored in inaccessible formats	Multiple disconnected systems; uneven, form-based data collection practices
Segmentation	Characteristic generalizations based on assumptions	Broad, silo-specific segment characterizations; "inside-out" customer journeys with some data
Journey Models	None	High level, simplistic, unvalidated models
Technology Stack	Disconnected, standalone technology with fragmented data	Basic collection of customer data across technologies without reconciliation or harmonization
Customer Attributes	None	Basic static characteristics (for example industry, role, organization size, etc.)
Metrics & Governance	None	Lack of enterprise policies for customer data collection and compliance, manual data quality metrics and remediation

3-Competent	4-Synchronized	5-Choreographed
ustom multi-system uerying; non-normalized ata; linked offline/online lentities; third-party data tegration	360-degree omnichannel profiles; preprogrammed responses to behavioral signals	Insight-driven practices; real-time machine learning behavior response
udience clusters defined y attributes; validated ourneys supported by data vidence	Predefined rules for associating customer and context attributes; accurate journey stage recognition	Individual-in-the-moment; predictable customer behaviors leading to proactive engagement and decision-making
etailed, validated models, ntegrated with repre- entation of technology omponents	Detailed models with technology representation, enhanced with sophisticated audience models	High-fidelity journey models with intent rendered in metadata terms; supporting metrics and integrated knowledge models
ggregation of customer ata and near real-time nteractions across latforms	Cross-platform application of digital body language to real-time system responses	Customer data platform aggregation across technologies, channels, devices, and offline and online experience, with machine learning optimization
Aultiple audience haracteristics specific to oals, objectives, buying ycle, demographics, rmographics	Explicit and implicit audience attribute models informed by multiple system interactions	Multidimensional, static and dynamic metadata with real-time updates via upstream and downstream digital interactions
onsistent customer data olicies, first- and third- arty usage measured nd managed	Decisions linked to business outcomes support ongoing investments in customer data processes	Metrics-driven governance playbook for compliance, programmatic optimization, and human decision-making

Table 11-3: Maturity Model for Product Information

Capability \ Maturity	1-Unpredictable	2-Aware
Product Launch & Item On-Boarding	Cycle times in weeks or months; manual processes	Multiple out-of-synch systems need to be updated and reconciled
Product Data Management	Poor data quality; manual validation; limited transformation	Category hierarchies and attribut identified; semi-automated data quality processes
Information Architecture	Taxonomy is product hierarchy and web navigation	Taxonomy of hierarchy and attrib serves collection and display
Content & Digital Asset Management	Static content; poor digital asset control; handcrafted channels	Content ownership defined; aggregation from multiple source lifecycle monitored
Site Search & SEO	Basic site search without filtering; manual dictionary updates; no coordination with SEO	Curated site search categories aligned with navigation; SEO-friendly landing pages
Marketing & Merchandising	No coherent cross-channel marketing capabilities	Manual coordination of merchandiser, category manager, and brand manager silos
Governance	None in place	Brand, merchandiser, and eCommerce fiefdoms

3-Competent	4-Synchronized	5-Choreographed
ultiple content streams ggered by product launch	Tuned taxonomies for channels and devices; A/B testing for launches	Seamless cross-channel product launch; cycle times in days
usiness rules built into product ata quality; manual hierarchy apping to channels	Data quality feedback to vendors; consistent cross-channel mapping	Many-to-many vendor-to-channel cross-mapping; integration with domain analytics
ollection vs. display taxonomies re cross-mapped by channel	Taxonomy updates are harmonized across channels, drive search	Taxonomy optimized for dynamic content, devices, and languages
ontent tagging/reuse mod-ate; digital assets managed; ditorial guidelines in place	Content and assets coordinated across channels by audience	Dynamic content presented according to device, context, geo-location, and segment
creased precision; SEO nonyms in taxonomy; search imensions optimized	Attributes drive comparisons and cross-sell; associative relationships drive ways to shop and upsell	Multi-device search; mobile geo-location; third-party site search is competitive advantage
nd-to-end workflows defined cross processes and channels	Consistent messaging and branding across channels	Seasonal placement; agile campaigns; flash sales are automated
entralized, managed, and nded	Competencies support maintenance processes and workflow	Integrated practices operationalized, impact analysis is proactive

Table 11-4: Maturity Model for Knowledge Management

Capability \ Maturity	1-Unpredictable	2-Aware
Core Collaboration	Rudimentary, random, and haphazard	Intentional, ineffective knowledge capture and codification
Expertise Location	Who you know	Word of mouth
Content Curation	Haphazard and application-limited	Pockets of curated content, sub-optimized across processes
Information Architecture	IA is navigation; inconsistent metadata; few standards; poor usability	Application and department locali taxonomies
Infrastructure	Foundational; few to no collaborative tools; CM rudimentary	Foundational tools in place but with out-of-the-box deployment
User Proficiency & Content Practices	Poor or minimal usage; lack of awareness of capabilities or content practices	Early adopters and power users using out-of-box features; little control of content
Governance	Non-existent	Initial attempts lead to fiefdoms

3-Competent	4-Synchronized	5-Choreographed
...ctices identified; formal ...vesting and promotion ...utput	Integrated into processes with creation, access, and reuse mapped	Seamless and habitual with collaboration processes integrated with business needs and downstream uses
... skills identified and ...tured	Formal expertise directories leveraged	Expertise derivation through text analytics, community participation, and group interactions
...ntent aligned with platform ...d process; governance-driven ...ormation concierge	Workflow-driven integration with hybrid tagging and entity extraction processes	Value added at each touch point; core metadata flows with content; lifecycles managed, retention enforced
...ssification structures applied ...upport dynamic knowledge	Multi-channel, device-and format-independent cross-application architecture	Upstream supply chain and downstream syndication with partner and customer processes
...owledge harvesting ...egrated with collaboration ...d reuse	Expertise location; community management; intentional knowledge optimization	Multiple tools mapped to detailed requirements and use cases with ongoing tuning and enhancement
...partmental collaboration ...h basic content control	Cross-team project-oriented collaboration with information lifecycle management	Automated workflows and reporting for compliance with enterprise content standards
...peatable, defined knowledge ...nagement governance	Integrated, cross-functional managed processes	Business value–driven; enterprise-wide deployment

Table 11-5: Maturity Model for Orchestration

Maturity / Capability	1-Unpredictable	2-Aware
Content Management	Information sprawl: chaotic, inconsistent, and unguided	Stable and labor-intensive rudimentary lifecycle; siloed activities with department-level incentives; one-off experiments; low reuse
Content Component Architecture	Static, monolithic documents; tool- and device-specific content structures	Templates and copies with burdensome tagging requirements
Offer Architecture	One size fits all	Basic audience segmentation and understanding of personalization drivers
Audience Architecture	Characteristic generalizations based on assumptions	Broad, silo-specific segment characterizations; "inside-out" customer journeys with some data
Customer Data Management	Identity hard to determine; unknowable data quality; data stored in inaccessible formats	Multiple disconnected systems; uneven, form-based data collection practices
Product Information Management	Unreliable manual processes and data; navigation-only taxonomy; few useful attributes	Out-of-sync systems; few data quality processes; onboarding templates; classification taxonomy with category-specific attributes
Knowledge Management	Haphazard; application-limited; no collaborative tools	Intentional but inefficient; basic collaborative tools; knowledge silos; inconsistent reuse; labor-intensive reactive asset creation
Governance & Metrics	Reactive involvement, no effective measures or stewardship structures	Departmental expectations; siloed and inconsistent standards; few champions
Orchestration	None: manual processes; acts of heroics; technological dead ends	Ineffective use of data sources and signals; multiple one-off projects; brittle integration and customization; tool customizations at capacity

Table 11-5 (continued)

3-Competent	4-Synchronized	5-Choreographed
omprehensive content ecycle; rudimentary haring; broad audience egmentation	Adaptive content repurposed across applications and channels; content effectiveness reporting	Automation-supported production enables meaningful personalization; accountability for content effectiveness
ase-driven component euse; rules-based tagging; nited customization	Multidimensional modeling of content in selected channels for few defined customer groups	High-fidelity multidimensional content model across multiple content asset types and channels
Multidimensional audience egmentation applied limited, manual offer ombinations	Dynamic audience segmentation based on explicit and hidden dimensions; foundational messaging framework	Offer components dynamically recombine for range of business outcomes (registration, conversion, retention)
udience clusters defined y attributes; validated ourneys supported by ata evidence	Predefined rules for associating customer and context attributes; accurate journey stage recognition	Individual-in-the-moment; predictable customer behaviors leading to proactive engagement and decision-making
ustom multi-system uerying; non-normalized ata; linked offline/online dentities	360-degree omnichannel profiles; preprogrammed responses to behavioral signals	Insight-driven practices; real-time machine learning behavior response
ontent workflows triggered by product launch; ormalized and controlled ttribute values	Attributes-driven cross-sell and merchandising; vendor data collaboration	Seamless cross-channel launch; responsive, personalized product content
ctive asset harvesting nd distribution; reuse of ampaign components; xpertise networks; taxono-y for knowledge curation	Intentional knowledge operations integrated into business processes; community management; global sharing of best practices	Frictionless and efficient knowledge access and application to all aspects of customer experience lifecycle; ongoing feedback loops
unded and centralized versight, policy, and ana-tics; repeatable process-s; assigned responsibilities	Metrics-driven governance playbook; center-of-excellence model with cross-functional decision-making	Metrics-driven culture; accountability prioritized by value; process governance automation
nterprise taxonomy; prod-ct and content workflows ligned with some custom-r signals; system-specific nformation sharing	Enterprise ontology; scalable services with some automation; workflow synchronization; non-destructive data streams	Comprehensive unified attribute models; 360-degree customer view with real-time analytics and insight activation; personalization at scale

You can adapt these representative models for your industry and organization by identifying the critical support processes and dimensions that underlie the digital capabilities that enable your vision for the future state. Each of these dimensions (the table rows) can be broken down into finer detail. For example, data analytics are broad capability areas that each can be defined with their own models.

To assess maturity, you must determine which characteristics describe the current state as well as those of the desired future state. Maturity can be uneven—one part of the organization or process can be more advanced than another. One goal of the exercise is to harvest practices in parts of the organization that are most mature and apply the lessons learned elsewhere.

WHY PROJECTS FAIL

Despite your best efforts and careful benchmarking of maturity, challenges lurk around every corner when you are implementing information and AI programs. Implementation is especially challenging in the case of emerging technology initiatives, as approaches and tools are still being developed and refined. So here's what to look out for:

- **The wrong approach to "moonshot" projects.** AI and machine learning can enable you to consider changing paradigms, reinventing the value chain, and completely rethinking the business. This can inspire, energize, and motivate the organization and its leadership. It can also lead to career-limiting outcomes: highly visible, expensive, and embarrassing failures. It is important to manage the expectations on the ground and in the C-suite so as not to disillusion the organization and fatigue stakeholders.
- **Unrealistic expectations and budgets.** Stakeholders (both on the business side and on the technical side) may have expectations that are out of alignment with reality. This lack of congruity can stem from their not understanding the nature of the problem or not understanding what it takes to solve the problem. One organization I ended up working with had a product catalog of over 200,000

items, and a vendor who had a relationship with the senior managers there proposed to revamp their taxonomy for $150,000. That was a fantasy. In the end, addressing the product information challenges (which includes taxonomy work) cost about $4 million. Executives sometimes propose budgets inadequate for the complexity of the task or in response to lowballed estimates of the challenge. An under-resourced project will take longer than promised, be delivered without needed functionality, go over budget, or fail outright.

- **Overpromised functionality.** Vendors or program champions often promise more than is possible. In the AI space, because many solutions are new and emerging, it is easy to fall into this trap. During times of significant change in technologies (as we are experiencing with AI), there is a great deal of fear and confusion in the marketplace. Experimentation may be necessary to determine how to apply emerging technologies. It is important to separate what is real and practical within a short time frame and what is a *distant* future stated vision. The "moonshot" AI projects can be part of ideation and a long-term vision of the future, but you can't count on them as an operationalized capability.
- **Incorrect resources devoted to initiative.** At a recent AI conference in New York, Vodafone discussed the fact that they could not find "cognitive engineers" on the market and had to "grow their own." These resources consisted of business analysts, subject matter experts, linguists, information architects, user experience specialists, and knowledge management experts. Because cognitive and AI projects appear to be completely new approaches, organizations may forget to tap into the people in their organization who already know the customer, understand the details of processes, and have been trained in approaches that are necessary to prepare knowledge sources for AI. It is a mistake to try to hire data scientists to address a user experience problem.
- **Overly broad scope.** Scope issues are always a challenge when you are considering organizational processes holistically. If you're trying to develop an enterprise architecture, the scope will appear to be too broad to be practical. But you can start with a high-level

perspective, model a domain, implement archetype scenarios that are representative of the broader scope, and drill down into specific areas for detailed development. This zooming in and zooming out will allow for the enterprise scope to be chunked into pieces even as it respects the overall unified architecture vision.

- **Overly complex technology stack.** Some AI vendors have collections of discrete systems that require costly integrations to create an "AI" solution. In reality, many problems can be solved using limited applications of AI and machine learning or by integrating specific functionality rather than an overly broad set of technologies.

- **Inclusion of rebranded legacy products.** Beware the complex suites of independent technologies that came from a technology vendor's string of acquisitions. Sometimes these "suites" use different architectures, programming languages, and approaches that add unnecessary cost and complexity to deployments.

- **Lack of "training data."** This commonly cited challenge confounds many AI projects. In the end, success is less about the algorithm and more about the data. For example, data for cognitive assistants or chatbots has to be curated and structured for the specific use cases under consideration. Machine learning requires data appropriate to the process and objectives—one cannot "throw all the data at the AI" and expect meaningful results. Often data sources are noisy and dirty—cleanup may require tuning of the algorithm as well as manual remediation.

Fragmentation

One consequence of the lack of foundational planning is that organizations end up with too many disconnected initiatives, a condition known as "digital fragmentation." These initiatives need to be aligned before the organization can realize the full potential of its vision. This alignment can be difficult to achieve because each initiative often has its own business justification, funding, and, in many cases, decision-making process.

The problem with fragmented initiatives is they may not align with strategic goals. Groups may have conflicting objectives. One organization I worked with had a group looking for efficiencies while another searched for new markets for their information products. New markets required more thoughtful upstream production processes that ran counter to the efficiency goal. As this organization learned, short-term motivators, metrics, and incentives may conflict with longer-term investment.

There will always be some degree of fragmentation in large, complex enterprises because decision-making and responsibilities are distributed among business units, functions, and departments. The best approach is to have visibility in multiple initiatives, provide guidance around decision-making and measurements, and ensure that reusable elements are in fact reused across initiatives.

SOME KEY QUESTIONS FOR A REALISTIC ASSESSMENT

I once attended a presentation for an organization that was investing an enormous amount of money in a phased approach to personalization. A slide in the strategy deck for the leadership team showed the following process:

- Phase one—limited personalization implemented
- Phase two—personalization with demographic and interest specific content
- Phase three—dynamic machine-learning-based personalization
- Phase four—predictive personalization enabled by machine learning
- Phase five—AI-driven personalization with advanced prescriptive algorithms

Regrettably, while these terms were jargon-filled and buzzword-compliant, they meant very little in terms of a practical approach. Leadership always has to ask the questions, "So what? What does that mean?" In this instance, specific questions included, What is "limited personalization? What will it look like? What will it mean for the customer? For the departments that have to support the capability? What is the difference between "dynamic personalization" and "predictive personalization"?

When pressed, the author of the content on this slide could not articulate the differences between each of these "phases."

After your technology vendor describes functionality in tangible, specific terms with actual examples, your next question should be, "How is this next phase going to be different?"

If the answer makes sense, terrific. If it doesn't, it's time to pause and look for what's real and what's noise. So let's look at some questions you should be asking.

How Much Do You Need to Understand?

Part of investigation is exploring what you don't yet fully understand. But there has to be a foundational explanation that makes sense, with a range of options to explore and questions to answer. If you can't attain a basic understanding, and this is just a pure exploration of something completely new, be prepared to make an investment in building a foundational understanding rather than taking a leap of faith based on the promises of zealous champions.

In the personalization scenario I just described, when the design team began to develop content architecture to support personalization even at a basic level, the company had no idea how its various audiences differed from each other or what content to use to personalize the message. Their message was really the same across their different audiences. The company lacked both the digital tools and the strategy to develop personalized content, let alone build "advanced, predictive, IoT-enabled smart machine-learning dynamic AI-enabled prescriptive capabilities" (blah blah blah). But no one asked the hard questions, and no one would say that the emperor (technology vendor) had no clothes.

Again, the question that always needs to be asked is, "So what?" More specifically, What difference will this (approach, tool, technology, methodology, term, even data element) make? Why do we need it? What will it do for us, the user, our customer, the process, system, model, or whatever element it is supposed to improve? When you define a requirement to capture data for a process, ask, "What will we do with the data when we have it?" In other words, what is the justification for the requirement?

What Does the User Really Need?

At the end of the day, all of this comes down to use cases and user scenarios—the day in the life of the user. What are the things that they need to do to solve their problem or achieve their goal? It is very easy to lose sight of the day-to-day tasks and activities of the people whom our technology is serving.

I once worked with a large Medicare administrative contractor—one of the insurance processing organizations that handle Medicare claims. Entire departments of people were churning out hundreds of documents about claims regulations and processes each week. When we asked these people who they were creating the content for and what the purpose was, no one knew. Further investigation (through measurement of user behaviors) revealed that much of the content was never even read or downloaded by anyone!

Do You Really Need All Those Applications?

Technology and business processes have become so complex in large enterprises that it is difficult to understand the reasons why many of them exist. They exist mainly because they are part of someone's job or part of a legacy environment. One distributor of retail goods used 600 applications to run their business. No one understood that ecosystem and the underlying complexity. In one financial services firm, nearly an entire department of people who managed data was eliminated. Guess what? No one complained. This is why digital transformations are such incredible opportunities to question everything and to continue to ask, "So what?"

What the business needs is not a new application but the questioning of fundamental assumptions about the things that are in place and that everyone accepts as part of the process. When a new application is being considered, that question is even more important.

DIGITAL TRANSFORMATION

The natural endpoint of all this digital thinking is digital transformation: the complete reimagining of the workings of business in digital terms. AI and digital transformation initiatives are already a top priority for board-room executives. The question is how to make these programs visionary yet realistic and achievable.

While most companies know that digital transformation is vital to sur-vival, many organizations are embarking on these efforts without detailed knowledge of the customer. In its "State of Digital Transformation" report for 2019, the Altimeter Group found that 41% of organizations are pro-ceeding with digital transformation without thorough customer research.[6] They define digital transformation as "the evolving pursuit of innovative and agile business and operational models—fueled by evolving technolo-gies, processes, analytics, and talent capabilities—to create new value and experiences for customers, employees, and stakeholders." With that defi-nition, one would think that knowledge of the customer journey would be important. Agile business and operational models are enabled by mastery of the elements of orchestration.

The results of the study suggest that many companies are making either tactical or isolated investments in digital technology in the absence of a formal, overarching strategy for how the business can optimize the cus-tomer experience. To fully achieve successful digital transformation, companies must build a digital vision and strategy, as well as create an information architecture to guide technology choices and to fully leverage investments.

You must also ask, is there a solid foundation for a successful transi-tion to AI technologies and your future digital business? In order to suc-ceed, you need to understand the limitations and maturity of the current state, identify gaps, and define the actions and resources required to fill those gaps along the paths of data and architecture, technology and infra-structure, and execution and governance. While technology supports all aspects of the customer lifecycle, the processes that generate the external experience are often disconnected and data is fragmented.

In fact, everything in your technology efforts can be viewed as a pre-diction engine that surfaces the right information for the right user at the right time. No matter what the context, the problem that the organization needs to solve is an information flow problem, a findability problem, and a knowledge and insight problem. Customers, from their initial exposure to the organization through their final act of purchase, are presented with a series of information journeys, both online and offline. Whether and how easily they can locate what they need when they need it determines whether you win their business.

Selling is an information problem: deciding who to call, what to say, and what information is needed to move the prospect forward and turn them into a customer. Product development is a series of information problems: understanding market needs and customer preferences, determining gaps, assessing the competitive landscape, solving problems in a unique or higher-value manner, and communicating that value to targets in the marketplace. Manufacturing is a series of information problems: ·Conceiving of a physical solution to a real-world problem, designing and evaluating options, modeling and prototyping, manufacturing most efficiently, identifying quality issues and their root causes, and designing the information flows for products in the field. Researching new drugs and treatments for diseases is a series of information problems.

In each case, the technology is augmenting human creativity and our inherent ability to make new associations between diverse fields and to synthesize new approaches and solutions. Too often we get hung up on the technology and fail to take a step back, re-examine the problems we are trying to solve, and build a flexible data and process foundation for it. The organization gets caught up in limited thinking and looks at ways to improve current processes. There is little appetite for long-term thinking about how the organization can disrupt itself before it is disrupted.

An inflexible infrastructure is a major impediment. It is difficult to change legacy processes because they are ingrained in organizational habits and embedded in technologies that were deployed years or decades earlier. It is difficult to recombine information and content into new service or sales models because of fragmented data and brittle tool integrations. Digital transformations are meant to clear out those impediments and rethink the organization and its value proposition. Trying to add AI to a transformation that does not address these core issues will not create an agile business that can react quickly to the marketplace.

Digital Thinking at a Unicorn Startup

A young, rapidly growing company worth over $1 billion faced a problem with help tickets and support communications. The volume of tickets was in the tens of millions per month. The organization had to route them to the correct person, match them with a response, and in some cases provide a credit for the service (along with the appropriately sincere apology for the issue).

The problem was that it was difficult to interpret the issue and provide the answer without a great deal of manual review. The company's data scientists came up with several algorithms that did a better job of understanding the core issue and routing the ticket. They used a deep-learning convolutional neural network, which improved the ability to route the tickets.

One challenge was that the taxonomy of issues was poorly developed to begin with, and it evolved organically and without formal decision-making or testing. In other words, the organization was very immature in a core information process. The fact that they were using AI to solve an information architecture problem was very surprising. They were making up for their sins in information architecture by using advanced machine learning AI algorithms! They were using an AI sledgehammer rather than an IA flyswatter to kill their trouble-ticket-routing fly.

One reason why we need to apply machine learning and AI to our information is because of our terrible, unstructured information management hygiene. Over the past couple of decades, organizations have been inundated with content and data but have lacked the formal processes to manage them. Collaboration tools were unleashed on the corporate world and no one looked back. This is why so much of the world's data is inaccessible. It was not designed in an accessible way, so now text analytics, semantic search, and neural networks are attempting to sort, organize, and classify this ocean of unstructured information.

Leading the Change

Leaders who are undertaking complex, risky projects like digital transformation must have the organizational capital to be credible and to inspire others to follow their lead. They need to have both a realistic vision of where they are taking the organization and a track record of success. People need to believe in the vision and see a path to the goal. The leader must also build a coalition of support from across the organization, must be able to convince their peers that they will be successful, and must bet their own reputations on the outcome. In political, risk-averse cultures, this is very difficult. Here are some principles that can help with this transformation.

- **Project a "must do or be left behind" attitude.** Data-focused transformation is not a nice-to-have or an option. As author and business expert Jeffrey Hayzlett says, "your organization has to continually reinvent itself, disrupt itself, and create new sources of value and competitive advantage." Be clear that disruption is required, or like the paper-catalog-based company in chapter 6, you will be disrupted by others.
- **Start with measured risks.** The transformation need not be all or nothing. A large, risky project can be broken down into a series of lower-risk components that are developed using known approaches. Lower-profile projects based on new approaches will enable learning from experiments with new vendors, software, processes, and business models.
- **Determine what is most important for the business in the short and longer term.** Long term, the business needs to be trans-formed. Short term, it needs to address problems that provide immediate value but lead toward the longer-term vision. The reason for developing the grand vision is to establish the North Star and travel toward it while solving day-to-day problems and improving efficiencies and effectiveness.
- **Pursue success rather than avoiding failure.** A success mindset is important to maintain so that your organization can move toward the vision of success. This is far more likely to result in planned and orchestrated progress than moving based on a fear of failure or disruption.
- **Set priorities based on multiple dimensions.** As we discussed in chapter 3, these dimensions could include visibility (highly visible versus off the radar), breadth and scope (narrow versus broad), internal versus external focus, clear ROI versus cost of doing

business, number of processes supported or enabled (few versus many), level of complexity (simple versus complex), degree of integration, cost, use of internal resources, nature of the process supported, and other factors. For example, you might want a pilot with a high probability of success to be highly visible and broad in scope in order to demonstrate a capability.

- **Conduct experimental projects out of the spotlight.** If a project has many unknowns, then a quiet, narrow-scope, low-visibility project is more likely to move you in the direction of your goal.

- **Create throwaway projects to acquire learning.** In many cases, it is necessary to learn from and build on experiments. These experiments will not be deployed and will likely be thrown away. This mindset allows for risk-taking and fast failures. Every failure is a step toward a solution.

- **Agility is not an excuse for not planning.** I once suggested setting a foundational architecture for a project and the customer responded, "We don't use taxonomies; we are an agile shop." That's like saying, "I don't eat ice cream; I ride a bicycle." The two are not opposites. Some planning of an architecture is needed, including for agile projects. Reference data and consistent terminology can support multiple agile iterations.

- **Consider what can be developed iteratively.** Iterative, agile development allows for successive generations of application that can leverage lessons from experimentation and provide progressive levels of functionality and performance, even as they maintain constant labels for concepts and data.

- **Evaluate current state versus future state (and the maturity of supporting processes).** The difference between your business's current state and its future state is the capability gap. Advanced capabilities need to be supported by the appropriate level of maturity in supporting processes. If organizational maturity is too rudimentary, more work has to be done to build the foundation. Otherwise, the program will not be sustainable, will not be economically feasible, or will not scale. Acts of heroics do not scale.

- **Develop an orchestration model.** An orchestration model includes content processes, customer experience, product data, and knowledge architecture. Orchestration requires a holistic view of enterprise processes, the customer relationship, business strategy, differentiators and value proposition, core and aspirational competencies, well-integrated tools, unified and aligned content, mature supporting processes, and a continuous-improvement mindset. Build the capabilities that will lead to competitive differentiation on a rock-solid foundation of well-architected data and technologies. Don't incur technical debt for the sake of rapid deployment.

- **Implement metrics-driven governance.** Metrics and metrics-driven governance are the key to course corrections and ensuring a return on investment of resources and funding. KPIs ensure that course corrections represent actual progress and allow the balancing of conflicting objectives—for example, keeping control of customer support costs versus having high levels of customer satisfaction.

- **Assess maturity.** As we described earlier in the chapter, perform this assessment across multiple dimensions including product data, onboarding, architecture, governance, content processes, customer data, search, findability, customer experience, customer journey, knowledge processes, messaging architecture, and componentization. These supporting dimensions need to be at a sufficient stage of maturity to support the desired level of target process capability.

- **Align technology.** Assess existing and potential tools and technologies in the context of the engagement strategy at each stage of the lifecycle. As I described in chapter 3, you need to determine the fitness to purpose of your technology infrastructure based on how the organization interacts with prospects and customers.

- **Focus on doing what's hard and essential versus what's fun and interesting.** It's fun to buy shiny new technology but hard to make current systems work. New tools are a distraction from the hard work that is required regardless of the technology stack.

- **Build the right team.** Focus on roles, responsibilities, metrics, right person in the right seat, internal versus external skills, developing new core competencies, and IP, depending on the core value proposition. You cannot outsource the talent behind your core value proposition—it is too critical to the survival of your organization. According to veteran marketer Carla Johnson, "organizations are not realizing the full potential [of AI technologies] because they are not looking at the talent transformation behind [digital transformations]." Even so, some organizations are attempting to outsource critical human elements or not reskilling their people to fully leverage the technology. Consider how the organization's people need to change along with the technology to deliver the value promised by AI.

- **Grow capabilities.** Vodafone had to develop its own "cognitive engineers." Give your team the ability to learn new skills and evolve and reinvent themselves. For example, train component content experts (usually found in the tech docs department) in virtual assistant technologies. Enlist your user experience experts in designing AI interactions. Train business analysts in use case development for analytics and machine learning applications. Bring marketers and content creators into the process for creating training content for cognitive AI systems. Create an internal center of excellence to share practices and build familiarity and competency with emerging AI technology.

- **Plan a moonshot—versus risking everything on a moonshot.** You don't want to bet your career on a high-visibility, high-cost, risky venture. However, planning what a moonshot project might entail and then breaking it down into bite-sized chunks will allow for exploration of risk, options, capabilities, and learnings. Consolidate those learnings.

- **Pursue organizational readiness.** What tells you who is ready to lead the way and blaze new trails for the organization? Who is most enthusiastic? Who is willing to take a risk to learn new approaches (and fail along the way)? What part of the organization recognizes the need to adapt and evolve and has the incentive, resources, or use cases to proceed?

- **Manage old-school mindsets.** Banish old-school thinking during ideation. Bring the old-school thinkers back in during execution (after the trailblazers commit to the unsexy stuff).

- **Manage change.** Budget for education, socialization, and change management. You may have warehouses full of change management material; you may even have a department to do it. Communicate, bring in stakeholders—or, if your organization is large or public, the influencers (use organizational/social network analysis[7] to find them)—and involve them in system design, requirements, and validation of the solution. Always ask, "Who else needs to be brought on board?" Or, when working with an executive, "Who from your team should represent your interests? We want to make sure you have a seat at the table." Ask that question during every interview and working session.

- **Understand the cost of mistakes versus the cost of experiments.** Experiments are intentional. Mistakes are not. Encourage experiments that are calibrated to risk, potential reward, investment, and appetite. If a project is strategic and you need to learn lessons, do it with the small providers who will invest with you. (The big vendors and system integrators will charge full price to learn on your dime.) If there are mistakes, learn why they happened. Get to the root without (detailed) explanation. If there is a pattern, learn and move on.

- **Manage risk factors.** Worry about what Donald Rumsfeld referred to as the "known unknowns." They are what you can plan for.

- **Build a test bed.** Build sandboxes with three to five tools. All of the major players in natural language processing—Amazon Lex, Google Dialogflow, Microsoft LUIS, Apple's Siri—have overlapping functionality. Try mixing dialog design from one with utterance classification from another. Try tools like Twilio for omnichannel development.

- **Investigate what's practical versus what's possible.** Distinguish the possible from the practical by asking about scaling, integration, data sources, and content processing. What works in the innovation lab may be impractical to deploy in production.

These recommendations show how organizations need to measure the impact of architectural changes and begin with a clear understanding of the results gleaned from good data hygiene and consistent measures. Once these pieces are put into place, it will be possible to apply automated approaches to some steps in the process.

The future is out there, and it will be different. Go—do your part to usher in the robot apocalypse.

TAKEAWAYS FROM CHAPTER 11

Digital transformation is a challenging goal—you might even call it a moonshot. Pursuing it means changing to a digital mindset and clearly understanding the state of your organization's maturity. These are the main points in this chapter.

- Planning a moonshot approach to digital transformation can generate many benefits along the way.
- Your approach to AI will determine if your organization thrives in today's fast-moving digital world.
- Laying the foundation for quality data and an ontology isn't sexy, but it's essential.
- Your management needs to adopt a digital mindset to succeed; this is a cultural shift.
- Your AI roadmap depends on a disciplined approach to assessing your organization's maturity in supporting processes and capabilities.
- AI projects fail for multiple reasons, including believing vendor promises, a lack of attention to proper training data, a lack of success measures, and fragmented corporate technologies
- Ask the "So what?" question at the start of any project. Why does it matter? What does the user actually need? and Why do you need another application?
- Digital transformation success depends on a determination to move forward, a sober assessment of risks, appropriate priorities, and metrics-driven governance, among other factors.

GLOSSARY

"ABOUT-NESS." Characteristic that describes the classifications and qualities of data elements in an ontology; metadata "about" content, documents or any source or piece of information. *See also* "is-ness."

ACCIDENTAL ONTOLOGIES. Data architectures that arise naturally from individual technology projects, but without an overarching organizational principle.

ARTIFICIAL INTELLIGENCE (AI). A broad term representing multiple classes of algorithm that identify patterns in data and emulate some aspects of human judgment to draw non-obvious conclusions from them.

ARTIFICIAL NEURAL NETWORKS (ANNS). *See* neural networks.

ATTRIBUTE MODEL. The set of descriptors (metadata) that describe content, products, customers, knowledge, or structured data sources. *See also* customer attribute model.

AUDIENCE. A collection of users (for example, customers or employees) attempting to solve a problem (for example, finding a product to buy or verifying a policy).

AUGMENTED REALITY. A technology that allows a visual display to overlay digital information on a view of the real world.

BANTS CRITERIA. An acronym for the five criteria used to qualify leads: budget, authority, need, timeline, and strategic fit.

BIG DATA. Massive collections of information that can't be analyzed with traditional methods due to demanding levels of volume, variety, and velocity.

BOTS. Automated tools that perform activities or interface with customers or employees. *See also* chatbots.

CAD/CAM (COMPUTER AIDED DESIGN/COMPUTER AIDED MANUFACTURING). A set of tools that enables the virtual creation, visualization, and manipulation of objects to be manufactured.

CATEGORIZATION. Classification applied to similar types of data, such as product descriptions or documents.

CDP. *See* customer data platform.

CHATBOTS. A class of bots that can conduct conversations with customers or employees.

CHIEF DATA OFFICER (CDO). A C-suite executive whose responsibility is to improve the consistency and quality of data in an enterprise.

CLUSTERING. Identifying similar content or documents—for example, to help contextualize search queries.

COBOT (COLLABORATIVE ROBOT). A robot that provides assistance working alongside a human.

COGNITIVE LOAD. The amount of mental effort that a customer or employee needs to invest to accomplish a task. Interfaces that pay too little attention to user experience often end up generating an increase in cognitive load.

CONFIGURE-PRICE-QUOTE (CPQ) SYSTEM. A tool that allows selection of product options to meet user needs and preferences, and that can streamline the selection and quoting process by recommending and pricing appropriate combinations of features.

CONTENT MANAGEMENT SYSTEM (CMS). A system for managing, assembling, and distributing content on a website or other customer engagement application.

CONTENT MODEL. A structured representation of concepts within a document, defined as metadata regarding "is-ness" and "about-ness".

CONTENT MARKETING. A marketing practice that creates useful content for customers to attract and retain their attention.

CONTEXT. The environment in which data or content is considered or applied; to operate on the data, AI algorithms often need to know the context to operate on the data. Users need content in the context of their goal.

CONTEXTUALIZATION. The process of identifying the context in which data is considered or applied.

CONVERSATIONAL MARKETING. A practice in which automated tools use natural language interactions to converse with customers.

CRM. *See* customer relationship management system.

CROWDSOURCING. A process that uses shared comments in an online social network to gather information and ideas for a project.

CUSTOMER ATTRIBUTE MODEL. A set of descriptors that represent the customer's interests, needs, tasks, objectives, role, history, propensity to buy, and so on;

the "is-ness" and "about-ness" of a customer described in metadata terms.

CUSTOMER DATA PLATFORM (CDP). A system that aggregates customer data (the customer's "digital body language") from multiple sources for the purpose of improving engagement.

CUSTOMER EXPERIENCE (CX). The sum total of all experiences the customer has in their interaction with an organization—both online and offline; the discipline of analyzing such experiences.

CUSTOMER JOURNEY. The path that a customer takes as they interact with the company. *See also* high-fidelity customer journey, journey map.

CUSTOMER LIFECYCLE. The set of broad stages a customer goes through as they interact with your organization—for example, learn, choose, purchase, use, maintain, and recommend.

CUSTOMER MODEL. A description of the customer in terms of everything the organization knows about them. *See also* customer attribute model.

CUSTOMER RELATIONSHIP MANAGEMENT (CRM) SYSTEM. A system that holds information about customers and their interactions with an organization.

DARWIN INFORMATION TYPING ARCHITECTURE (DITA). A document component architecture that makes information more easily consumable by computers.

DATA DICTIONARY. A description of the contents, format, structure, and relationships contained in a database.

DATA HYGIENE. The discipline of keeping data accurate and up to date to avoid errors, costs, and inefficiencies.

DATA MODEL. A broad term used to represent the makeup of structured, unstructured, and semi-structured information throughout the enterprise.

DATA QUALITY. A measurement of the trustworthiness, completeness, accuracy, and timeliness of a set of data.

DIGITAL ASSET MANAGEMENT (DAM) SYSTEM. A software system used to manage rich media digital content (such as images, video, drawings, and photos) for deployment in marketing communications, for example.

DIGITAL TRANSFORMATION. A corporate initiative to reengineer a company's processes and culture to be fully digital and integrated.

DIGITAL TWIN. A virtual representation of a physical product that can be used in tests and simulations.

DISPLAY TAXONOMY. A product classification design used to aid site navigation. *See also* navigational hierarchy.

DOMAIN MODEL. A structured view of data and content in a given information area (such as customers, vendors, products, or finance) or process (such as product onboarding, marketing campaign development, or customer service).

EMPLOYEE JOURNEY. The steps an employee takes to solve a problem; analogous to customer journeys.

ENGAGEMENT STRATEGY. How your organization differentiates from the competition through messaging, channels used to reach its audience, how it delivers value, and the character of the customer relationship.

ENTERPRISE RESOURCE PLANNING (ERP) SYSTEM. A software system that companies use to manage resources and integrate other systems, such as accounting, inventory management, and procurement systems.

ENTITY EXTRACTION. An AI technique that identifies concepts and associated terms in text.

EQUIVALENCE TERMS. Different terms referring to the same concept in the ontology.

EXPLICIT (CUSTOMER) DESCRIPTORS. Facts about customers stored in customer systems. *See also* implicit (customer) descriptors.

EXPLICIT KNOWLEDGE. Knowledge documented in knowledge bases.

FACETS. Options presented in a search that refine search queries for faster resolution. Facets use product and content attribute models.

FEATURES. In the context of customer attribute models, a feature is a type of customer or product descriptor. Also described as attributes or metadata. In the context of text analytics, it refers to ways of describing the information in a document. In machine learning, a feature is a property or characteristic in the data. Feature engineering is the selection of characteristics that have a meaningful impact on the output of the algorithm.

FRICTION. Anything that impedes the efficient functioning of an enterprise.

GROUPWARE. A category of software, now largely obsolete, that was designed to improve information sharing. Example: Lotus Notes.

HELPER BOT. A bot designed to aid employees—for example, call center workers.

HEURISTICS. Rules of thumb, standards, and rubrics for evaluation—for example, in the context of a maturity assessment, user experience, data structures, or content organizing principles

HIERARCHY. A classification system, such as a taxonomy, consisting of parent–child or whole–part relationships. *See also* navigational hierarchy.

HIGH-FIDELITY CUSTOMER JOURNEY. A representation of the customer's needs in data terms, including attributes and descriptors that indicate their role, buying state, interests, demographics, goals, and even state of mind.

HIGH-FIDELITY (CUSTOMER) JOURNEY MAP. A validated model of the high-fidelity customer journey featuring data elements about the customer at every stage.

IMPLICIT (CUSTOMER) DESCRIPTORS. Inferences about customers based on other data. *See also* explicit (customer) descriptors.

INFERENCE ENGINE. A mechanism that can answer questions beyond those originally programmed into it.

INFORMATION ARCHITECTURE (IA). The structural design of information that comprises the user experience or that enables digital capabilities.

INFORMATION METABOLISM. An analogy used to describe the flows of information within businesses.

INFRASTRUCTURE PROGRAMS. Programs that improve the basic functioning of technology within an enterprise but that do not have a direct line of sight to the customer.

INTELLIGENT VIRTUAL ASSISTANT. *See* virtual assistant.

INTENT. The task a user of a system is trying to accomplish, typically identified from a finite list of possible desires.

INTERNET OF THINGS (IOT). The broader computing environment that results from the proliferation of connected devices.

"IS-NESS." Characteristic that describes the fundamental nature of data elements in a content model and the ontology. *See also* "about-ness."

JOURNEY MAP. A high-level description of the customer journey. Also called a customer journey map. *See also* high-fidelity journey map.

KNOWLEDGE ARCHITECTURE. An ontology and associated content models for organizing knowledge.

KNOWLEDGE BASE. A collection of information that a human or AI system can draw on to solve problems.

KNOWLEDGE DOMAIN. The complete set of knowledge a particular company operates within, as determined by the industry in which it participates.

KNOWLEDGE ENGINEERING. The process of revealing the structure of information for best use by humans or artificial intelligence.

KNOWLEDGE GRAPH. The relationship between various concepts and data elements in an ontology used to describe the knowledge domain.

KNOWLEDGE MANAGEMENT SYSTEM. A system that supports employee productivity by making the best information available to, and easily findable for, employees who need it.

KNOWLEDGE PORTAL. A structured knowledge base that supports employee productivity and customer self-service by making the best information available and easily findable in the context of an employee or customer's task.

KPIS (KEY PERFORMANCE INDICATORS). Metrics used to measure the level of success of a system.

LABORATORY INFORMATION MANAGEMENT SYSTEMS (LIMS). A technology that collects, manages, and analyzes masses of data from laboratory instrumentation.

LEGACY SYSTEMS. Older technology systems that an enterprise depends on but that may not be configured to work easily with modern AI algorithms.

LUMPERS. People who have a tendency to gather things together into larger groups. *See also* splitters.

MACHINE LEARNING. An umbrella terms for AI applications that identify patterns, make predictions, find anomalies, and classify images or data.

Machine learning algorithms solve problems by using increasingly accurate approximations as input to improve the output.

MARKETING AUTOMATION. A technology that manages marketing campaigns and customer engagement activities across channels.

MARKETING QUALIFIED LEAD (MQL). A lead that meets two of the five BANTS criteria.

MARKETING TECHNOLOGY STACK. The collection of interconnected marketing technologies that, together, enable a company to attract and interact with customers.

MASTER DATA. A consistent set of identifiers that describe elements of an ontology and how they are applied to enterprise applications.

MATURITY. The level of sophistication of a technology system or organization, measured against a rubric.

MENTAL MODEL. How a customer or other user thinks about a problem and how to solve it.

MERCHANDISER. A person whose job is to make changes in the presentation of products in a retail store or site so as to maximize sales.

MESSAGING ARCHITECTURE. A framework that allows for the systematic customization and personalization of marketing messages.

METADATA. Data about data or descriptions of data; "is-ness" and "about-ness" of content and information. For example, a video is data, while information about the length, author, format, and date of creation of the video would be called metadata. Also called features, attributes, facets, properties, fields, and columns.

METRICS-DRIVEN GOVERNANCE. A framework that allows executives, managers, and front-line employees to make decisions and execute them based on careful analysis of data and KPIs about the enterprise.

MODEL-BASED DESIGN. The process of conceiving, creating, and testing products through virtual simulations.

MULTIPHYSICS. A term for simulations that involve multiple models or simulation systems for any given product.

NATURAL-LANGUAGE PROCESSING (NLP). Machine algorithms that parse text or speech to generate meaning.

NAVIGATIONAL HIERARCHY. A product taxonomy used to aid site navigation. *See also* display taxonomy.

NET PROMOTER SCORE (NPS). A simple likelihood-to-recommend metric that organizations use to measure customer satisfaction.

NEURAL NETWORK. A computing structure that generates optimal outputs by identifying patterns in broad and varied input data. Neural networks loosely mimic biological processes with artificial "neurons" that compute an approximate output based on changing the weights associated with each element in a network. The output of each "neuron" is used as an input to generate the next iteration of adjustments.

OMNICHANNEL MARKETING/MESSAGING. A marketing practice that coordinates messaging to a given customer across channels and devices.

ONBOARDING. The process of adding new products to a product information system.

ONTOLOGY. The master knowledge scaffolding of an organization: a complete, consistent data model of the customers, products, processes, and relationships that make a business work.

ORCHESTRATION. The coordination and synchronization of marketing activities that happens in a mature digital marketing environment.

PERSONA. An iconic or archetypal representation of a specific type of customer.

PERSONALIZATION. Customization of site content or marketing messages for each individual customer.

PERSONALIZATION ENGINE. Software components that determine which data and content should be delivered in each channel to each customer on each device.

PIM. *See* product information management system.

PLANOGRAM. A diagram showing how products are organized in a retail store.

POLYHIERARCHY. A classification system in which some items are located in more than one place.

PREDICTIVE ANALYTICS. A process that anticipates future states by analyzing current information and past patterns of behavior.

PREDICTIVE OFFERS. An ecommerce technique that tries to anticipate the offer most likely to entice a given customer, based on past actions of similar customers.

PRIMARY (CUSTOMER) RESEARCH. The practice of talking to, interviewing, or observing customers in their actual environment.

PRODUCT INFORMATION MANAGEMENT (PIM) SYSTEM. A database that holds information about products.

PRODUCT LIFECYCLE INTELLIGENCE (PLI). The use of advanced analytics to optimize innovation across all stages of the product lifecycle. The successor to product lifecycle management (PLM).

PROMISEWARE. AI tools that promise functionality but don't actually deliver it.

PROPENSITY-TO-BUY MODEL. A scoring algorithm that models the likelihood that a prospect will make an actual purchase.

RACI CHART. A chart that tracks which entities and people are responsible, accountable, consulted, or informed for any given decision or responsibility.

REFERENCE DATA. Standard definitions and values used to ensure consistency of information across systems. The ontology contains reference data for enterprise systems, applications, and processes.

RIGHTS MANAGEMENT. A process that ensures that use of content respects the rights of the original creator or licensor of the content.

ROBOTIC PROCESS AUTOMATION (RPA). Automation technology that duplicates the activities of a human in moving data among systems.

ROT. An acronym for redundant, out-of-date, and trivial content.

SALES QUALIFIED LEAD (SQL). A prospect that sales has qualified for three of the five BANTS criteria.

SCENARIOS. In the context of an ontology, a description of how a problem is solved as a series of steps. In the context of site design, a description of steps that a particular type of customer might take to solve a problem.

SCHEMA. A structure for data, content, or knowledge in a database.

SEARCH ENGINE OPTIMIZATION (SEO). The activity of modifying website content to enable pages to appear higher in search engine results.

SEED DATA. Initial contexts and examples used to train intelligent virtual assistants.

SEMANTIC LAYER. Ontology elements that translate inconsistent information structures into a common language.

SEMANTIC SEARCH. A mechanism for integrating diverse structured and unstructured information sources to provide appropriate data to aid in a task leveraging the semantic layer.

SHOPPING BASKET ANALYSIS. An ecommerce technique that makes suggestions based on past purchases of customers who have bought similar items.

SMART OBJECTS. Sensor-enabled physical goods that can communicate data about themselves.

SMART SPACES. Instrumented buildings that track activity within their spaces.

SOFTWARE AS A SERVICE (SAAS). A model in which companies subscribe to software services for various technology needs.

SPLITTERS. People who have a tendency to separate things into smaller and smaller subcategories. *See also* lumpers.

STRUCTURED KNOWLEDGE. Knowledge that is explicitly created for reuse and retrieval from a knowledge base.

TACIT KNOWLEDGE. Knowledge that is generated through experience but not documented.

TAGGING. The application of metadata attributes to enable the location of data and content relevant to a particular problem or situation.

TAXONOMY. A clearly defined hierarchical structure for categorizing information of a given type using parent–child and whole–part relationships. *See also* display taxonomy.

TECHNICAL DEBT. Friction and challenges created by technology systems that were not well documented, kept up-to-date, or integrated with other systems.

TEXT ANALYTICS. A set of algorithms that read text and identify patterns or elements within the text, for tagging, sentiment analysis, categorization, and other purposes.

TEXT MINING. The process of deriving insights from unstructured collections of text.

TRAINING DATA. A subset of a collection of data that an AI algorithm uses to identify patterns.

UNSTRUCTURED KNOWLEDGE. Knowledge generated through ongoing collaboration activity that is not designed for reuse.

UTTERANCE. A bit of sound or text that a user generates, which is then analyzed by an AI system to extract meaning and intent.

VIRTUAL AGENT. A domain-specific, task-oriented, and contextualized algorithm that can respond to user queries. *See also* virtual assistant.

VIRTUAL ASSISTANT. An algorithm that uses AI to generate information to make a human's job easier. Includes virtual sales assistants that help customers with ecommerce and intelligent virtual assistants that answer support questions.

VIRTUAL REALITY. A technology that displays a digital world that people can move through and interact with, typically on a visual headset.

VOICE-OF-THE-CUSTOMER. Term to describe programs that gather customer feedback to provide insights into a business.

ACKNOWLEDGMENTS

Writing *The AI-Powered Enterprise* has been quite a journey over the past two-plus years. I want to thank my wife, Lisa, for putting up with my weekday (and even weekend) evening working sessions and supporting me throughout the process.

This was a team effort, starting with Josh Bernoff who helped me at the start and has continued with extended editorial effort throughout the development process, and Maggie Langrick, the publisher and founder of LifeTree Media, who helped to rework my stream-of-consciousness writing into a structured, logical flow. Kudos to both of you for your hard work and patience. This book would not exist without you. Thanks also to the whole LifeTree Media team, including Sarah Brohman and Tara Tovell.

I am grateful for the help and support of my colleagues at Earley Information Science. In the past few years, we have done a great deal of prototyping, proof of concept development, and technology investigation. My current and former EIS colleagues who contributed to those efforts include Jeannine Bartlett, Dennis Connolly, Eli Cooley, John Dolce, Dino Eliopulos, Donna Fritzsche, Jeanna Giordano, Tobias Goebel, Gustavo Gonzalez, Prakash Govind, Bryan Kohl, Mac McBurney, Carla Pealer, Vivek Shivaprabhu, Ash Subramanian, and Henry Truong (who also provided the examples from TeleTech). The other members of the EIS team whose hard work make everything we do possible include Mike Anthony, Rachel Benson, Ian Galloway, Jeremy Grubman, Jason Hein (to whom I also owe the fuzzy socks metadata example), Chantal Schweizer, Dave Skrobela, Melissa Wilkins, and Laura Wright. Special thanks to Sharon Foley.

This book would not have been possible without the fascinating stories of the people doing great AI work and the people who introduced me to them. They were kind to allow me to include them here. These include the folks at PR 20/20, including Mike Kaput, who runs their Marketing AI Institute; Paul Roetzer, founder of the agency and the terrific Marketing AI conference; and Sandie Young, who set up multiple meetings and who introduced me to rasa.io, MarketMuse, and Pandata. I'd also like to thank Cal Al-Dhubaib, Jane Alexander, Mike Barton, the late Darcy Belanger, Jeff Coyle, Nadine Harder, Brett Knight, Jared Loftus, Stephanie McCay, Ryan Miller, Niall Murphy, Melanie Nuce, Molly Soat, Wes Sprinkle, Robert Tercek, and Erik Wolf.

My research and analysis are better because of the smart people I've spoken with over the years. These include Scott Abel, Prith Banerjee, Mathieu Bernard, Ursula Cottone, Brice Dunwoodie, Siobhan Fagan, Jim Gilligan, Jeffrey Hayzlett, Rick Hutton, Carla Johnson, Pete Johnson, Marina Kalika, Gene Kolker, Rebekah Kowalski, Dan Miller, Piero Molino, Mark Nance, Steve Orrin, Steven Keith Platt, Devashish Saxena Kinjal Shah, Laks Srinivasan (who really understood the need for IA in machine learning AI applications), David Talby, Brandon Thomas, Gwen Thomas, Derek Top, Steve Walker, and Rich Wendell. Their insights and stories about analytics, machine learning, chatbots, and AI have inspired me.

A special thank you to Joyce Gavenda, one of my first clients over 25 years ago, whose help over the years has been critical to the company.

I also want to express appreciation for the long-time colleagues who worked on some of our best projects: Jeff Carr, architect for PCL and Applied Materials, who co-developed the IA and ontology development methodologies discussed in *The AI-Powered Enterprise*; Seth Maislin, who contributed to the future scenario that opens the book; Amber Swope and Paul Wlodarczyk, who were instrumental in the success of the Allstate and Applied Materials projects; Branka Kosovac, who worked on many marquis customers; and Stephanie Lemieux, who made contributions to taxonomy methodologies and programs over the course of her tenure with EIS.

Thanks to the hundreds of EIS customers I have had the privilege to work with over the past 30 years and the many people who have passed through the virtual and physical doors of EIS, who are too numerous to mention but have contributed to the lessons, the learning, and the knowledge encompassed in this book.

Looking back, thanks to Gary Kahn, who mentored me early in my career on knowledge management projects with Lotus and then joined EIS to help us become successful.

Finally, thanks to Tom Davenport, not only for writing the foreword and providing candid feedback on the manuscript, but also for participating in EIS webinars and knowledge salons, being part of my research, and making various introductions to folks in the AI space—as well as endangering himself in Falmouth Harbor while experiencing the Thundercat.

NOTES

Chapter 1: The Promise and the Challenge of AI

1. This meaningless statement is from "AI Will Bring About the Biggest Transformation in Human History," Futurism.com, March 9, 2017, https://futurism.com/ai-will-bring-about-the-biggest-transformation-in-human-history.

2. For more detail, see David Rotman, "AI is reinventing the way we invent," *Technology Review,* February 15, 2019, www.technologyreview.com/s/612898/ai-is-reinventing-the-way-we-invent.

3. I wrote about this in an article: Seth Earley, "There Is No AI Without IA," *IT Professional* 18, no. 3 (2016): 58–64, https://ieeexplore.ieee.org/document/7478581.

4. Here's a review of Gareth Morgan's metaphor: Iman Tohidian and Hamid Rahimian, "Bringing Morgan's metaphors in organization contexts: An essay review," *Cogent Business & Management* 6, no. 1 (2019). See https://www.tandfonline.com/doi/full/10.1080/23311975.2019.1587808.

5. While some progress has been made in having AI fix the data that's fed into it, the use cases are fairly narrow and significant preparation is needed to make them work. This includes adding "reference data" and numerous examples of what the output should look like.

Chapter 2: Building the Ontology

1. This description is from the company's home page at appliedmaterials.com.

2. This example is inspired by the research article from IBM about using multiple specialist bots to solve complex problems: Sethuramalingam Subramaniam and Garbi B. Dasgupta, "COBOTS—A Cognitive Multi-Bot Conversational Framework for Technical Support," in *Proceedings of the AAMAS 2018 Conference* (Stockholm, Sweden, July 10–15, 2018), 597–604 http://ifaamas.org/Proceedings/aamas2018/pdfs/p597.pdf.

3. Quote from P.V. Kannan, *The Age of Intent: Using Artificial Intelligence to Deliver a Superior Customer Experience* (Herndon, VA: Amplify, 2019), 26.

4. The game is played by finding the shortest list of movies that link an arbitrarily selected actor and Kevin Bacon. See https://en.wikipedia.org/wiki/Six_Degrees_of_Kevin_Bacon.

5. Albert Einstein is quoted as saying, "If I had an hour to save the world, I would spend 59 minutes identifying the problem and 1 minute solving it," in Dwayne Spradlin, "Are You Solving the Right Problem?" *Harvard Business Review,* September 2012, https://hbr.org/2012/09/are-you-solving-the-right-problem.

Chapter 3: Customer Experience: The Front Line of the Battle

1. Based on Jill Avery, Susan Fournier, and John Wittenbraker, "Unlock the Mysteries of Your Customer Relationships," *Harvard Business Review,* July–August 2014, https://hbr.org/2014/07/unlock-the-mysteries-of-your-customer-relationships.

Chapter 5: Making Ecommerce Smarter

1. Jason Hein used this example in a conference keynote address.

2. According to Salesforce, personalized product recommendations boost revenue. Statistics from Heike Young, "Personalized Product Recommendations Drive 7% of Visits but 26% of Revenue," *Salesforce Blog,* November 2, 2017, https://www.salesforce.com/blog/2017/11/personalized-product-recommendations-drive-just-7-visits-26-revenue.html.

3. Quoted in Jared Spool, "When It Comes to Personas, The Real Value Is In The Scenarios," UIE, September 11, 2018, https://articles.uie.com/when-it-comes-to-personas-the-real-value-is-in-the-scenarios.

Chapter 6: Sharpening the Sales Process

1. A short list of such tools appears in Mike Kaput, "4 Scary Smart AI Tools That Will boost Sales Productivity," Marketing Artificial Intelligence Institute, October 8, 2018, https://www.marketingaiinstitute.com/blog/ai-for-sales.

2. The EverString claim is documented in "The World's Best Data," a marketing piece posted at http://xd07g309cu21kppg63qolt4t-wpengine.netdna-ssl.com/wp-content/uploads/2018/01/EverString_WorldsBestData.pdf.

Chapter 7: Customer Service: Delivering Higher Quality at a Lower Cost

1. Data from the "Customer Service Representatives" page on Deloitte's Data USA website: https://datausa.io/profile/soc/customer-service-representatives.

2. See IA Staff, "70% of Buying Experiences are Based on How the Customer Feels They are Being Treated," Industry Analysts, Inc., December 5, 2017, https://www.walkerinfo.com/knowledge-center/featured-research-reports/customers-2020-a-progress-report; Glance, *Counting the Customer: The Complete Guide to Dynamite Customer Care*, http://ww2.glance.net/wp-content/uploads/2015/07/Counting-the-customer_-Glance_eBook-4.pdf.

3. Adam Cheyer remarks are from BigSpeak Speakers Bureau, "Adam Cheyer—Siri, Back to the Future," YouTube video, 55:37, April 27, 2016, See https://www.youtube.com/watch?v=UBHgj9TuHXM.

4. Ontologies such as this can use a specific structural system called DITA—Darwin Information Typing Architecture. DITA is a component architecture, developed originally by technical documentation professionals to make information more consumable by computers and more accessible for people to use in various contexts. Once the knowledge is in this format, it can fuel an AI system, which can pick out the exact information a customer is looking for.

5. For more on the ongoing challenges with training Watson, see Jason Bloomberg, "Is IBM Watson A 'Joke'?" *Forbes,* July 2, 2017, https://www.forbes.com/sites/jasonbloomberg/2017/07/02/is-ibm-watson-a-joke/#4dfb0577da20.

6. This is from P.V. Kannan, *The Age of Intent: Using Artificial Intelligence to Deliver a Superior Customer Experience* (Herndon, VA: Amplify, 2019), 143.

7. More detailed analysis in Susan Hash, "Chatbots in the Call Center," *Contact Center Pipeline*, March 2019, https://www.contactcenterpipeline.com/Article/chatbots-in-the-contact-center.

Chapter 8: Accelerating Employee Productivity

1. TeleTech changed its name to TTEC in 2018.

Chapter 9: Physical Meets Digital: Manufacturing, Supply Chain, and Logistics

1. Thanks to Cal Al-Dhubaib, Managing Partner at Pandata, for making us aware of the work of the Cleveland Museum of Art.

2. A description of digital twins appears on the "Digital Twin" page on Siemens' website: https://www.plm.automation.siemens.com/global/en/our-story/glossary/digital-twin/24465.

3. The study appeared in the IEEE transactions journal: S.H. Huang and Hong-Chao Zhang, "Artificial neural networks in manufacturing: concepts, applications, perspectives," *IEEE Transactions on Components, Packaging, and Manufacturing Technology: Part A* 17, no. 2 (1994): 212–228, https://ieeexplore.ieee.org/document/296402.

4. More detail in Robert Gebelhoff, "Sequencing the Genome Creates So Much Data We Don't Know What To Do with It," *Washington Post,* July 7, 2015, https://www.washingtonpost.com/news/speaking-of-science/wp/2015/07/07/sequencing-the-genome-creates-so-much-data-we-dont-know-what-to-do-with-it/?utm_term=.6585c7ec7969.

5. For more on simulations, see Carlos Gonzalez, "The Impact of Simulation and the Future of Manufacturing," *Machine Design*, February 1, 2017, https://www.machinedesign.com/fea-and-simulation/impact-simulation-and-future manufacturing.

6. Quote from Insights Team, "How AI Builds A Better Manufacturing Process," *Forbes Insights,* July 17, 2018, https://www.forbes.com/sites/insights-intelai/2018/07/17/how-ai-builds-a-better-manufacturing-process/#6b19aff41e84.

7. The video describing this is Jordan Reynolds and Ryan Whittle, "KNOW/The Future of Product Data Analytics," *Viewpoints on Innovation,* January 10, 2019, http://viewpoints.io/entry/know-the-future-of-product-data-analytics.

8. Quote from Luigi Alberto Ciro De Filippis, Livia Maria Serio, Francesco Facchini, and Giovanni Mummolo, "ANN Modelling to Optimize Manufacturing Process," IntechOpen, December 20, 2017, https://www.intechopen.com/books/advanced-applications-for-artificial-neural-networks/ann-modelling-to-optimize-manufacturing-process.

9.   For more insights, see Zohar Yami, Golan Meltser, and Rotem Greener, "Supply Chain Complexity—Dealing with a Dynamic System," *Tefen Tribune*, Spring 2010, http://tefen.com/uploads/insights/1456214433_ZyuFmdCdXJ.pdf.

10.   Cited from Howard Slusken, "Four million parts, 30 countries: How an Airbus A380 comes together," CNN, December 2018, https://www.cnn.com/travel/article/air-bus-a380-parts-together/index.html.

11.   Cited from Jonathan Webb, "How Many Suppliers Do Businesses Have? How Many Should They Have?" *Forbes*, February 28, 2018, https://www.forbes.com/sites/jwebb/2018/02/28/how-many-suppliers-do-businesses-have-how-many-should-they-have/#1ad2fbc9bb72.

Chapter 10: AI-Powered Strategy and Governance

1.   More on this in Jen Booton, "Under Armour Launches Ecosystem of Connected Fitness Products," *SportTechie*, January 16, 2019, https://www.sporttechie.com/under-armour-launches-ecosystem-of-connected-fitness-products.

2.   More on this in Kate Grosch, "John Deere—Bringing AI to Agriculture," *HBS Digital Initiative*, November 7, 2018, https://digital.hbs.edu/platform-rctom/submission/john-deere-bringing-ai-to-agriculture.

Chapter 11: Leading into the Future

1.   Data from Evan Andrews, "10 Things You May Not Know About the Apollo Program," History.com, September 1, 2018, https://www.history.com/news/10-things-you-may-not-know-about-the-apollo-program.

2.   For more detail, see Burton Dicht, "The Greatest Engineering Adventure Ever Taken," ASME, December 28, 2010, https://www.asme.org/engineering-topics/articles/history-of-mechanical-engineering/the-greatest-engineering-adventure-ever-taken.

3.   For more detail, see Rhuaridh Marr, "To the Moon and Back on 4KB of Memory," *Metro Weekly*, July 24, 2014, https://www.metroweekly.com/2014/07/to-the-moon-and-back-on-4kb-of-memory.

4.   For more detail, see Sasjkia Otto, "Apollo 11 moon landing: top 15 Nasa inventions," *The Telegraph*, July 22, 2009, https://www.telegraph.co.uk/news/science/space/5893387/Apollo-11-moon-landing-top-15-Nasa-inventions.html.

5.   This refers to Robert Tercek's book *Vaporized: Solid Strategies for Success in a*

Dematerialized World (Vancouver: LifeTree Media, 2015).

6. More detailed analysis available in Brian Solis, "The State of Digital Transformation," Altimeter, 2019, https://insights.prophet.com/the-state-of-digital-transformation-2018-2019.

7. Patti Anklam, an expert and consultant in ONA, wrote an informative book on the topic: *Net Work: A Practical Guide to Sustaining Networks at Work and in the World* (Oxford, UK: Butterworth-Heinemann, 2007).

INDEX

ABOUT THE AUTHOR

Throughout his career, Seth Earley has been passionate about the crucial role that information management would play in a world hurtling toward digital transformation. He provides challenging insights to executives who are tasked with leading their organizations forward in an age in which the digital experience offered to customers determines the winner.

As CEO of Earley Information Science, a consulting firm he founded more than 25 years ago, Seth guides some of the world's most recognized brands on how to leverage their information assets to deliver state-of-the-art customer experiences through integrated enterprise architectures. Seth has a long history of contributing to industry education and research in emerging fields. His current work contributes to a better understanding of topics including cognitive computing, knowledge engineering, data management systems, taxonomy, ontology, and metadata governance strategies.

He coined the phrase "There's no AI without IA," which calls out the need for a foundational information architecture for AI projects. His phrase was repeated by IBM CEO Ginni Rometty at the World Economic Forum in Davos, Switzerland, in 2019, when she was interviewed about the challenges of AI.

Seth Earley is a sought-after speaker, writer, and influencer. His writing has appeared in IEEE's *IT Professional* magazine, where, as former editor, he wrote a regular column on data analytics and information access issues and trends. He has also contributed to the *Harvard Business Review*, *CMSWire*, and *Applied Marketing Analytics*. He co-authored *Practical Knowledge Management* from IBM Press.

ABOUT EARLEY INFORMATION SCIENCE

Earley Information Science is a professional services firm. For 25 years, we have made it our mission to support business outcomes by organizing data—making it findable, usable, and valuable.

Earley Information Science specializes in structuring and organizing enterprise information with service offerings around four pillars: Product Data Management (PD), Knowledge Engineering (KE), Content Optimization (CO), and Customer Engagement (CE).

Our service offerings include:

- **AI strategy and roadmap** (all pillars). Learn how to best leverage AI for business value.
- **Current state maturity** (all pillars). Understand your current state to develop a realistic roadmap and action plan.
- **Conversational commerce readiness** (PD). Prepare for conversational commerce; don't get left behind.
- **Chatbot proof of capability** (PD, KE). As you evaluate chatbots, separate hype from reality.
- **Product data optimization** (PD). Optimize online catalogs for ecommerce and build the correct foundation for advanced capabilities.
- **Readiness for personalization** (all pillars). Review current state of readiness for marketing and ecommerce personalization.
- **Knowledge architecture for AI** (KE). Separate hype from reality, solve problems today while preparing for the future.

- **Metrics-driven governance** (PD, CO, CE). Measure your return on investments, build a metrics-driven playbook, show linkage to business value.
- **Configure/price/quote** (all pillars). Improve efficiencies, reduce overhead, speed responsiveness, and remain competitive.
- **Technology selection** (all pillars). Control the procurement process, don't be manipulated by the vendor sales process, and make decisions that will advance your career.
- **Taxonomy and ontology design** (all pillars). Realize the value of next generation information architecture to support AI and legacy technologies (since there's no AI without IA).

Looking for help? Contact us at +1-781-812-5551 or info@earley.com.